Home Cooking

CONTENTS

COOKING WITH TASTE

America's Best Homemade Recipes!

OVER 600 FAMILY-PROVEN RECIPES!

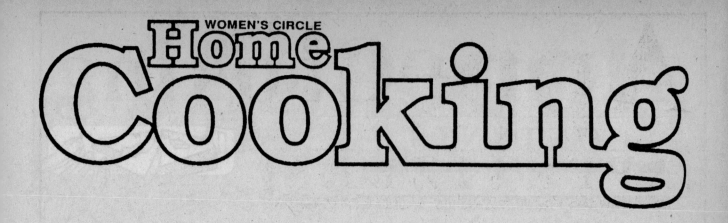

WOMEN'S CIRCLE
Home Cooking

EDITOR
JUDI K. MERKEL

PRODUCTION
PATRICIA ELWELL
BEVERLY WEILAND
DARLENE ZEHR

PHOTOGRAPHY
RHONDA DAVIS
MARY JOYNT
NANCY SHARP

PUBLISHERS
CARL H. MUSELMAN
ARTHUR K. MUSELMAN

CHIEF EXECUTIVE OFFICER
JOHN ROBINSON

MARKETING DIRECTOR
SCOTT MOSS

(219) 589-8741
FAX: (219) 589-8093

Women's Circle Home Cooking cookbook is a collection of recipes obtained from *Women's Circle Home Cooking* magazine, published by House of White Birches, 306 East Parr Road, Berne, Indiana 46711.

Exclusively distributed by:

P.S.I. & Associates, Inc.
13322 SW 128th St.
Miami, Florida 33186
(305) 255-7959

Appealing
APPETIZERS

SALMON LOG

1 (1-pound) can salmon
1 (8-ounce) package cream cheese, softened
1 tablespoon lemon juice
2 tablespoons grated onion
1 teaspoon prepared horseradish
1/4 teaspoon salt
1 teaspoon liquid smoke seasoning
1/2 cup chopped walnuts
3 tablespoons snipped parsley

Drain and flake salmon, removing skin and bones. Combine salmon with the next 6 ingredients; mix well. Chill several hours. Combine walnuts and parsley. Shape salmon mixture into 8x2-inch log, or use a fish mold. Roll in nut mixture. Chill well. Serve with crisp crackers.

Brenda Peery, Tannersville, Va.

DILL WEED DIP

2/3 cup real mayonnaise
2/3 cup sour cream
1 tablespoon dried onion
1 tablespoon dried parsley
2 teaspoons dill weed
1 teaspoon Lawry's seasoning salt
Dash pepper
2 drops Tabasco sauce
1/2 teaspoon Worcestershire sauce
1/2 teaspoon Accent

Mix together and let set at least 2 hours before serving. Fresh vegetables and bread cubes are great to serve with the dip.

Loriann Johnson, Gobles, Mich.

SAUSAGE BALLS

1 pound hot or mild sausage
2 cups Bisquick mix
10 ounces sharp cheese, grated

Combine all ingredients. Roll into small balls. Bake at 375 degrees for 10–15 minutes, or until lightly browned.

You may add more cheese, if you desire.

Helen Harlos, Ethel, Miss.

SAUSAGE TEMPTERS IN APPLESAUCE
Makes 4 dozen

1 pound pork sausage
2 cups applesauce
1 ounce cinnamon red candies
2 drops red food coloring

Form sausage in ¾-inch balls. Brown and cook meatballs in a skillet. Turn them so they brown evenly. Place a toothpick in each ball. Heat applesauce, candies and food coloring until candies dissolve. Place sausage balls in sauce, toothpick side up. Serve hot.

Note: A chafing dish would be ideal in which to keep sausages hot while serving.

Carmen Bickert, Dubuque, Iowa

ISLAND MACADAMIA NUTS

1 cup macadamia nuts
1/3 cup margarine
2 tablespoons soy sauce

Melt margarine and add soy sauce. Toss nuts gently to coat. Bake at 400 degrees, stirring often for about 10 minutes. Drain on paper towels.

CRAB PUFFS

1 cup water
1 stick margarine
1 cup flour
4 eggs

Bring water to boil and add margarine, return to boil. Add flour all at once. Remove from heat and beat in 1 egg at a time. Then add all the following ingredients:
3 scallions, chopped
1 teaspoon dry mustard
1 (6½-ounce) can crabmeat
1 teaspoon Worcestershire sauce
½ cup sharp cheddar cheese, grated

Drop on cookie sheet by spoonfuls. Bake at 400 degrees for 15 minutes. Turn oven down to 350 degrees and bake 10 additional minutes.

These can also be frozen.

Rosie E. O'Connell, Greensburg, Pa.

CHEESE-COCONUT BALLS

Makes about 30

2 packages (3 ounces each) Roquefort cheese
1 package (4 ounces) shredded cheddar cheese
1 package (8 ounces) cream cheese, softened
1 package (3 1/2 ounces) flaked coconut

Mash cheeses and combine them thoroughly with electric mixer. Chill for at least one hour. Shape into 1-inch balls and roll in coconut. Serve with fresh apple slices.

Mrs. Agnes Ward, Erie, Pa.

PINEAPPLE CHICKEN WINGS

Serves 4

12 chicken wings
3 tablespoons butter
1 small onion, sliced
8 1/2-ounce can pineapple chunks, drained, juice reserved
Orange juice
1/4 cup soy sauce
2 tablespoons brown sugar
1 tablespoon vinegar
1 teaspoon ground ginger
1/2 teaspoon salt
1/2 teaspoon ground mace
1/2 teaspoon hot pepper sauce
1/4 teaspoon dry mustard
1 1/2 tablespoons cornstarch

Fold chicken wing tips under to form triangles. Melt butter in large skillet; add wings and onion. Cook until wings are brown on both sides, about 10 minutes. Measure reserved pineapple syrup and add enough orange juice to make 1 1/4 cups liquid. Blend in soy sauce, sugar, vinegar, ginger, salt, mace, hot pepper sauce and mustard. Pour over chicken.

Cover and simmer 30 minutes, or until chicken is tender, basting top pieces once or twice. Remove chicken to hot plate. Add a small amount of water to cornstarch, blending to dissolve. Add slowly to the hot liquid in pan, stirring, and bring to boil to thicken. Return chicken to skillet, along with pineapple chunks.

Serve chicken wings and sauce with steamed rice.

Mrs. Betty L. Herrick, Nokomis, Fla.

BROILED CHICKEN LIVER ROLL-UPS

2 cans water chestnuts
1 pound chicken livers
1/2 pound bacon (cut each slice into thirds)
1 bottle soy sauce
1/2 cup brown sugar

Drain water chestnuts and slice each into 3 pieces. Wrap each water chestnut with a small piece of chicken liver and bacon piece. Secure with a toothpick and marinate in soy sauce for at least 4 hours.

Just before serving, remove roll-ups from soy sauce and roll each in brown sugar. Place on broiler rack and broil for about 10 minutes, or until crisp. Serve at once.

TASTY CHICKEN BASKETS

Makes 40-50 baskets

Baskets (directions follow)
Filling:
2 cups chopped cooked chicken meat
5 slices bacon, fried and crumbled
3 tablespoons diced, pared apple
1/2 teaspoon salt
1/8 teaspoon pepper
1/4 cup mayonnaise
1/4 cup finely chopped pecans
4-ounce can mushrooms, chopped

Combine and mix all filling ingredients. Cover and refrigerate for 2 hours. Makes 2 1/2 cups filling, enough for 40-50 baskets.

To make Baskets:

Cut 90-100 rounds from regular sliced bread using a 1 1/2-inch round cookie cutter. Spread half the rounds with softened butter.

Cut a small hole from the centers of remaining bread rounds, "doughnut" fashion. Place each "doughnut" atop a buttered round, and fill center with chicken filling, mounding high. Garnish with sprigs of parsley.

Louise Beckner

ROLLED SANDWICHES

Makes 25-30 sandwiches

1 loaf of bread, sliced into lengthwise slices
Filling:
1/4 pound (1 stick) butter, softened
4 ounces cream cheese
1/4 teaspoon paprika
1/4 teaspoon salt
1 tablespoon mayonnaise
3/4 cup minced nuts, raisins, dates and/or figs

Slice crusts from long pieces of bread. Combine *Filling* ingredients well. Spread on bread slices. Roll up from narrow ends. (Before rolling, strips of sweet pickles or olives may be placed over filling for colorful variations.) Press end of roll firmly and wrap each roll tightly in plastic wrap. Store in refrigerator overnight.

Before serving, slice each roll into 1/4-inch slices. Arrange on serving plate.

Note: Instead of the nuts-and-dried-fruit filling, you can use one of the following: 1 1/2 cups tuna salad, crab, shrimp, salmon, finely chopped raw vegetables, grated cheddar cheese, chicken, turkey or ham filling.

Sue Hammer

SHRIMP PUFFERS

Makes 60 appetizers

8 tablespoons softened butter or margarine
2 eggs, separated
3 cups shredded sharp cheddar cheese
15 slices white bread (thin-sliced)
60 cooked shrimp, shelled and deveined

Blend butter, cheese and egg yolk until smooth. Beat egg whites until stiff; fold into cheese mixture.

Trim crusts from thinly sliced bread; cut each piece in quarters diagonally. Top each slice with a shrimp and 1 teaspoon of the cheese mixture. Bake in a preheated 350-degree oven on lightly greased cookie sheets for about 15 minutes, or until puffy and golden.

CANAPE PUFFS

Makes about 25 puffs

1/2 cup water
1/4 cup (1/2 stick) butter
1/2 cup flour
2 eggs

Heat water and butter to boiling; reduce heat and stir in flour all at once. Stir about 1 minute until mixture forms ball around spoon. Remove from heat and beat in eggs, one at a time, until mixture is smooth.

Place by rounded teaspoonsful onto ungreased cookie sheets. Bake in a preheated 400-degree oven for about 25 minutes or until golden. Remove and cool on racks.

Slice off tops; remove any doughy insides. Fill with any sandwich filling; chill until serving time.

Blanche Towner

EGG & HAM HORS D'OEUVRES

Makes 20 appetizers

5 hard-cooked eggs
1 teaspoon minced chives
Salt and paprika
1-2 drops hot pepper sauce
Mayonnaise
1/2 pound boiled ham

Separate yolks and whites of eggs. Force yolks through a sieve; add chives, seasonings and mayonnaise to moisten. Beat to a smooth paste. Chop egg whites and ham together and mix with yolks. Form into 1-inch balls and garnish with additional mayonnaise.

Mrs. Agnes Ward, Erie, Penn.

BLUE CHEESE MUSHROOMS

1 pound mushrooms (1-1 1/2 inches in diameter)
1/4 cup green onion slices
2 tablespoons butter or margarine
1 cup (4 ounces) crumbled blue cheese
1 small package (3 ounces) cream cheese, softened

Remove stems from mushrooms; chop stems. Saute stems and green onion in margarine until soft. Combine with cheeses, mixing well. Stuff mixture into mushroom caps. Place on a broiler pan rack and broil for 2-3 minutes or until golden brown. Serve hot.

Mrs. Agnes Ward, Erie, Penn.

SWEET AND SOUR MEATBALLS

1 pound lean ground beef
1 envelope dry onion-soup mix
1 egg
  Combine beef, soup mix and egg and form into tiny meatballs. Brown in skillet; discard all but 1 tablespoon fat.

Sauce:
8-ounce can tomato sauce
16-ounce can whole-berry cranberry sauce

Combine ingredients for sauce with reserved tablespoon of fat from meat in saucepan. Heat; add meatballs. Cover and simmer for about an hour. Serve with toothpicks.

Bonnie La Roche, Bensalem, Penn.

PEPPERONI BALLS

1 package hot roll mix
1/4 pound mozzarella cheese, cut in cubes
1/4-1/2 lb. pepperoni, thinly sliced

Prepare roll mix according to package directions, but *omitting egg* and using *1 cup water*. Dough does *not* need to rise. Place one cheese cube on one pepperoni slice. Pinch off a piece of dough and shape carefully around cheese and pepperoni, forming a ball. Repeat until all ingredients are used.

Fry in deep hot oil for about 5 minutes, or until golden brown, turning once. Drain on paper towels and serve warm.

BLUE CHEESE BITES

Makes 40 appetizers

1 package (10-count) refrigerated biscuits

1/4 cup margarine
3 tablespoons crumbled blue cheese or grated Parmesan cheese

Cut each biscuit into four pieces. Arrange pieces on two greased 8x1 1/2-inch round baking pans. Melt margarine; add cheese and stir to blend. Drizzle cheese mixture over biscuits. Bake in 400-degree oven for 12-15 minutes.

Mrs. Robert T. Shaffer, Middleburg, Penn.

CHICKEN WINGS

1 pound chicken wings
1/4 pound (1 stick) butter
1/4 teaspoon garlic powder
2 tablespoons parsley
1 cup fine, dry bread crumbs
1/2 cup Parmesan cheese
1 teaspoon salt
1/4 teaspoon pepper

Cut off tips from chicken wings and discard; split remaining portion of wing at joint to form two pieces. Melt butter, mixing in garlic powder. Combine bread crumbs, Parmesan cheese and seasonings. Dip chicken wing portions in seasoned butter, then roll in crumbs. Bake on a greased baking sheet (use one with edges) in a preheated 325-degree oven for about 50 minutes.

These can be frozen and baked later.

Nancy Lesky, LaCrosse, Wis.

DEVILED EGGS

4 hard-cooked eggs
1/3 cup grated Parmesan cheese
1 teaspoon prepared mustard
Pepper
Skim milk
Paprika

Halve the eggs lengthwise; remove yolks and mash. Add the cheese, mustard, few grains pepper, and enough milk to moisten well. Beat until fluffy and refill the egg whites. May want to garnish with paprika for added color. (65 calories per egg half)

Shari Crider, Stoughton, Wis.

Beverages
REFRESHING

PACIFIC FRUIT PUNCH

1 large can orange juice
1 large can apriocot nectar
1 large can pineapple juice
1 quart ginger ale
1 cup fresh strawberries
1 quart orange sherbet, soften in refrigerator

Combine juices and ginger ale in punchbowl. Add sherbet, strawberries, and ice. Garnish individual glasses with pineapple spears and small umbrellas.

SPICED TEA MIX
Makes ¾ cup

⅔ cup Tang Orange Flavored Breakfast Beverage Crystals
3 tablespoons instant tea
1 teaspoon nutmeg
1 teaspoon allspice

Combine all ingredients and blend well. Store in tightly covered jar. For 1 serving, combine ½ cup *each*, water and apple juice in saucepan, and bring just to a boil. Pour over 1 well-rounded teaspoon Tea Mix in mug and stir until dissolved. Serve hot or over ice. For 1 quart, combine 2 cups each water and apple juice, and bring just to a boil. Add ⅓ cup mix; stir until dissolved. Serve hot or over ice.

Diane Cole, Cleveland, Ohio

LOW-CAL SPICED TEA MIX
Makes 48 servings

1 cup lemon-flavored instant tea, sweetened with NutraSweet
1 tablespoon Tang, sweetened with NutraSweet
1 tablespoon apple pie spice
1 (1 1/2-ounce) package lemonade drink mix, sweetened with NutraSweet

Combine all ingredients in a bowl and mix well. Store mixture in air-tight container. For each serving, place 1 1/4–1 1/2 teaspoons mix in cup. Add 3/4 cup hot water. Stir well. (3 calories per serving)

Brenda Peery, Tannersville, Va.

HOLIDAY PUNCH
Serves 50

3 cups sugar
3 cups water
4 cups cranberry juice cocktail
3 cups lemon juice
2 cups orange juice
2 cups unsweetened pineapple juice
2 quarts ginger ale

Combine sugar and water in saucepan; stir over heat until sugar dissolves. Bring to boiling point; let boil, without stirring, for about 7 minutes. Cool; add fruit juices. When ready to serve pour over ice; add ginger ale. Garnish with sprigs of mint.

Jennie Lien, Stoughton, Wis.

PINEAPPLE-ORANGE PUNCH
Makes 5 quarts

½ gallon orange sherbet
1 (46-ounce) can pineapple juice, chilled
1 (33½-ounce) bottle ginger ale, chilled
3 cups orange-flavored drink, chilled
3 cups lemon-lime carbonated beverage, chilled

Place sherbet in a large punch bowl; add remaining ingredients and stir well. Chunks of orange sherbet will remain in punch.

Sharon Case, Chicago, Ill.

HOT CHOCO-MALLOW MIX
Makes 6 cups

4 cups dry non-fat dry milk
1 cup dry non-dairy creamer
¾ cup sugar
¾ cup cocoa
1 cup colored, miniature marshmallows

Stir together dry non-fat milk, non-dairy creamer, sugar and cocoa in large bowl. Stir in marshmallows.

Spoon mix into glass jar with tight-fitting lid. Use smaller containers, if desired. Attach instruction label: For each serving combine ¼ cup mix and 6 ounces boiling water in mug. Stir and serve.

Sally Simpson, Detroit, Mich.

EASY PARTY PUNCH

3-ounce package raspberry gelatin
3-ounce package cherry gelatin
3 cups boiling water
5 cups cold water
3 cups pineapple juice
12 ounces frozen orange juice
2 pints pineapple or lemon sherbet

Dissolve gelatins in boiling water; add next 3 ingredients. Stir in one tray ice cubes until melted. Spoon in sherbet. Serve immediately or let stand at room temperature.

Barbara Brittain, San Diego, CA

GOOD LUCK PUNCH
Makes 1 gallon

1 quart fresh rhubarb
Water to cover
3 cups sugar
2 cups water
Juice of 6 lemons
1 cup pineapple juice
1 quart gingerale

Cut rhubarb into 1-inch pieces; cover with water and cook until soft, about 12-15 minutes. Drain through cheesecloth. Should be about 3 quarts of juice. Dissolve sugar in the 2 cups water and cook 10 minutes to make a syrup.

Combine all juices, except ginger ale, pouring over chunk of ice in punch bowl. Just before serving, add ginger ale.

PARTY PINK PUNCH

1 (46-ounce) can pineapple juice
1 large bottle lemon lime pop
1 small can pink lemonade, frozen
1 can water
2 large bottles strawberry pop
Sugar, if desired
Raspberry sherbet

Mix first six ingredients. Drop spoonfuls of sherbet on top before serving. Delicious!

Barbara Brittain, San Diego, Calif.

AUTUMN PUNCH
Makes 7-1/2 quarts

1-1/2 cups honey
3/4 cup lemon juice
6 whole cardamom seeds
3 (3-inch) sticks cinnamon
1 teaspoon whole allspice
2 teaspoons whole cloves
1-1/2 quarts cranberry juice
5 cups apple juice
5 cups apricot nectar
3 quarts ginger ale
Crushed ice

Combine first 6 ingredients in a saucepan; bring to a boil; reduce heat; simmer 10 minutes. Strain and discard spices. Chill. Combine chilled mixture with remaining juices and ginger ale. Serve over ice.

Mrs. Bruce Fowler, Woodruff, S.C.

RHUBARB PUNCH

1 quart diced rhubarb
1 quart water
3/4 - 1 cup sugar
1/4 cup lemon juice

Cook rhubarb in water until very tender. Let drain through cloth-lined colander or strainer. Add sugar; stir to dissolve. Add lemon juice. Chill to serve.

This recipe makes a delicious soft pink punch.

May Ann Kooker, Bluffton, OH

SHERBERT PUNCH

3 (2-liter) bottles 7-Up, chilled
1/2 gallon orange or raspberry
  sherbet

Soften sherbet. Add by large scoops to punch bowl. Pour chilled 7-Up over the sherbet and serve.

Sue Thomas, Casa Grande, Ariz.

SPICY CALIFORNIA PUNCH

4 cups unsweetened grapefruit juice
4 cups orange juice
2 cups honey
1/4 cup lime juice
1 teaspoon allspice
1 teaspoon nutmeg

In a 3-quart container, combine 4 cups each of both grapefruit juice and orange juice, then add honey, lime juice, and spices. Let stand at room temperature for 1 hour to allow flavors to blend. Chill. To serve, pour over ice in a punch bowl or several pitchers.

Agnes Ward, Erie, Pa.

TROPICAL FRUIT SMOOTHIE
Makes 5 cups

1 (15-ounce) can cream of coconut
1 medium banana
1 (8-ounce) can juice packed
  crushed pineapple
1 cup orange– juice
1 tablespoon bottled lemon juice
2 cups ice cubes

In blender, combine all ingredients, except ice; blend well. Gradually add ice; blend until smooth. Serve immediately; refrigerate leftovers.

Peggy Fowler Revels, Woodruff, S.C.

COFFEE COOLER

4 quarts strong coffee, cold
1 cup sugar
2 quarts vanilla ice cream
1 tablespoon vanilla
1 quart whole milk

Combine coffee, milk, and vanilla. Add sugar and stir until dissolved. Chill thoroughly and pour over ice cream that has been spooned into a punch bowl. Serves about 50 small punch cups.

Sue Thomas, Casa Grande, Ariz.

Brunch
BUFFET

BREAKFAST SANDWICH

4 eggs, hard-cooked and finely chopped
4 bacon slices, browned crisp and chopped
1/4 cup mayonnaise
1 cup Swiss cheese, grated
1 teaspoon tarragon
1-1/4 teaspoons mustard
8 slices bread

Mix together all ingredients, except bread. Spread mixture evenly between 8 slices bread, forming 4 sandwiches. Spread melted butter on outside surfaces of top and bottom of sandwiches. Brown on both sides in heavy skillet or on a microwave browner for 30 seconds; flip over and cook 1-1/2 minutes on the second side.

Mildred Sherrer, Bay City, Texas

ALL-TIME FAVORITE PANCAKES

1-1/4 cups flour
2 teaspoons baking powder
1/2 teaspoon soda
1/2 teaspoon salt
1 egg, beaten
1 cup buttermilk
2 tablespoons salad oil

Blend egg, milk, and oil. Measure flour after stirring. Blend dry ingredients together. Add to liquids; beat with rotary beater until all flour is moistened. Grease heated griddle, if necessary, and pour batter from pitcher or tip of large spoon in pools slightly apart. Turn pancakes as soon as they are puffed and full of bubbles, but before bubbles break. Turn and brown on other side. Serve at once with blueberry sauce or syrup.

Suzan Wiener, Spring Hill, Fla.

SAUSAGE SCRAPPLE
Serves 9

This is a shortcut version of a country cooking favorite. Serve fried slices for breakfast, brunch or dinner, plain or with maple syrup or ketchup.

½ pound well-seasoned bulk pork sausage
1½ cups water
⅓ cup yellow cornmeal
⅓ cup water
½ teaspoon salt
¼ teaspoon crumbled sage (optional)

Spray a large saucepan with pan release; add sausage and 1½ cups water. Heat to boiling; stir to crumble sausage; reduce heat; simmer about 20 minutes.

Meanwhile, in a small bowl stir together cornmeal, ⅓ cup water, salt and sage if using; set aside. Line an 8-inch square pan with foil long enough to also cover contents when pulled over.

Drain cooked sausage in a strainer, reserving broth. Spoon grease from broth; return 1 cup stock to saucepan. Vigorously stir in moistened cornmeal; bring to boiling, stirring. Cover; cook over low heat about 10 minutes, stirring occasionally. Stir in sausage; return to boiling. Pour into prepared pan; spread until smooth on top. Refrigerate; when cold cover closely with foil. Freeze, if desired, in meal-size units.

To serve, cut into squares; flour lightly. It can be fried in a skillet glazed with butter, or until crisp in deep fat. Serve hot with maple syrup or ketchup.

Note: Scrapple is usually poured into a loaf pan then sliced to fry. My friend, Anne Beaven, discovered and shared this wonderful timesaving idea of spreading scrapple in a shallow pan—no messy slicing, just cut into squares.

SUNDAY OVEN OMELETTE
Serves 4

2 tablespoons butter
7 eggs
1/4 teaspoon salt
1/3 cup dairy sour cream
1/4 cup milk
3/4 cup diced ham
1/2 cup shredded cheddar cheese

Melt butter in 9x9x2-inch glass baking dish. Whip eggs; add remaining ingredients and whip again. Pour into baking dish. Bake at 350 degrees for 40-45 minutes; test with a knife for doneness.

Angie Biggin, Lyons, Ill.

P.D.Q. COFFEE CAKE

1 compressed yeast cake
2-1/2 cups lukewarm milk
1/2 cup shortening (part butter adds
    flavor)
1/2 cup sugar
1 egg
2 teaspoons salt
5 cups flour
1 stick butter or margarine, melted
Cinnamon and sugar mixture

Crumble yeast cake into a bowl and add milk. Stir until dissolved. In separate bowl combine shortening, sugar, egg, and salt. Combine the two mixtures. Add 1 cup of flour at a time to combined yeast mixture; beat after each addition. Beat dough until smooth and blended. Cover bowl and let rise until double. Punch dough down by giving it a stir with a spoon. Divide dough into 3 layer cake pans. Melt 1 stick of butter or margarine. Drizzle on top of cakes. Sprinkle mixture of sugar and cinnamon over cakes. Let rise again. Bake 20 minutes in a 450-degree oven.

Jane Williams, Columbus, Ohio

APPLE SCHMARREN

¼ cup flour
2 teaspoons sugar
⅜ teaspoon salt
⅔ cup milk
2 eggs
1 medium tart apple,
    peeled and thinly sliced
1½ teaspoons raisins,
    optional
    Cinnamon and confec-
    tioners' sugar
3 tablespoons butter

Combine first 3 ingredients. Whisk in milk and eggs. Peel the apple; slice into batter. Add raisins; fry batter in the butter. I use an 8-inch non-stick fry pan. It should be nicely browned on all sides, so don't stir too often. Serve with cinnamon and confectioners' sugar sprinkled over the top.

Linda Taylor, Gravois Mills, Mo.

PUMPKIN PANCAKES
Makes 16

2 cups biscuit mix
2 tablespoons brown
    sugar
2 teaspoons cinnamon
1 teaspoon allspice
1½ cups milk
½ cup canned pumpkin
2 tablespoons vegetable
    oil
2 eggs
1 teaspoon vanilla extract

Combine biscuit mix, brown sugar, allspice and cinnamon. Add milk, pumpkin, oil, eggs and vanilla. Beat until smooth. Cook on lightly greased and heated griddle. This is a moist and tender pancake!

Vickie Vogt, Kewaskim, Wis.

HAM & EGGS CASSEROLE
Serves 6

3 cups cooked ham, diced
5 hard-cooked eggs, sliced
1 (6-ounce) can button mushrooms,
    drained
1 (10-1/2-ounce) can cream of
    onion soup
1/2 cup milk
1 teaspoon prepared mustard
2 cups Swiss cheese, grated
1 tablespoon Worcestershire sauce
1/2 teaspoon liquid hot sauce
1 cup dry bread crumbs
4 tablespoons butter or margarine,
    melted
2 tablespoons parsley, chopped

Grease a 2-quart casserole. Make alternate layers of ham, eggs, and mushrooms; start and finish with ham. In a saucepan combine soup, milk, and mustard. Add cheese, Worcestershire sauce, and hot sauce; heat until cheese melts, stirring constantly. Pour over layered mixture in casserole. Mix crumbs and butter; sprinkle over top. Bake at 325 degrees for 25 minutes until hot and crumbs are golden; scatter parsley over individual servings.

Gwen Campbell, Sterling, Va.

FRENCH TOAST
Serves 2

1 egg white
1 tablespoon skim milk
1 teaspoon sugar
1 tablespoon butter,
    melted
2 slices bread

Mix all ingredients, except bread. Soak bread in mixture. Cook on lightly oiled griddle over low heat. Turn frequently to brown evenly. Serve with sugar and cinnamon mixed together, maple syrup, honey or jam. (90 calories per slice)

Edna Askins, Greenville, Texas

CINNAMON TOAST COFFEE CAKE
Serves 10-12

2 cups flour
1 cup sugar
2 teaspoons baking powder
1 teaspoon salt
1 cup milk
2 tablespoons melted butter
1 teaspoon vanilla
1/4 teaspoon cinnamon
1/4 teaspoon nutmeg
1/2 cup seedless raisins

Topping:
1/2 cup melted butter
1/2 cup sugar
1-1/2 tablespoons cinnamon

Combine dry ingredients; stir in milk, 2 tablespoons butter, and vanilla until batter is smooth. Add raisins. Spread evenly into well-greased and lightly floured 15x10x1-inch jelly roll pan or sheet cake pan. Bake at 350 degrees for 20-25 minutes until lightly browned. While coffee cake is baking, combine 1/2 cup sugar and cinnamon. Remove cake from oven after 10 minutes of baking; drizzle 1/2 cup melted butter evenly over top of hot cake; sprinkle with sugar-cinnamon topping mixture and return to oven. Bake 10-15 minutes more. Serve warm.

Dee L. Getchell, Old Lyme, Conn.

CHOCOLATE LOVER'S BREAKFAST BREAD

Makes 2 loaves

3 cups flour
3 eggs
2 cups sugar
1 cup oil
1 teaspoon vanilla
1 teaspoon *each* ground cinnamon, baking soda and baking powder
½ cup sour cream
2 cups shredded zucchini
1 cup semisweet chocolate bits

Combine flour, eggs, sugar, oil, vanilla, cinnamon, baking soda, baking powder and sour cream in mixer bowl. Beat at medium speed for 2 minutes, or until well-blended. Stir in zucchini and chocolate bits. Pour batter into 2 well-greased (8 x 4-inch) loaf pans and bake at 350 degrees for 1 hour and 15 minutes.

HEATH BAR COFFEE CAKE

2 cups flour
1/4 cup brown sugar
1/4 pound butter or margarine
6 chilled Heath candy bars
1 egg
1 cup milk
1 teaspoon vanilla
1 teaspoon baking soda
1-1/2 teaspoons salt
1-1/2 cups nuts, chopped

Grease and flour a 9x13-inch pan. Mix together flour, sugar, soda, salt, and butter to the consistency of pie dough (reserve 1 cup for topping).

Beat together egg, vanilla, and milk; add to first mixture. Pour into prepared pan. Break up Heath bars into small pieces, using a rolling pin. Add Heath bars and chopped nuts to reserved cup of first mixture; sprinkle on top of cake. Bake at 350 degrees for 40 minutes.

Agnes Ward, Erie, Pa.

SAUSAGE CORN BREAD APPLE PIE

Serves 8

1 pound pork sausage
1 tablespoon vegetable oil
1 egg, beaten
1 1/2 cups buttermilk
1 3/4 cups corn bread mix
1 can apple pie filling
1/8 teaspoon cinnamon
1 tablespoon sugar

Cook sausage over medium heat until browned; stir to crumble; drain well and set aside. Place oil in a 10-inch cast-iron skillet or heavy 10-inch baking pan. Heat at 400 degrees for 5 minutes, or until hot. Combine egg, buttermilk and corn bread mix in a large mixing bowl; stir until mixture is smooth. Stir in crumbled sausage; pour into skillet. Bake at 400 degrees for 25–30 minutes. Place sugar, cinnamon and pie filling in a small saucepan. Cook over low heat, stirring constantly, until heated. Spread over corn bread. Serve hot. This is a good brunch main dish or for breakfast.

Leota Baxter, Ingalls, Kan.

CHOCOLATE CHIP STREUSEL COFFEE CAKE

Streusel:
1/2 cup brown sugar
1/2 cup flour
1/4 cup margarine
1/4 cup chopped walnuts
1 cup chocolate chips

Cake:
1 (8-ounce) package cream cheese
1-1/2 cups sugar
3/4 cups margarine
3 eggs
3/4 teaspoon vanilla
2-1/2 cups flour
1-1/2 teaspoons baking powder
3/4 teaspoon baking soda
1/4 teaspoon salt
3/4 cup milk

For streusel, combine brown sugar and flour. Cut in margarine until mixture resembles coarse crumbs. Stir in walnuts and chocolate chips. Set aside. Grease and flour a 13x9x2-inch pan. Combine cream cheese, sugar, and margarine, mixing at medium speed until well-blended. Blend in eggs and vanilla. Add combined dry ingredients alternately with milk, mixing well after each addition. Spoon batter into prepared pan. Sprinkle with crumb mixture. Bake at 350 degrees for 40 minutes. Cool.

Great for large crowds! If you like cheese filling, you'll love it!

Mrs. George Franks, Millerton, Pa.

NO-FRY DOUGHNUTS

Makes 1½–2 dozen

2 packages yeast
1½ cups lukewarm milk (scalded then cooled)
½ cup sugar
1 teaspoon nutmeg
2 eggs
4½ cups flour
¼ cup warm water
1 teaspoon salt
¼ teaspoon cinnamon
⅓ cup shortening
¼ cup margarine, melted
Cinnamon and sugar

In large mixer bowl, dissolve yeast in warm water. Add milk, sugar, salt, spices, eggs, shortening and 2 cups flour. Blend ½ minute on top speed, scraping bowl occasionally. Stir in remaining flour, until smooth, scraping sides of bowl. Cover. Let rise in warm place until double, 50–60 minutes. Turn dough onto well-floured, cloth-covered board; roll around lightly to coat with flour (dough will be soft to handle). Roll dough to about ½-inch thickness. Cut with a 2½-inch doughnut cutter. Place 2 inches apart on baking sheet; brush doughnuts with melted margarine. Cover; let rise until double, about 20 minutes. Heat oven to 425 degrees. Bake 8–10 minutes, or until golden brown. Immediately brush with melted margarine and shake in sugar and cinnamon or use doughnut glaze.

Sharon Crider, Evansville, Wis.

BREAKFAST EGG DISH

Serves 6

8 slices bread
1/2 cup melted butter
1 cup grated Cheddar cheese
Bacon or ham bits
Chopped green pepper
Sliced mushrooms, optional
2 cups milk
1/4 teaspoon salt
1/8 teaspoon pepper

Cut crust off the slices of bread and cube bread. Put in a 9x13 inch buttered pan. Pour the melted butter over the bread cubes; sprinkle on bacon bits, green pepper, and mushrooms.

Separate the eggs. Beat the yolks with the milk, salt, and pepper; pour over ingredients in the pan. Beat egg whites until stiff. Seal above mixture with egg whites. Cover and keep in the refrigerator overnight.

Bake at 325 degrees for 40-45 minutes.

EGG 'N' CHIPS

Serves 6

6 hard-boiled eggs, chopped
2 tablespoons chopped green pepper
1/2 teaspoon salt
2/3 cup mayonnaise or salad dressing
1-1/2 cups diced celery
3/4 cup coarsely chopped walnuts
1 teaspoon minced onion
1/4 teaspoon pepper
1 cup grated Cheddar cheese
1 cup crushed potato chips

Combine eggs, celery, walnuts, green pepper, onion, salt, pepper and salad dressing or mayonnaise. Toss lightly, but thoroughly, so ingredients are evenly moistened. Use additional salad dressing if needed. Place in a greased 1-1/2 - quart baking dish. Sprinkle with cheese and top with crushed chips. Bake at 375 degrees for about 25 minutes or until thoroughly heated and cheese has melted.

Shirley Anne Crist, Marion, IN

FOOLPROOF SCRAMBLED EGGS

Serves 3-4

6 eggs
1/3 cup light cream
3/4 teaspoon salt
1/8 teaspoon pepper
1/2 teaspoon Worcestershire sauce

Beat eggs; beat in cream and seasonings. Cook in upper part of double boiler, over hot water, until just set, stirring often. Serve at once with toast.

Agnes Ward, Erie, PA

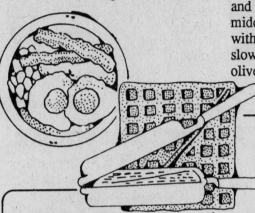

SCRAMBLED BAGEL ROYALE

Serves 2

2 bagels
1-1/2 tablespoons butter
    or margarine
4 eggs
2 tablespoons milk
3 tablespoons chopped onion
1/4 cup lox pieces or smoked salmon
2 ounces cream cheese
2 slices tomato garnish

Slice bagels in half horizontally. Lightly spread with one tablespoon of butter or margarine; toast lightly. Over medium high heat, saute chopped onion in remaining half tablespoon of butter or margarine until translucent. Beat eggs with milk; add to onions. Stir eggs. When eggs are almost set, add lox pieces and cream cheese that has been cut into small chunks; scramble in pan until cheese begins to melt.

Spoon mixture over bagels. Garnish with tomato slices.

TOLEDO HAM AND EGGS

Serves 6

1 cup chopped, cooked ham
1 tablespoon olive oil
2 cups cooked peas
2 canned pimentos, chopped
1/4 cup chopped green olives
Salt and pepper, if desired
6 eggs
2 tablespoons olive oil

Saute ham in olive oil for 2-3 minutes. Combine with peas, pimento, and olives. Heat well; add salt and pepper if desired. Put in the middle of a hot platter and surround with the eggs, which have been slowly cooked in the 2 tablespoons of olive oil.

Agnes Ward, Erie, PA

TUNA STUFFED EGGS

Makes 24 halves

12 eggs
6 slices bacon
1 - 3-1/4 to 3-1/2 - ounce can tuna,
    drained and finely flaked
3/4 cup mayonnaise
1 tablespoon lemon juice
1/2 teaspoon hot pepper sauce
1/2 teaspoon salt

In 4-quart saucepan, place eggs and enough water to come one inch above tops of eggs over high heat; heat to boiling. Remove saucepan from heat; cover tightly and let eggs stand in hot water 15 minutes; drain.

Meanwhile, in 10-inch skillet, cook bacon until browned, remove to paper towel to drain. Crumble bacon, set aside.

Peel and slice eggs lengthwise in half. Remove yolks and place in medium bowl. With fork, finely mash yolks. Stir in tuna, mayonnaise, lemon juice, hot pepper sauce and salt until smooth. Pile egg yolk mixture into egg whites center. Sprinkle with bacon. Cover and refrigerate.

Dorothy K. Garms, Anaheim, CA

Casseroles

CREATIVE

RANCHO SAUSAGE SUPPER
Serves 6

1 pound pork sausage
1 cup chopped onions
1 green pepper, chopped
2 cups stewed tomatoes
2 cups dairy sour cream
1 cup uncooked elbow macaroni
1 teaspoon chili powder
1 teaspoon salt
1 tablespoon sugar

In a large skillet fry sausage until pink color disappears. Drain. Add onions and green pepper; cook slowly for 5 minutes. Stir in tomatoes, sour cream, macaroni, chili powder, salt and sugar. Cover. Simmer 30 minutes, stirring frequently, until macaroni is done. Serve hot.

Serve with a green salad and hard rolls.

Betty M. Burt, Winnemucca, Nev.

BEEF-ONION RING CASSEROLE
Serves 4–6

1-1/2–2 pounds ground chuck
Salt and pepper
1 can condensed cheddar cheese soup
1 can condensed cream of mushroom soup
1 package frozen Tater Tots
1 package frozen onion rings

Press raw meat into bottom of casserole; season with salt and pep-per. Combine the 2 soups and spread half over meat. Add Tater Tots. Pour rest of soup over Tater Tots. Top with onion rings. If canned onion rings are used, stir them into last half of soup mixture. Bake at 350 degrees for 1–1-1/2 hours.

Leota Baxter, Ingalls, Kan.

JIFFY MINESTRONE
Serves 8

4 cups coarsely chopped cabbage (½ medium-size head)
1 medium onion, coarsely chopped
¼ cup parsley, chopped
1 clove garlic, chopped
1 teaspoon salt
1 teaspoon oregano
¼ teaspoon pepper
3 tablespoons oil
5 cups beef broth
1 (16-ounce) can tomatoes *or* 2 cups chopped fresh
¼ pound spaghetti, broken up
1 medium zucchini, sliced
1 (16-ounce) can red kidney beans

In Dutch oven, over medium heat, sauté cabbage, onion, parsley, garlic ,salt, oregano and pepper in oil, stirring often, 5 minutes, or until cabbage is crisp-tender. Add broth and tomatoes; bring to boil. Stir in spaghetti, zucchini and beans. Cook, stirring occasionally, for 10 minutes, or until spaghetti is of desired doneness. (200 calories per serving)

Nadia Boreiko, Dearborn, Mich.

ZUCCHINI AND CHICKEN SKILLET

2 medium zucchini, sliced
2 tablespoons shortening
½ cup tomatoes, drained
2 pounds chicken
1 can cream of celery soup
1 teaspoon paprika
1 teaspoon basil
Salt and pepper to taste

In skillet brown chicken in shortening. Pour off excess fat. Add soup, tomatoes and seasonings. Cover. Cook on low heat for 30 minutes. Add zucchini. Cook about 15 minutes longer.

Sheila Symonowicz, Loganville, Pa.

SMOKED SAUSAGE AND SAUERKRAUT
Serves 4

1 pound smoked sausage
1 can sauerkraut
1 tablespoon cooking oil
1/2 pint water
1 potato, grated
1 carrot, grated
Pinch salt
1/3 cup sugar
2 onions, chopped

Heat oil in skillet and fry chopped onions; add sauerkraut and simmer for 2 minutes. Add water and sausage; cook until done. Add grated potato, salt, sugar, and grated carrot. Cook 4-5 additional minutes.

Lucy Dowd, Sequim, Wash.

CHEESY SPAGHETTI

1 (12-ounce) package thin spaghetti
1/4 pound bacon, cut in small pieces
1 large onion, chopped
1 pound ground beef
2 cups (2 8-ounce cans) tomato sauce
1 (4-ounce) can sliced mushrooms, drained
1 teaspoon salt
1/2 teaspoon Italian seasoning
1/2 teaspoon garlic salt
1/8 teaspoon pepper
1 cup (4 ounces) shredded cheese
1/2 cup shredded Provolone cheese

Cook spaghetti; drain. Fry bacon slowly until browned. Drain off grease. Add onion and beef; cook until meat is brown; mix in tomato sauce and seasonings. Simmer 15 minutes. In large bowl, combine sauce and spaghetti. Place half of mixture in a buttered 2 quart casserole. Top with half of the Cheddar and half of the Provolone cheese. Repeat layers. Bake in pre-heated 375 degree oven for 20-25 minutes.

Betty L. Perkins, Hot Springs, AR

PORK CHOP CASSEROLE

6 pork chops
1 cup uncooked brown rice
6 slices onion
6 tomato slices
6 green pepper rings
1 teaspoon salt
1/8 teaspoon pepper
2 cups tomato juice

Spray 12-inch skillet with vegetable cooking spray. Brown pork chops on each side. Transfer to plate.
Place rice over bottom of skillet. Arrange chops on top. Stack slices of onion, tomato, and green pepper on top of each chop. Sprinkle with salt and pepper. Pour tomato juice over chops. Cover; simmer 45 minutes or until chops are tender.

Ella Evanicky, Fayetteville, TX

BACON AND RICE CREOLE

1 pound bacon
1 green pepper, diced
3 small onions, chopped
2-1/2 teaspoons salt
1/8 teaspoon pepper
2 cups canned tomatoes
1 cup raw rice (not quick-cooking)

Simmer vegetables and spices in a sauce pan. At the same time, fry the bacon. When bacon is done, remove from pan and crumble into small pieces. Drain off all but 3 tablespoons of fat, to which add the raw rice. Let rice brown lightly. Add the vegetables and bacon; let simmer over very low heat for 30 minutes. Check after 20 minutes to see if it is drying out, if so, add more tomatoes, or some water, or a combination of both.

Linda Taylor, New Lenox, IL

FIESTA CORN CASSEROLE
Serves 4-6

3 tablespoons butter
3 cups corn flakes
1 pound lean ground beef
3/4 teaspoon seasoned salt
1 (8-ounce) can tomato sauce
1 (1-1/4 ounce) package Lawry's Taco Seasoning Mix
1 (17-ounce) can whole kernel corn, drained (save 1/4 cup liquid)
2 cups grated Cheddar cheese.

Combine butter and 2 cups corn flakes in bottom of a shallow 1-1/2 quart baking dish. Crush remaining corn flakes; set aside. In skillet, brown beef until crumbly; drain. Add seasoned salt, tomato sauce, taco seasoning mix, and reserved liquid from corn; mix well. Layer 1/2 each; corn, meat mixture, and cheese over buttered corn flakes in baking dish; repeat layers. Sprinkle crushed corn flakes over top in diagonal strips.

Agnes Ward, Erie, PA

CHICKEN ALMOND CASSEROLE

5 cups diced, cooked chicken breasts
2 cups diced celery
3 cups cooked rice
1 (8-ounce) can sliced water chestnuts
2 cans cream of chicken soup
1/2 cup sour cream
1/2 cup mayonnaise
2 tablespoons chopped onion
2 tablespoons lemon juice
1 tablespoon salt
3/4 teaspoon white pepper
1 cup sliced almonds

Mix above ingredients and put into buttered 9x13 inch baking dish.

Topping:
1/2 cup sliced almonds
3 cups crumbled corn flakes
2/3 cup butter

Mix above ingredients and sprinkle on top of casserole. Bake at 350 degrees for 35-45 minutes. Can be prepared ahead and refrigerated until baking.

Sharon Sisson, Longview, Was

GERMAN SUPPER
Serves 4-5

5-6 potatoes, scrubbed (not peeled)
1/4 cup chopped onion
1/4 teaspoon garlic powder
1/2 teaspoon salt
1/3 teaspoon pepper
3 cups cubed beef Hillshire Farms sausage or Eckrich smoked sausage
1 (7-ounce) can sauerkraut

Cut potatoes into thumb-size pieces. Add onion, garlic powder, salt, and pepper. Brown in a small amount of oil for 25 minutes until tender. Add sausage; heat; stir occasionally. Drain kraut and spread on top surface. Do not stir. Cover and heat.

Ann Sterzer, Lynch, Neb.

FRESH CORN CASSEROLE

Preheat oven to 350 degrees. Generously butter a 2-quart rectangular baking dish. In blender puree:

1 cup corn (fresh or frozen, thawed)
1/2 cup butter, softened
2 eggs

Pour into bowl; blend in:

1 cup corn
4-ounce can green chilies; drained, seeded, and chopped
1 cup sour cream
1 cup diced Monterey Jack cheese
1/2 cup cornmeal
1-1/2 teaspoons salt

Spread above ingredients in baking dish. Bake 50 - 60 minutes. Serve with sliced tomatoes. This is delicious and very light!

Patricia Staley, Westmont, IL

STUFFED SHELLS

Serves 8-10

1 (12-ounce) package jumbo shells for stuffing
2 tablespoons butter
1 clove garlic, crushed
1/2 cup finely-chopped onion
2 beaten eggs
2 pounds Ricotta cheese
1/2 cup Parmesan and Romano cheese, mixed
1/3 cup parsley flakes
1/8 teaspoon nutmeg
1 cup shredded Mozzarella cheese (4 ounces)
2-3 pounds Italian meat sauce
1/2 cup Parmesan and Romano, mixed for topping

Preheat oven to 350 degrees. Cook shells according to package directions. Rinse with cold water; drain. Melt butter; sauté garlic and onion until soft. Mix together onion, garlic, eggs, ricotta, Parmesan, Romano, parsley, and nutmeg. Stir in Mozzarella, stuff shells with filling. (At this point, the shells may be frozen for future use).

Cover the bottoms of two 13x9x2-inch baking dishes with meat sauce.

Place shells on top of sauce and sprinkle with Parmesan and Romano. Bake, covered with foil, at 350 degrees for 30-40 minutes or until hot and bubbly.

This is a dish that is easy to prepare; and receives many compliments at potluck dinners.
Betty Perkins, Hot Springs, Ark.

DEVILED HAM AND RICE CASSEROLE

Serves 6

1 medium onion, chopped
1/2 medium green pepper, chopped
1/2 cup finely diced celery
2 tablespoons butter or margarine
1 cup raw rice
2 chicken bouillon cubes
2 (4-1/2 ounce) cans deviled ham
3 cups boiling water
Chopped parsley

Sauté first 3 ingredients in butter for 2-3 minutes. Place mixture in 1-1/2 quart casserole with remaining ingredients, except parsley. Mix with fork. Cover and bake for 45 minutes in pre-heated moderate oven at 350 degrees, stirring twice at 15-minute intervals, or until rice is tender. Sprinkle with parsley.

Mrs. Robert Shaffer, Middleburg, PA

ANOTHER HAMBURGER CASSEROLE

1 pound hamburger
1 green pepper, chopped
1 (8-ounce) package of 1/4 inch noodles, cooked
1 can cream of mushroom soup
1 can evaporated milk

Fry hamburger with green pepper, then blend in soup and milk. Combine with cooked noodles and bake 45-60 minutes at 350 degrees. Do not alter any of these ingredients. It takes this combination for the special flavor.

Linda Taylor, New Lenox, IL

CHICKEN LIVER CASSEROLE

Serves 5-6

2 (10-ounce) packages frozen French-style green beans
4 slices bacon, diced
1 pound chicken livers, cut in half
1/2 teaspoon seasoning salt
2 tablespoons sherry
1 (10-ounce) can cream of mushroom soup
1/2 cup sour cream
3/4 cup crushed barbecue potato chips

Cook green beans according to directions. Drain and spread in greased 9x6 or 8x8 inch baking dish. Sauté bacon until crisp; scatter over beans. Stir-fry chicken livers in bacon fat until pinkness disappears. Add next 4 ingredients, as soon as heated; pour over bacon. Top with potato chips. Bake at 375 degrees for 15 minutes, or until bubbly.

This is a very tasty dish and easy to make!

Lillian Smith, Montreal, Que., Canada

ZUCCHINI CASSEROLE

Serves 12

2 cups bread crumbs
1/4 cup butter or margarine, melted
1/4 teaspoon Italian seasonings
1/4 cup Parmesan cheese
2 pounds zucchini; sliced, parboiled, and drained
1 medium carrot, shredded
10-1/2-ounce can cream of chicken soup
1 cup sour cream
1/4 cup chopped green onion

Combine crumbs, butter, seasonings, and cheese; spread half in bottom of 13 x 9 x 2-inch pan. Combine zucchini and carrot; spread over crumbs. Mix soup, sour cream, and onion; pour over vegetables. Top with remaining crumbs. Bake at 350 degrees for 1 hour.

Lisa Varner, Baton Rouge, LA

HAM, POTATO, AND ONION CASSEROLE

Serves 8-10

6 tablespoons ham drippings or butter
6 tablespoons enriched flour
3 cups milk
2 teaspoons salt
1/4 teaspoon pepper
1/4 pound Cheddar cheese, grated
1 pound diced cooked ham
4 cups cubed cooked potatoes
12 small cooked onions
1/2 cup buttered bread crumbs

Melt drippings or butter. Blend in flour and add milk, stirring constantly. Cook mixture until thickened, boiling about 3 minutes. Add seasonings and grated cheese. Cook slowly until cheese melts. Add cooked ham, potatoes, and onions. Pour mixture into a greased casserole. Sprinkle with buttered bread crumbs. Bake, uncovered, in a 350 degree oven for 30-40 minutes or until crumbs are lightly browned.

Ruby Walsh, West Chicago, Ill.

VEGETABLE CASSEROLE

1 can whole kernel corn, drained
1 can French green beans, drained
1 cup finely chopped celery
1 cup finely chopped onion
1/2 cup green pepper, finely chopped
4 cups grated sharp cheese
1 container sour cream
1 can cream of celery soup

Mix well and pour into a very large casserole.

Topping:
3/4 box Cheese-It crackers, crumbled into 3/4 stick melted margarine. You may add a can of slivered almonds. Bake at 350 degrees for 45 minutes. This makes a large amount. Great for a covered-dish supper!!

Peggy Fowler, Woodruff, SC

CHICKEN-PASTA HOT DISH

Serves 6-8

1/2 pound elbow or spiral pasta (2 cups uncooked)
1/4 cup butter or margarine
1/4 cup finely chopped onion
3 tablespoons all-purpose flour
1-1/2 teaspoons salt
1/8 teaspoon pepper
3 cups milk
3 cups shredded cheddar cheese
2 cups diced cooked chicken or turkey
1 (9-ounce) package frozen Italian-cut green beans, thawed and drained
1 (2-ounce) jar diced pimiento, drained
3 tablespoons cornflake crumbs

Cook pasta according to package directions; drain. In large saucepan, melt butter; add onion and cook until tender. Stir in flour, salt, and pepper. Blend in milk. Cook, stirring constantly, until thickened and bubbly. Add cheese; stir until melted. Combine pasta, cheese sauce, chicken, green beans, and pimiento; mix well. Pour into a 3-quart casserole. Top with cornflake crumbs. Bake in a 350-degree oven until hot, about 30 minutes. Refrigerate leftovers.

** National Pasta Association

ONE-POT TUNA PASTA

Serves 4

3-1/2 cups water
4 chicken bouillon cubes
1/8 teaspoon pepper
1 teaspoon basil leaves
2 cups (8 ounces) elbow pasta or spiral pasta
1 (4-ounce) jar pimiento
1 (9-ounce) package frozen cut green beans
2 cups milk
1 cup (4 ounces) process American cheese
1 (7-ounce) can tuna, drained and broken into chunks

1/4 cup chopped parsley

Bring water, bouillon cubes, pepper and basil leaves to a boil in a 4-quart pot. Gradually add uncooked pasta so that water continues to boil. Cover and simmer for 7 minutes, stirring occasionally.

Meanwhile, dice pimiento. Stir diced pimiento, beans, and milk into pot; cover and simmer 6 to 8 minutes longer or until pasta and beans are tender. Stir in cheese, tuna, and parsley until cheese is melted. Serve from pot or turn into serving dish. Serve immediately.

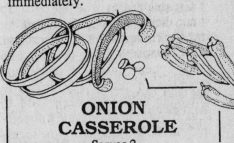

ONION CASSEROLE

Serves 2

2 large or 3 medium onions
1/4 teaspoon salt
Dash of pepper
2 or 3 tablespoons whipping cream (see directions)
1/3 cup buttered bread crumbs
Garlic powder (optional)

Grease or spray with pan release a small baking dish, about 2-cup capacity.

Peel onions; cut in half lengthwise; place cut-side down on board; cut in 1/4-inch slices. Use your hands to separate layers. Drop into saucepan of cold salted water. Bring to boil over high heat; boil until onions are transparent but barely fork tender, about 3 minutes. Drain thoroughly. (If doing ahead, set aside.) Return to pan. Sprinkle on salt and pepper. Add 2 tablespoons cream; toss to mix; if onions seem dry, add another tablespoon cream (this depends on how well drained onions were). Spread evenly in prepared dish. Top with crumbs; sprinkle crumbs lightly with garlic powder, if desired.

Bake at 325 or 350 degrees (depending on what else may be cooking in the oven) until heated through and crumbs are golden. 20 to 25 minutes.

WINTER SQUASH CASSEROLE
Serves 2

1 cup mashed squash, thawed if frozen
1 or 2 slices bacon (use two if you can afford the calories)
1/4 cup chopped onion
1/3 cup grated Cheddar cheese
1/4 teaspoon salt
Dash Tabasco or use black pepper
1/4 cup buttered bread crumbs

Grease or spray with pan release a small baking dish, one quart or smaller. Put squash into medium bowl. Fry bacon until crisp; crumble into squash. Leave about 1 tablespoon drippings in skillet. Fry onions in drippings until transparent; add to squash. Add cheese (I grate it directly into the bowl, estimating the measure). Add salt and Tabasco or pepper; mix well. Transfer to prepared baking dish; top with bread crumbs.

Bake at 325 or 350 degrees (depending on what else may be cooking in the oven) until heated through and crumbs begin to brown, 25 to 30 minutes.

TAGLIARINA

1 pound hamburger
1 onion, chopped
2 tablespoons butter
1 (8-ounce) can tomato sauce
1-1/2 cups water
2 cups uncooked noodles
1 (1-cup) can corn
1 large jar whole mushrooms
1 (No. 2) can pitted ripe olives
1 cup Parmesan cheese
Salt to taste

Mince and brown onion in butter in large skillet. Add meat and brown. Add tomato sauce, water and noodles; stir until noodles are tender. Add more water, if needed. Add salt and rest of ingredients. Pour into 11x11x2-inch glass baking dish and sprinkle with Parmesan cheese. Bake 45 minutes in 350 degree oven. Let stand in oven with door open for 15 minutes before serving.

MOCK OYSTER CASSEROLE

1 medium eggplant
1 stick margarine
1-1/2 cups Ritz cracker crumbs
1 egg, beaten
1 (6-1/2 ounce) can minced clams, drained (reserve liquid)
Salt, pepper, Tabasco sauce to taste

Peel eggplant; cut into 1-inch cubes and parboil 3 minutes. Drain well; set aside. Melt margarine and add Ritz crackers; mix well. Reserve 1/3 cup cracker crumb mixture for topping.

Gently mix beaten eggs, drained clams, and eggplant. Add crumbs, salt, pepper, and Tabasco sauce. Then add enough clam liquid to make quite moist, but not soupy. Pour into buttered casserole. Top with remaining crumbs and bake at 350 degrees for 45 minutes.

Rebecca Preston, Weare, N.H.

LUNCHMEAT AND NOODLE CASSEROLE

1/4 cup margarine
1/4 cup all-purpose flour
1/2 teaspoon salt
Dash of pepper
2-1/2 cups milk
1 can lunch meat, cubed
2 cups cooked noodles
1 teaspoon mustard
3/4 cup bread crumbs
2 tablespoons melted margarine
1 (16-ounce) can peas and carrots

Preheat oven to 375 degrees. Melt margarine in a skillet. Blend in flour, salt, pepper, and gradually stir in milk. Cook over medium heat, stirring constantly, until mixture is smooth and thick.

Add meat, noodles, mustard, and peas and carrots. Mix well. Spoon into a greased 1-1/2 quart casserole. Combine crumbs and melted butter; sprinkle over noodles. Bake 25 minutes.

Alpha Wilson, Roswell, N.M.

CORNED BEEF SCALLOP CASSEROLE

1 (3-ounce) package potato soup mix
1-1/2 cups milk
1 cup water
1 cup American cheese, grated
1/2 teaspoon Worcestershire sauce
1 (12-ounce) can corned beef, shredded
3/4 cup carrots, sliced and cooked
1/2 cup celery, sliced and cooked
1/4 cup green peas, cooked
2 tablespoons pimiento, chopped
1 teaspoon parsley, chopped
3/4 cup soft bread crumbs

Empty potato soup mix into saucepan; add milk and water; stir constantly until blended. Cook until mixture comes to a boil; remove from heat. Add cheese and Worcestershire sauce; mix well. Stir in corned beef shreds, carrots, celery, green peas, and pimiento. Turn into a well-greased 1-1/2 quart ovenproof casserole. Sprinkle parsley over the top, then bread crumbs; cover. Bake 350 degrees for 20 minutes; uncover; bake 12 minutes longer until top is golden.

Gwen Campbell, Sterling, Va.

MAIN DISH NOODLES
Serves 2

2-1/2 cups uncooked medium noodles
2 tablespoons butter or margarine
2 tablespoons half-and-half or cream
2 tablespoons Parmesan cheese
1 (6-ounce) can boneless salmon or tuna

Cook noodles in boiling, salted water according to directions on package.

Meanwhile, in a medium saucepan, melt butter. Stir in half-and-half and cheese; leave over low heat. Drain fish; break into lumps; add to butter mixture. Drain cooked noodles; immediately add to saucepan; toss to mix. Serve with additional Parmesan cheese.

LADIES' LUNCHEON LAYERED DISH

1 cup crushed potato chips
4 hard-cooked eggs, sliced
1 onion, sliced thin and separated into rings
1/3 cup parsley, chopped
1 (10-1/2-ounce) can cream of mushroom soup
1/4 cup sour cream
3/4 cup milk
1/2 teaspoon paprika

Spread 1/3 of potato chips in bottom of a greased 1-1/2 quart ovenproof baking dish. Cover with 1/3 of the egg slices, 1/3 of the onion rings and chopped parsley. Repeat layers until potato chips, egg slices and onion rings are all used. Combine soup with sour cream, milk, and paprika; mix well; pour over all; cover. Bake 350 degrees for 30 minutes; uncover, bake 10 minutes longer until hot, bubbly, and golden.

Gwen Campbell, Sterling, Va.

BAKED RICE WITH HERBS
Serves 4-6

2 tablespoons butter
1 green onion, minced
1/4 cup parsley, chopped fine
1/4 teaspoon thyme
1/4 teaspoon sage
Salt and pepper to taste
1 cup brown rice
2-1/2 cups water
1/2 teaspoon garlic powder

Preheat oven to 350 degrees. Place butter in ovenproof baking dish with lid. Heat butter and sauté green onion until golden. Add parsley, thyme, and sage. Sprinkle with salt and pepper; add rice. Pour 2-1/2 cups water over rice and then stir in garlic powder. Bring to a boil for about 45 minutes or until liquid is absorbed and rice is tender.

This rice goes well with turkey, goose, or duck.

Suzan L. Wiener, Spring Hill, Fla.

LASAGNA SURPRISE
Serves 6-8

3/4 cup chopped onion
2 cloves garlic, finely chopped
2 tablespoons vegetable oil
2 (26-ounce) jars prepared spaghetti/pasta sauce or prepare about 2 quarts of your own tomato-based spaghetti/lasagna sauce recipe (add ground meat or sausage, if desired)
1 (15- or 16-ounce) container ricotta or cottage cheese
1 (10-ounce) package frozen chopped spinach, thawed and well-drained
1 pound mozzarella cheese, shredded
1/2 cup grated Parmesan cheese
2 eggs
1 (1-pound) package lasagna noodles, cooked according to package directions

In a large pan, cook onion and garlic in oil. Add prepared pasta sauce. (If you cook your own sauce, it may not be necessary to add more onion and garlic.) Simmer 15 minutes. In bowl, mix ricotta, spinach, and *1 cup* mozzarella, all the Parmesan, and eggs. In 15x9-inch baking dish (or smaller dishes as needed), layer *2 cups* sauce, half the lasagna, half the remaining sauce, all the spinach mixture, half the mozzarella, remaining lasagna and sauce. Cover; bake at 350 degrees for 45 minutes or until hot. Uncover; top with remaining mozzarella. Bake 15 minutes. Let stand 15 minutes before serving.

PORK PAGODA

1 cup diced cooked pork
1/2 cup sliced celery
1 cup cooked bean sprouts
1/2 cup sliced mushrooms
1/2 cup sliced carrots
1/4 cup sliced green onions
2 tablespoons oil

1 (10-ounce) can condensed cream of asparagas soup
1/4 cup water
2 teaspoons soy sauce
1 (10-ounce) box frozen chopped spinach, thawed and squeezed dry.

In large skillet, sauté pork and all the vegetables in oil until meat is brown and vegetables are tender. Blend in soup, water, soy sauce, and spinach. Heat, stirring occasionally. Serve hot over chow mein noodles. I have substituted beef for the pork and any other creamed soup, also.

Mrs. Laura Hicks, Troy, Mont.

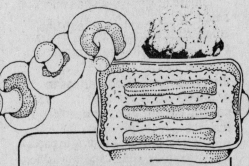

CROWD PLEASER CASSEROLE
Serves 10-12

1 (20-ounce) package frozen broccoli flowerets
1 (20-ounce) package frozen cauliflower flowerets
4 tablespoons butter or margarine
3 tablespoons flour
3 cups milk
6 ounces (or 1-1/2 cups) shredded cheddar cheese
1 cup Parmesan cheese, shredded or grated
1/2 teaspoon salt
3 cups chopped ham
3 cups fresh bread crumbs tossed with 4 tablespoons butter

Cook broccoli and cauliflower in slightly salted water. Cook slightly underdone. Drain; set aside. Melt 4 tablespoons butter in a 1-quart saucepan; add flour; blend well. Add milk, stirring constantly, until thickened. Add cheddar, Parmesan, and salt. Stir over low heat until cheese melts. Place vegetables in an ungreased 4-quart casserole. Sprinkle with chopped ham. Pour cheese sauce mixture over ham. Make a border of buttered bread crumbs around edge of casserole. Bake uncovered at 350 degrees for 30 minutes.

PASTA PRIMAVERA
Makes 4-6 servings

8 ounces uncooked spaghetti
1 cup tender green beans, cut in
   1-inch pieces
2 small zucchini, sliced
2 small yellow squash, sliced
1 cup thinly sliced carrot
1 cup cauliflower flowerets
1 tablespoon olive oil
2 garlic cloves, minced
1/8 teaspoon crushed red pepper
   flakes
1/4 cup chicken broth
1/4 cup lightly packed fresh basil
   leaves, chopped
1/4 cup oil-packed, sun-dried
   tomatoes
3 tablespoons grated Parmesan
   cheese
1/4 cup chopped fresh parsley

Cook spaghetti according to package directions, drain and set aside. Steam vegetables only until crisp-tender, drain and chill. Sauté garlic in olive oil until light brown. Add crushed red pepper, stir; then add chicken broth and simmer 1 minute. Add chopped basil, spaghetti and vegetables; toss. Arrange on platter. Garnish with sun-dried tomatoes, Parmesan cheese and parsley. Serve at room temperature.
***Recipe provided by the courtesy of the National Pasta Association

BAKED MACARONI AND CHEESE WITH SOUR CREAM
Serves 2

3/4 cup macaroni, uncooked
1/3 cup sour cream
1 cup grated sharp Cheddar cheese
1/3 cup milk
Paprika

Preheat oven to 325 degrees. Cook macaroni in boiling, salted water according to package directions until barely tender. Drain well. Return to saucepan. Add sour cream, cheese, and milk; mix well. Turn into a small greased baking dish; sprinkle on paprika. Bake at 325 degrees for about 25 minutes.

HARVEST SWEET POTATO CASSEROLE
Serves 6

1 (23-ounce) can sweet potatoes or
   yams, drained, *or*
1 (18-ounce) can vacuum-packed
   sweet potatoes
7 tablespoons butter, melted
1 apple, cored and thinly sliced

Topping:
1/4 cup firmly packed brown sugar
1 tablespoon all-purpose flour
1/4 teaspoon cardamom
1 tablespoon cold butter
2 tablespoons chopped pecans

Preheat oven to 350 degrees. In 1-quart round casserole, mash sweet potatoes until smooth. Stir in the 7 tablespoons melted butter. In small bowl cut 1 tablespoon cold butter into brown sugar, flour, and cardamom. Stir in pecans and sprinkle one-half of the mixture over potatoes. Arrange apple slices on top. Sprinkle with remaining mixture. Bake for 35-40 minutes or until apples are crisp/tender.

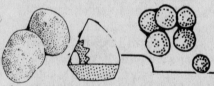

POTATO AND HAM CASSEROLE
Serves 6-8

1 (5-1/2 ounce) package au gratin
   potatoes
2-1/2 cups diced cooked ham
1 cup canned or frozen peas
1 small onion, chopped
1 small green pepper, chopped
1/3 cup chopped celery
1 cup shredded Cheddar cheese

Preheat oven to 400 degrees. Mix potatoes as directed on package in a 2-quart ovenproof dish. Mix together ham, peas, onion, green pepper, celery, and add to casserole. Sprinkle cheese on top.

Bake 30 minutes and serve hot. This is a great dish for working women who have to cook "hurry-up" dinners.
Mrs. H. W. Walker, Richmond, Va.

REUBEN CASSEROLE

1 can corned beef—or 1 pound deli
1/2 cup thousand island dressing
1 can sauerkraut, drained
6 slices rye bread, cut in cubes or
   crumbled
1/2 pound Swiss cheese, grated
1/2 cup margarine, melted

Crumble corned beef into well-greased 12x8-inch glass dish. Spread dressing, then sauerkraut. Cover with cheese. Toss crumbled bread with melted margarine; sprinkle on top. Bake at 350 degrees for 30 minutes or until hot and bubbly.
Laura Morris, Bunnell, Fla.

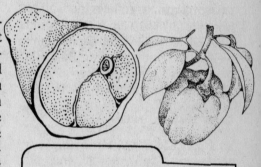

SAUCY SAUSAGE SUPPER
Serves 4

1 (16-ounce) can applesauce (2
   cups)
1 (16-ounce) can sauerkraut,
   drained and snipped (2 cups)
1/3 cup water
2 tablespoons brown sugar, packed
1/2 teaspoon salt
4 small onions, quartered
4 small potatoes, peeled and
   quartered
1 (12-ounce) Polish sausage, cut
   diagonally to desired lengths
Snipped parsley

In a 3-quart saucepan, combine applesauce, sauerkraut, water, brown sugar, and salt; add onions and potatoes. Cover and simmer 20 minutes, stirring occasionally. Add sausage; simmer, covered about 20 minutes longer, stirring occasionally. To serve, spoon sauerkraut mixture onto a platter and top with sausage. Sprinkle with parsley.
Agnes Ward, Erie, Pa.

Celebrate
WITH CAKES

RUSSIAN TEA CAKES
Makes 36

1 cup margarine, softened
1/4 cup confectioners' sugar
1 teaspoon vanilla extract
2 cups flour
1/2 cup toasted pecans, chopped
Confectioners' sugar

Cream margarine, 1/4 cup confectioners' sugar and vanilla together until light and fluffy. Mix in the flour and pecans. Chill 2 hours. Pinch off small pieces of dough and roll into 1-inch balls. Place on greased baking sheet. Bake at 375 degrees until lightly brown, 10-12 minutes. Cool on wire rack. Roll in confectioners' sugar before serving. Store in airtight container.

Edith Ruth Muldoon, Baldwin, N.Y.

GLAZED APRICOT CAKE
Serves 16-20

4 eggs, separated
2 sticks (1 cup) butter, softened
2-1/3 cups sugar, divided
1-1/3 cups apricot nectar, divided
Grated rind of 1 lemon
1-1/2 teaspoons vanilla extract
2-1/2 cups **plus** 1 tablespoon flour
2-1/2 teaspoons baking powder
1/4 teaspoon salt

Beat egg whites until stiff. Set aside. In a large bowl, cream butter with 2 cups sugar. Beat in egg yolks. Then beat in 1 cup apricot nectar, lemon rind, and vanilla. In another bowl, stir together flour, baking powder, and salt. Beat into the creamed mixture, then fold in egg whites, gently but thoroughly. Turn batter into greased and floured angel food or tube cake pan. Bake at 350 degrees for 1 to 1-1/4 hours, or until toothpick inserted in center comes out clean. Just before cake finishes baking, heat remaining 1/3 cup sugar with remaining 1/3 cup apricot nectar, just to a boil (stir to dissolve sugar). When cake is done, transfer to rack and slowly pour hot apricot syrup over all. Let cake remain in pan until cool.

Sharon McClatchey, Muskogee, Okla.

LEMON PUDDING CAKE
Serves 6

2 eggs, separated
1 teaspoon grated lemon peel
1/4 cup lemon juice
2/3 cup milk
1 cup sugar
1/4 cup all-purpose flour
1/4 teaspoon salt

Heat oven to 350 degrees. Beat egg whites until stiff peaks form; set aside. Beat egg yolks. Blend in lemon peel, juice and milk. Add sugar, flour and salt; beat until smooth. Fold into whites. Pour into ungreased 1-quart casserole. Place casserole in pan of very hot water (1 inch deep). Bake 45–50 minutes. Serve warm or cool and, if desired, with whipped cream.

PUMPKIN POUND CAKE
Serves 12

3 cups sifted flour
4 teaspoons baking powder
1/4 teaspoon baking soda
1/2 teaspoon salt
1 cup butter or margarine
1 cup sugar
1 cup brown sugar, packed
2 eggs
1 cup canned or mashed, cooked pumpkin
1 teaspoon lemon extract
1/2 cup milk
1 cup chopped walnuts
Sifted powdered sugar

Sift together flour, baking powder, baking soda and salt; set aside. Cream together butter, sugar and brown sugar in mixing bowl until light and fluffy, using electric mixer at medium speed. Add eggs, one at a time, beating well after each addition. Blend in pumpkin and lemon extract (total beating time 10 minutes). Add dry ingredients alternately with milk to creamed mixture, beating well after each addition, using electric mixer at low speed. Stir in walnuts. Pour batter into greased 10-inch tube pan. Bake in 325 degree oven 1 hour and 20 minutes, or until cake tester inserted in center comes out clean or top springs back when lightly touched with finger. Cool in pan on rack 10 minutes. Remove from pan; cool on rack. Sprinkle with powdered sugar.

Barbara Beauregard - Smith, Northfield, S. A., Australia

PRALINE CHEESE CAKE

1 cup graham cracker crumbs
3 tablespoons sugar
3 tablespoons melted butter
3 (8 ounce) packages cream cheese
1-1/4 cups dark brown sugar, firmly packed
3 eggs
2 tablespoons flour
1/2 cup chopped pecans
1-1/2 teaspoons vanilla
Maple syrup

Mix crumbs, sugar and butter, and press into 9-inch springform pan. Bake at 350 degrees for 10 minutes. Cool. Beat cream cheese and brown sugar until fluffy. Beat in eggs, one at a time. Sift in flour, add pecans and vanilla. Pour mixture into pan. Bake at 350 degrees for 55 minutes or until set. Cool in pan, remove to serving plate, and brush with maple syrup and garnish with chopped pecans. Chill for at least 3 hours.

Patricia Habiger, Spearville, Kan.

GOLDEN CARROT CAKE

2 cups sugar
1-1/2 cups salad oil
3 eggs
1 teaspoon vanilla
3 cups flour
1 teaspoon soda
1/2 teaspoon salt
1 teaspoon cinnamon
1 cup crushed pineapple
2 cups raw carrots, finely grated
1 cup nuts, chopped

Mix together sugar, salad oil, eggs, and vanilla. Add combined flour, soda, salt, and cinnamon. Mix well. Add pineapple, grated carrots, and nuts, mixing well. Place into a 13x9-inch pan and bake in a 350-degree oven for 1 hour and 15 minutes or until tested done. Frost with a cream cheese icing. **Note:** Use as a dessert, snack, or coffee cake.

Agnes Ward, Erie, Pa.

ONE-STEP COCOA CAKE
Serves 12

2-1/2 cups all-purpose flour
1-3/4 cups sugar
1/2 cup cocoa
2 teaspoons baking soda
1/2 teaspoon salt
1 cup milk
2/3 cup softened butter or margarine
2 teaspoons vanilla
3 eggs
1/4 cup sliced almonds

Heat oven to 350 degrees. Grease and flour 13x9-inch pan. In large bowl, combine all ingredients, except almonds. Beat 1 minute at low speed; beat 3 minutes at highest speed. Pour into prepared pan; sprinkle almonds over top. Bake at 350 degrees for 35-45 minutes, or until center tests done. Cool; cut into squares.

Agnes Ward, Erie, Pa.

PINEAPPLE CRUSH CAKE

1 package Duncan Hines Pineapple Cake or Lemon Cake
1 (8-ounce) package cream cheese
1 (4-ounce) box instant vanilla pudding
2 cups chilled milk
1 (4-ounce) can crushed pineapple, drained
1 (8-ounce) carton Cool Whip or La Creme whipped topping

Make cake according to directions on package. Bake in a 9x13x2-inch pan which has been greased and lined with waxed paper. Let cake cool and place in refrigerator for several hours. Split the cake, making 2 layers. Cooling makes it easier to split.

Filling:
Beat cream cheese until fluffy; add to this the package of instant vanilla pudding and 2 cups cold milk. Mix or beat mixture in a small bowl, 2 minutes on medium speed. Spread on cooled half of cake. Spoon over filling mixture one (4-ounce) can of crushed (drained) pineapple. Top with the other half of the cake. Spread whipped topping over sides and top of cake.

Store in refrigerator overnight. It is especially nice since you can make it the day before you plan to serve it.

May Folden, San Jose, Calif.

CARROT CAKE

2/3 cup fructose
3/4 cup cooking oil
2 eggs
1 1/2 cups cake flour
1/2 teaspoon salt
1/2 teaspoon cinnamon
1 teaspoon baking powder
1 teaspoon baking soda
1 cup cooked carrots

Mix all ingredients together with electric beater. Bake in a greased and floured 8x8-inch pan, at 375 degrees for approximately 45 minutes.

TUTTI-FRUTTI CREAM CAKE

3 cups cake flour, sifted
4 teaspoons baking powder
1 teaspoon baking soda
1/4 teaspoon salt
3/4 cup shortening
1-1/2 cups sugar
2 tablespoons sour cream
1/4 cup flaked coconut
1/4 cup maraschino cherries, sliced
1/4 cup crushed pineapple, drained
1/4 cup mashed bananas
4 eggs
1-1/2 cups milk

Sift first 4 ingredients; cream shortening with dry ingredients. Add sugar, sour cream, coconut, cherries, pineapple, and mashed bananas. Beat in one egg at a time; mix thoroughly. Add flour alternately with milk; beat until smooth. Turn into a well-greased tube pan; bake at 350 degrees for 1 hour. When cool, dust with confectioners' sugar across top of cake.

Gwen Campbell, Sterling, Va.

FRUITED APPLESAUCE CAKE

Serves 10-12

1/2 cup margarine
1 cup brown sugar, firmly packed
1 cup canned applesauce
2-1/4 cups cake flour
1/2 teaspoon salt
1/2 teaspoon baking soda
1 teaspoon baking powder
1/2 teaspoon cloves, powdered
1/2 teaspoon cinnamon
1/2 teaspoon nutmeg
1/2 cup seedless raisins, washed
   and drained
1/2 cup dried currants
1/4 cup ground nuts

Cream together margarine and brown sugar until light and fluffy. Add applesauce; mix well. Sift together dry ingredients; add to applesauce mixture, mix well.

Add raisins, currants and nuts, mix until well incorporated. Turn into 9 x 5x3-inch loaf pan with paper cut to fit bottom. Bake at 325 degrees for 1 hour or until tested done. Cool 10 minutes; remove from pan and finish cooling on rack. Remove paper.

Agnes Ward, Erie, Pa.

LEMON PECAN CAKE

Serves 16

2 cups butter
4 cups brown sugar, firmly packed
6 eggs, separated
4 cups flour
1 teaspoon baking powder
3 tablespoons lemon extract
1 pound pecans, chopped
1/2 pound candied cherries,
   chopped
1/2 pound candied pineapple,
   chopped

Cream butter and sugar; beat in egg yolks one at a time. Sift 2 cups flour and baking powder together; add to creamed mixture alternately with lemon extract, beating well. Dredge pecans and fruits in remaining flour in large bowl. Pour batter over fruit mixture. Stir well. Fold in

stiffly-beaten egg whites. Cover; let stand overnight. Spoon batter into greased and floured 10-inch tube pan. Bake tube cake in 275 degree oven for 2 hours. Remove cake from pan. Cool, cover and age for 24 hours.

Agnes Ward, Erie, Pa.

SOUR MILK GINGERBREAD

Serves 8-10

1-1/2 cups flour
1/2 teaspoon soda
1/2 teaspoon baking powder
1/4 teaspoon salt
1 tablespoon ginger
1/4 teaspoon ground cloves
2 teaspoons cinnamon
1/3 cup shortening
1/2 cup brown sugar, firmly packed
1 egg, beaten
1/2 cup light molasses
1 cup buttermilk

Sift together first 7 ingredients. Cream shortening by beating until soft and smooth. Gradually add sugar, beating thoroughly after each addition. Continue beating until light and fluffy. Add egg and beat until mixture looks light and fluffy again. Add molasses and beat thoroughly. Add flour and milk alternately to molasses mixture by adding 1/3 of the flour and 1/2 of the milk at a time, beginning and ending with flour. Stir after each addition until well blended. Pour into well-greased and floured 9-inch square cake pan. Bake at 350 degrees for 20-25 minutes or until done. Serve plain, with lemon sauce, or with whipped cream.

Lemon Sauce:
1/2 cup sugar
Few grains salt
1 tablespoon cornstarch
1 cup boiling water
2 tablespoons butter
1-1/2 tablespoons lemon juice
Dash of nutmeg

Mix sugar, salt and cornstarch in saucepan. Add water gradually, stirring as you add. Let mixture come to boil and boil for 5 minutes, stirring constantly to prevent lumping. Remove from heat. Add butter, lemon

juice and nutmeg. Stir until well blended. Makes 1 cup.

Betty Lyke, Flower Mound, Texas

EASY COCONUT CAKE

1 box white cake mix
2 packages frozen coconut
2 (8-ounce) cartons sour cream
2 cups sugar
1 (8-ounce) container Cool Whip

Mix cake mix according to directions on box. Bake in 2 (8- or 9-inch) round cake pans; split into 4 layers. Mix packages of coconut with sour cream and sugar. (Set aside 1/2 cup of this mixture for later use.) Spread the rest of the mixture thickly between layers. Mix the 1/2-cup mixture with the whipped topping. Spread on top and sides.

Refrigerate 3 days in an airtight container before cutting. This is delicious and a super-great dessert than can be made ahead of time.

Joni Bowen, Belen, Miss.

SPICED APPLE RING

Serves 6–8

1 (20-ounce) can apple
   pie filling
1 (9-ounce) package
   yellow cake mix
   Cinnamon
   Brown sugar
   Chopped nuts (optional)

Spread apple pie filling on bottom of a round microwave-Bundt cake pan. Sprinkle a little cinnamon on the pie filling.

Prepare cake mix according to package directions. Pour cake batter over pie filling. Microwave on HIGH power for 9–10 minutes, turning 1/4 turn every 2–3 minutes until done.

Invert immediately on a large plate. Sprinkle with cinnamon, brown sugar, and chopped nuts. Cool slightly and served topped with whipped cream or Cool Whip. This is a very quick and easy microwave cake.

Kayleen Avers, Hastings, Neb.

CAROL'S GERMAN CHOCOLATE-CARAMEL CAKE

1 package German chocolate cake mix
1 can Eagle Brand sweetened condensed milk
1 (12.25-ounce) jar caramel ice-cream topping
1 small container Cool Whip
¼ cup chopped pecans

Bake a German chocolate cake as directed in a 9 x 13-inch pan. While still warm poke holes, with a wooden spoon handle, about every 1–2 inches apart. Pour and spread on sweetened condensed milk. Spoon on caramel ice-cream topping. When cool spread on container of Cool Whip and sprinkle with ¼ cup chopped pecans. Store in refrigerator before serving. Very rich!

Jody Piercy, Fort Morgan, Colo.

WHITE SPONGE CAKE

6 egg whites
1/2 teaspoon cream of tartar
2 cups sifted cake flour
2 cups sugar
2 teaspoons baking powder
1 cup hot milk
3/4 teaspoon almond extract
1 teaspoon vanilla

Beat egg whites until foamy; add cream of tartar and beat until stiff. Sift together cake flour, sugar, and baking powder. Add hot milk to dry ingredients and mix well. Blend in almond extract and vanilla. Fold beaten egg whites into mixture. Bake in ungreased 13x9x2-inch pan at 375 degrees for 25 minutes. *Do not* invert pan while cooling.

If you do not have cake flour, remove 2 tablespoons from each cup of flour.

Betty Slavin, Omaha, Neb.

GOLDEN DOLLAR ANGEL CAKE

1/2 cup sifted cake flour
3/4 cup sifted sugar
6 egg whites
3/4 teaspoon cream of tartar
1/4 teaspoon salt
1/2 teaspoon vanilla
1/4 teaspoon almond extract
3/4 cup sifted cake flour
1 teaspoon baking powder
6 egg yolks
3/4 cup sugar
1/4 teaspoon salt
1/2 teaspoon vanilla
1/2 teaspoon lemon extract
1/4 cup boiling water

Sift flour and sugar, separately, 4 times; set aside. Beat egg whites until frothy; add cream of tartar and salt, then beat until mixture stands in peaks. Add sugar gradually while continuing to beat. Add flavorings, and fold in flour. Pour into an ungreased tube pan and let stand while preparing the second mixture.

Sift flour and baking powder together. Beat egg yolks until they reach a lemon color and are fluffy. Add sugar and salt, beating continuously. Add flavorings. Fold in flour mixture alternately with hot water. Pour slowly over batter in pan. Bake in a preheated oven at 350 degrees for 30-35 minutes. Invert pan until cool. Frost and serve.

Julie Habiger, Spearville, Kan.

SIMPLE PINEAPPLE CAKE

1 large can crushed pineapple
1 can angel flake coconut
1 (19-ounce) box yellow cake mix
1 stick margarine or butter

In an 11x7-inch baking dish, combine pineapple, juice, and all other ingredients. Place coconut and dry cake mix on top and spread evenly. Cut butter in thin slices and place over mix. Bake at 425 degrees for 40 minutes, or until top is brown and crunchy. Let cool before cutting into squares and serve upside down.

Suzan L. Wiener, Spring Hill, Fla.

MAPLE POUND CAKE

1 cup white sugar
3/4 cup light brown sugar
4 large eggs
1 teaspoon vanilla
1/2 teaspoon lemon extract
1/2 teaspoon maple extract
1 cup margarine
1 cup milk
1/2 teaspoon baking powder
1/2 teaspoon baking soda
1/2 teaspoon allspice
3 cups white flour

In large mixer bowl, combine sugars, margarine, eggs and extracts. Beat well until light and fluffy. Sift together dry ingredients and add alternately with milk. Beat smooth. Pour into non-stick or greased and floured large tube pan and bake in preheated 325 degree oven for one hour. Test with toothpick for doneness. Bake until toothpick comes out clean. Cool in pan for a few minutes, then turn out on rack. Serve plain or with whipped topping.

Pearle M. Goodwin, South Ryegate, Vt.

APPLE CAKE

1-1/2 cups flour, sifted
1/2 teaspoon salt
3 teaspoons baking powder
2 tablespoons shortening
1/2 cup milk
1/2 cup sugar
4 small apples
1 teaspoon cinnamon

Sift and mix together flour, salt, and baking powder. Cut in shortening; add milk and sugar. Place dough on floured board and roll out to 1/2-inch thickness. Place in shallow greased pan. Pare and slice apples. Press apple slices into dough and sprinkle with cinnamon. Bake for 30 minutes at 350 degrees.

Suzan L. Wiener, Spring Hill, Fla.

COOKIE CRUST CRUNCH CAKE
(Makes 2 loaf cakes)

2-1/4 cups vanilla wafer crumbs
1-1/4 cups pecans, finely chopped
1/2 cup sugar
1/2 stick butter or margarine
1 (18-1/4-ounce) box yellow cake mix
3 large eggs
1 stick butter or margarine, softened
1 tablespoon orange extract
2/3 cup water

Combine vanilla wafer crumbs, pecans, and sugar in bowl. Add 1/4 cup butter; cut in until crumbs are fine. Divide evenly into 2 greased 9x5x3-inch loaf pans. In a large mixer bowl, combine cake mix, eggs, 1/2 cup butter, orange extract, and water. Mix cake as directed on package; divide batter evenly into pans. Bake at 350 degrees for 60 minutes or until tested done in center of cake. Cool in pans on rack 5 minutes; loosen cake from pans; turn upside down on rack; cool completely. These loaves freeze nicely.

Gwen Campbell, Sterling, Va.

ANGEL RIPPLE CAKE
(from prepared mix)
Serves 12-16

1 package angel food cake mix
1 tablespoon ground cinnamon

Cinnamon Cream Sauce:
3/4 cup whipping cream
1/2 cup milk
1/3 cup confectioner's sugar
1 teaspoon vanilla
1/2 teaspoon ground cinnamon

Preheat oven to 375-degrees. Mix cake as directed on package. Spoon 1/4 of batter into an ungreased 10-inch tube pan and spread evenly. With a fine small sieve, sprinkle 1/3 of cinnamon over batter. Repeat layering 2 or 3 times ending with cake batter. Bake and cool as directed.

For sauce, mix cream and milk in a chilled bowl. Beat with chilled beaters until thick. Blend in confectioner's sugar, vanilla and cinnamon. Serve sauce over cake slices.

EASTER RING CAKE

2 cups sifted flour
1-1/4 cups sugar
3 teaspoons baking powder
1 teaspoon baking soda
1/2 teaspoon salt
1/2 cup shortening
2/3 cup orange juice
1 cup sugar
2 eggs
1/4 cup sweet orange marmalade
Lemon Butter Fluff Icing (recipe follows)

Sift together flour, sugar, baking powder, soda, and salt; blend in shortening and 2/3 cup orange juice. Beat 2 minutes at medium speed of electric mixer. Blend in remaining orange juice with eggs, beat at medium speed 2 minutes. Fold in orange marmalade and turn into greased and lightly floured 9 inch tube pan. Bake in a 350 degree oven for 50-55 minutes or until tests done. Cool completely before removing from pan. Frost with Lemon Butter Fluff Icing, and decorate with flowers.

Lemon Butter Fluff Icing:
1 (3-ounce) package cream cheese
2 tablespoons cream
1/2 cup soft butter
4 cups powdered sugar
1 tablespoon lemon juice
2-3 teaspoons grated lemon rind
1 teaspoon vanilla

Soften cream cheese to room temperature; blend in cream and butter. Beat until soft and smooth. Gradually blend in powdered sugar, lemon juice, rind, and vanilla. Beat until light and fluffy. Tint mixture a delicate color, if desired.

NOTE: A bouquet of real spring flowers placed in center of this ring cake is a delightful touch.

Leona Teodori, Warren, Mich.

ANGEL CAKE DELIGHT
Serves 24

1 (20-ounce) can crushed pineapple
1 large angel food cake
8 cups prepared Dream Whip (may substitute Cool Whip)
2 envelopes Knox unflavored gelatin
3 tablespoons lemon juice
1 cup white granulated sugar
1 cup coconut

Pour four tablespoons cold water over gelatin. Stir and add 1 cup boiling water. Add pineapple, lemon juice, and sugar. Let stand until chilled. Prepare Dream Whip, or use Cool Whip. Mix with gelatin mixture. Add coconut. Pinch cake in fine pieces. Prepare cake, alternating with a layer of cake crumbs and a layer of Dream Whip mixture—ending with Dream Whip mixture. Chill. This cake keeps very well when prepared and stored in a lid-covered cake tray.

Great recipe for a party, a family gathering, or anytime!

–Faye Wilson, Maysville, Ky.

ORANGE PEANUT BUTTER CAKE

2 oranges
1 package yellow cake mix (with or without pudding)
1-1/4 cups water
3 eggs
1/2 cup peanut butter (smooth or chunky)
1 teaspoon ground cinnamon
1/3 cup packed brown sugar

Grate peel from oranges; reserve. Peel oranges and cut into bite size pieces; drain well. In large bowl, combine cake mix, water, eggs, peanut butter, and cinnamon; beat according to package directions. Stir in orange pieces and peel. Pour batter into a greased and floured 13x9 inch cake pan. Sprinkle brown sugar over top. Bake 350 degrees for 35-40 minutes. Serve warm.

Mrs. Kit Rollins, Cedarburg, Wis.

CREAM-FILLED RASPBERRY ROLL

3 eggs
1 cup granulated sugar
1/3 cup water
1 teaspoon vanilla
1 cup cake flour or 3/4 cup all-purpose flour
1 teaspoon baking powder
1/4 teaspoon salt
1/2 cup raspberry jelly, plus 1/3 cup for top of cake
Fluffy White Frosting (recipe follows)
Coconut
1 tablespoon raspberry gelatin powder

Heat oven to 375 degrees. Line jelly roll pan, 15x10x1-inch, with waxed paper; grease. Beat eggs in small mixer bowl on high speed until very thick and lemon colored, 3-5 minutes. Pour eggs into large mixing bowl; gradually beat in granulated sugar. On low speed, blend in water and vanilla. Gradually add flour, baking powder, and salt, beating just until batter is smooth. Pour into pan, spreading batter to corners. Bake until wooden pick inserted into center comes out clean, 12-15 minutes. Loosen cake from edges of pan; immediately invert onto towel generously sprinkled with powdered sugar. Carefully remove wax paper; trim stiff edges of cake, if necessary. While hot, roll cake and towel from narrow end. Cool on wire rack at least 30 minutes.

Unroll cake; remove towel. Beat jelly with fork just enough to soften; spread over cake. Carefully spread a layer of Fluffy White Frosting over jelly; roll up. Place coconut in a small jar (about 2/3 cup) with 1 tablespoon gelatin powder and shake to color coconut. Spread about 1/3 cup jelly over rolled up jelly roll and sprinkle coconut on top.

Fluffy White Frosting:
1/2 cup sugar
1/2 stick butter or margarine
1/2 cup shortening
1-1/2 tablespoons flour
1/3 cup warm milk (barely heated)

1 teaspoon vanilla

Cream sugar, butter, and shortening. Add flour, and gradually add milk and vanilla. Beat until thick. Has consistency of whipped cream.
Geneva Cullop, Ceres, Va.

COCONUT POUND CAKE

1 cup butter, softened
3 cups sugar
6 large eggs
3 cups all-purpose flour
1/4 teaspoon soda
1/4 teaspoon salt
8 ounces sour cream
1 cup frozen coconut, thawed
1 teaspoon vanilla
1 teaspoon coconut extract

Cream butter and add sugar. Beat until mix is light and fluffy. Add eggs, one at a time, beating well after each addition. Mix together flour, soda, salt; add flour mixture alternately with sour cream to creamed mixture, beginning and ending with flour. Stir in coconut and flavorings last. Grease and flour 10-inch tube pan. Bake at 350 degrees for 1 hour and 15 minutes. Remove from pan; cool completely; dust with powdered sugar. If you like pound cake you will love this!!

Renee Dennis Wells, Columbia, S.C.

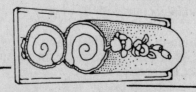

PINK AND PRETTY VALENTINE CAKE
(Serves 20)

1 cup sugar
3/4 cup butter or margarine, softened
2-1/3 cups cake flour
3/4 cup milk
2-1/2 teaspoons baking powder
1 teaspoon vanilla
3 eggs
1/2 teaspoon salt
Buttercream Frosting (recipe follows)
Chocolate Hearts (recipe follows)

1 cup raspberry preserves
3 tablespoons orange juice
Red food coloring

Preheat oven to 350 degrees. Grease and flour 10-inch springform pan. In large bowl, with mixer at high speed, beat sugar and butter until fluffy. At low speed, beat in flour, milk, baking powder, vanilla, eggs, and 1/2 teaspoon salt until blended. Beat 1 minute at medium speed. Spoon batter into pan. Bake 45 minutes or until toothpick inserted in center comes out clean. Cool in pan on rack 10 minutes. Remove side of pan. Cool completely.

Prepare Buttercream Frosting and Chocolate Hearts. Place raspberry preserves in bowl. Stir in orange juice.

Remove cake from pan bottom. Cut into 3 layers. Place 1 layer on cake plate. Spread with half of raspberry mixture. Top with another layer. Spread with remaining raspberry mixture. Top with remaining layer. Spread top and side of cake with about 2 cups frosting. Add coloring to remaining buttercream to tint pink. Place about 1/2 cup of pink buttercream in decorating bag with small writing tube. Use to pipe lattice on top of cake. Use remaining buttercream to pipe border around top and bottom of cake and decorate side. Attach chocolate hearts. Refrigerate.

Buttercream Frosting:
3 cups confectioners' sugar
1-1/2 cups butter or margarine, softened
4 egg yolks

In large bowl with mixer at low speed, beat sugar and softened butter until mixed. At high speed beat until fluffy. At medium speed beat in 4 egg yolks.

Chocolate Hearts:
1/4 cup semi-sweet chocolate pieces, melted

Spread chocolate pieces, melted, into 4x3-inch rectangle on waxed paper-lined cookie sheet. Refrigerate until firm. With heart-shaped cookie cutter, cut chocolate into hearts. Refrigerate.

GOOEY BUTTER CAKE

1/4 cup sugar
1/4 cup Crisco
1/4 teaspoon salt
1 egg
1 (6-ounce) cake of yeast
1/2 cup warm milk
2-1/2 cups all-purpose flour
1 tablespoon vanilla

Prepare a sweet dough by mixing sugar with Crisco and salt. Add egg and beat with electric mixer one minute until well blended. Dissolve yeast in warm milk. Add flour, then milk/yeast mixture, and vanilla to sweet dough batter. Mix 3 minutes with dough hooks or with hands. Turn dough onto floured board and knead for one minute. Place in a lightly-greased bowl; cover with a towel and let rise in a warm place for 1 hour.

M. Lanff, Philadelphia, Pa.

GOOEY BUTTER CAKE

1 yellow cake mix
4 eggs
1 stick butter, melted
1 pound box powdered sugar
1 (8-ounce) package cream cheese

Mix together the cake mix, 2 eggs, and butter. Spread batter into a 9 x 13 inch greased and floured pan. Batter will be thick. Blend remaining 2 eggs, powdered sugar, and cream cheese. Pour over batter. Bake at 350 degrees for 35 minutes or until top has a brown glaze and pulls from the sides of the pan.

Betty Ireton, Kingston, OH

APPLESAUCE CAKE

1-1/4 cups shortening (Crisco)
3 cups brown sugar
3 eggs
2-1/4 cups applesauce
4-1/2 cups sifted flour

1 teaspoon salt
2-1/4 teaspoons cinnamon
1 teaspoon ground cloves
2-1/4 teaspoons baking soda

Cream shortening, sugar, and eggs. Dissolve soda into the applesauce; add to egg mixture. Sift flour, salt, cinnamon, and cloves; add to egg mixture. Pour into tube pan; bake at 350 degrees for one hour. Let cool five minutes; invert on rack. No icing is needed.

Karin Shea Fedders, Dameron, MD

APPLE POUND CAKE

2 cups unsifted flour
1 teaspoon soda
1 teaspoon salt
1/2 teaspoon nutmeg
2 cups sugar
2 teaspoons vanilla
1 cup chopped pecans or walnuts
1/2 teaspoon cinnamon
1-1/2 cups corn oil
3 eggs
2 cups finely chopped apples
1/2 cup raisins

Preheat oven to 325 degrees. Combine flour, soda, salt, cinnamon, and nutmeg in a large bowl. With electric mixer at medium speed, beat together the oil, sugar, eggs, and vanilla until thoroughly combined. Gradually beat in the flour mixture until smooth. Fold in apples, pecans (or walnuts), and raisins. Turn into greased and floured 10-inch tube pan or bundt pan. Bake at 325 degrees for 1 hour and 15 minutes or until cake tester inserted in center comes out clean. Cool cake in pan on wire rack for 10 minutes, then remove from pan to cool completely. Store in air-tight container.

Mrs. H. W. Walker, Richmond, VA

MAPLE-FLAVORED GINGERBREAD
Serves 16

2-1/2 cups all-purpose flour
1-1/2 teaspoons soda
1 teaspoon ground cinnamon
1 teaspoon ground ginger
1/2 teaspoon ground cloves
1/2 teaspoon salt
1/2 cup shortening
1/2 cup sugar
1 egg
1/2 cup molasses
1/2 cup maple-flavored syrup
1 cup hot water
Whipped cream

Combine flour, soda, spices, and salt; set aside. Cream shortening and sugar until light and fluffy. Add egg, beating well. Gradually beat in molasses and syrup. Add dry ingredients alternately with hot water, beating well after each addition. Pour batter into greased 13 x 9 x 2 inch pan. Bake at 350 degrees for 30 minutes or until done. Cool thoroughly in pan. Serve with whipped cream.

Barbara Beauregard-Smith, Northfield, S. A. Australia

ONE-BOWL CHOCOLATE CAKE

Sift into large bowl:
3-1/2 cups flour
2 cups sugar
5 tablespoons cocoa
1 teaspoon cinnamon
2 teaspoons baking soda
1 teaspoon salt

To these 6 ingredients add:
1 cup cooking oil
2 teaspoons vinegar
2 teaspoons vanilla
2 cups water

Beat well. Pour into ungreased 9 x 13 inch pan. Bake at 350 degrees for 35-45 minutes. This is a very moist cake, easy to make, and no eggs needed.

Tom McNiel, Constantine, MI

NO-COOK FROSTING

1/4 teaspoon salt
2 egg whites
1/4 cup sugar
3/4 cup Karo syrup, red or blue label
1-1/4 teaspoons vanilla

Beat salt and egg whites until mixture peaks. Add sugar, 1 tablespoon at a time, beating until smooth and glossy. Continue beating and add Karo syrup gradually, until frosting peaks. Fold in vanilla. Add vegetable coloring, if desired; frost top and sides of two 9 inch layers.

Mrs. Olen Begly, West Salem, Ohio

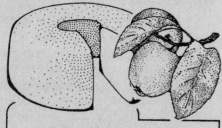

APPLE BUTTER CAKE

1/2 cup shortening
1 cup sugar
3 eggs
1 cup apple butter
2-1/2 cups sifted cake flour
3 teaspoons baking powder
1/2 teaspoon baking soda
1/2 teaspoon salt
1/2 teaspoon cinnamon
1/4 teaspoon nutmeg
1/2 cup apple butter
1 cup sour milk

Cream together shortening and sugar. Beat in eggs, one at a time; beat until light and fluffy. Stir in 1 cup apple butter. Sift together flour, baking powder, soda, salt, cinnamon, and nutmeg. Add dry ingredients to creamed mixture, alternately with sour milk. Turn into 2 greased and floured 9 inch cake pans. Bake at 350 degrees for 30-35 minutes. Cool thoroughly. Spread bottom layer of cake with 1/4 cup of remaining apple butter. Top with frosting. Cover with top cake layer. Frost top and sides with any marshmallow frosting. Swirl remaining apple butter on top for marbled effect.

Leah Daub, Milwaukee, Wis.

DUTCH APPLE CAKE
Makes 1 13 x 9-inch cake

1 (18-1/2 ounce) package spice cake mix
1/2 cup butter or margarine, melted
2 eggs
1 (21 ounce) can apple pie filling
3/4 cup brown sugar, firmly packed
1 teaspoon cinnamon
1/4 cup butter or margarine, softened
1/2 cup chopped nuts

In large bowl, combine dry cake mix, melted butter, and eggs. Blend well. Spread on bottom of 13 x 9 inch baking pan. Spoon pie filling evenly over batter. In small bowl combine brown sugar and cinnamon; cut in softened butter; stir in nuts. Sprinkle over pie filling. Bake at 250 degrees for 50 minutes or until cake springs back when lightly touched.

Agnes Ward, Erie, PA

APPLESAUCE CAKE

1 stick (1/2 cup) butter or margarine, softened
1 cup sugar
1 large egg
1-1/2 cups applesauce
2 cups all-purpose flour
2 teaspoons baking soda
1 teaspoon cinnamon
1 teaspoon nutmeg
1/4 teaspoon ground cloves
1 cup chopped, pitted dates
1/2 cup chopped walnuts

In a large bowl cream the butter, add the sugar, a little at a time. Beat the mixture until light and fluffy. Beat in the egg and add the applesauce. Into a bowl sift together the flour, soda, and spices, gently stir the mixture into the applesauce mixture with the dates and walnuts. Transfer the batter into a well greased baking pan, 12 x 8 x 2 inches, and bake in a preheated oven 350 degrees for approximately 45 minutes. Let the cake cool in pan on a rack. Frost if desired.

Very moist cake. Raisins may be used instead of dates.

Paula L. Walton, Fort Pierce, FL

APPLESAUCE LAYER CAKE

2 eggs
1-1/2 cups sugar
1-1/2 cups applesauce
1/2 cup butter or shortening
1 teaspoon soda
1 teaspoon salt
1 teaspoon cinnamon
1 teaspoon nutmeg
1/2 cup nut meats
2 cups flour
1 cup raisins (if desired)

Cream together the shortening and sugar. Add eggs, applesauce; and then sift the flour, soda, salt, and spices together. Add to creamed mixture; stir in raisins.

Grease (2) 8-inch round cake pans or use typing paper cut to fit inside pans. Pour batter into pans and bake at 325 degrees for 40 minutes or until cake tests done.

This cake is especially tasty with a mocha or caramel frosting.

Betty Slavin, Omaha, NE

SAUCY APPLE SWIRL CAKE
Serves 16

1/4 cup sugar
1 teaspoon cinnamon
1 package yellow cake mix (Pillsbury Plus best)
1 (15 ounce) jar (1-1/2 cups) applesauce
3 eggs

Heat oven to 350 degrees. Grease and flour 12-cup fluted pan or 10-inch tube pan. In small bowl, combine sugar and cinnamon; set aside. In large bowl, blend cake mix, applesauce, and eggs until moistened. Beat 2 minutes at high speed. Pour 1/2 of batter into prepared pan. Sprinkle with sugar mix. Cover with remaining batter. Bake 35-45 minutes until toothpick comes out of center clean. Cool upright in pan 25 minutes; turn onto serving plate. Cool completely. Dust with powdered sugar.

Judie Betz, Lomita, Calif.

OATMEAL CAKE

1 cup quick oatmeal
1 1/4 cups boiling water
1 stick butter or margarine
2 eggs, beater
1 cup white sugar
1 cup brown sugar
1 1/2 cups flour
1 teaspoon soda
1 teaspoon cinnamon
1/2 teaspoon salt
1 teaspoon vanilla

Stir together the oatmeal, boiling water and butter until butter melts. Let cool. Add the eggs and beat, then add sugar and beat mixture again. Sift together the flour, soda, cinnamon and salt and add to cake mixture with the vanilla. Beat all well.

Pour into greased and floured 9x 13" pan. Bake at 350-degrees for about 32 minutes.

When done and still hot, spread with the following topping. Mix together in heavy pan 3/4 cup brown sugar, 3/4 cup pecan pieces (or other chopped nuts), 6 tablespoons butter and 1/2 cup condensed milk (1/2 cup coconut, optional). Cream and cook until thick (but not too long).Evenly place mixture on cake. Place cake under broiler until topping becomes bubbly.

Karen Shea Fedders, Dameron, Md.

$100 CHOCOLATE CAKE

1/2 cup butter
2 cups sugar
4 ounces semi-sweet chocolate, melted
2 eggs, beaten
2 cups sifted cake flour
1/4 teaspoon salt
2 teaspoons baking powder
1-1/2 cups sweet milk
1 teaspoon vanilla
1 cup chopped nuts

Cream butter and sugar. Add melted chocolate. Add beaten eggs. Add flour, salt, baking powder mixture, and vanilla, alternately with milk. Beat with hand beater, not mixer, after addition. Put in 2 (9-inch) cake pans. Bake in 350 degree oven for 45 minutes. Batter is thin.

Frosting:
1/2 cup butter
2 ounces semi-sweet chocolate, melted
1 egg, beaten
1/4 teaspoon salt
1 teaspoon lemon juice
1 teaspoon vanilla
1-1/2 cups confectioners' sugar
1 cup chopped nuts

Mix first 6 ingredients, then stir in confectioners' sugar. Beat until thick enough to spread. (Beat by hand.) Sprinkle chopped nuts on top.
Sandra Russell, Gainesville, Fla.

ORANGE KISS ME CAKE

1 (6-ounce) can frozen orange juice, (3/4 cup thawed)
2 cups flour
1 cup sugar
1 teaspoon soda
1 teaspoon salt
1/2 cup shortening
1/2 cup milk
2 eggs
1 cup raisins
1/3 cup chopped walnuts

Preheat oven to 350 degrees. Grease and flour bottom of 9x13-inch pan. Combine 1/2 cup orange juice with remaining ingredients in large bowl. Blend at lowest speed of mixer for 30 seconds. Beat 3 minutes at medium speed. Bake 40-45 minutes. Drizzle remaining orange juice over warm cake and sprinkle with topping (recipe follows).

Topping:
1/3 cup sugar
1/4 cup chopped walnuts
1 teaspoon cinnamon
Combine in a bowl.
Susan Kirch, Dexter, N.Y.

SUNSHINE CAKE

7 egg yolks
1 teaspoon lemon extract
1-1/2 cups powdered sugar
10 egg whites
1 teaspoon cream of tartar
1 cup cake flour
1/4 teaspoon salt

Preheat oven to 325 degrees. Line bottom of a 10-inch tube pan with wax paper; cut to fit. Beat egg yolks; add lemon extract and 1 cup of the powdered sugar. Beat until thick and pale; set aside. Beat egg whites until foamy; add the cream of tartar, and beat until whites form soft peaks. Gradually, add remaining 1/2 cup powdered sugar and beat until stiff. Stir a fourth of the whites into the yolk mixture. Spoon remaining whites on top of the yolk mixture and sift flour and salt over them. Carefully fold until blended. Spoon into pan and bake for 50-60 minutes, until a toothpick comes out clean. Invert pan on a rack and let cake cool completely before removing from the pan. Frost with your favorite icing.
Lucille Roehr, Hammond, Ind.

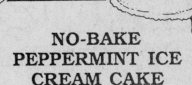

NO-BAKE PEPPERMINT ICE CREAM CAKE

10-inch angel food cake
6 chocolate peppermint patties
1/2 cup nuts
1/8 teaspoon peppermint extract
1 quart vanilla ice cream

Cut cake in 4 layers. Chop patties and nuts. Soften ice cream slightly. Stir in candy, nuts, and extract. Spread thick layer of ice cream mixture between cake layers and rebuild the cake. Cover top with ice cream mixture. Keep in freezer; no thawing necessary.
Sally Jonas, Lafayette, Ind.

CARROT CAKE

1/2 cup oil
1 cup sugar
2 eggs, well beaten
1/2 cup grated carrots, packed
1/2 cup crushed pineapple
1-1/2 cups sifted flour
1/2 teaspoon salt
1/2 teaspoon baking soda
1/2 teaspoon baking powder
1/2 teaspoon cinnamon
1 teaspoon vanilla
1/2 cup chopped walnuts

Combine oil and sugar; add well-beaten eggs, carrots, and crushed pineapple. Mix just to combine. Sift flour, salt, baking soda, baking powder, and cinnamon. Stir into oil mixture. Add vanilla and nuts. Mix to combine. Pour batter into a greased and floured 9x13-inch pan. Bake at 350 degrees for 30 minutes or until done. Cool.

Icing:

1 (3 ounce) cream cheese
3 ounces margarine
1-1/2 cups powdered sugar
1 teaspoon walnuts, chopped fine
1 teaspoon crushed pineapple

Mix together cream cheese, margarine, and powdered sugar. Beat until light and fluffy. Add nuts and pineapple. Ice cooled cake.

Leona Teodori, Warren, Mich.

NO-FUSS FRUITCAKE

3/4 cup brown sugar
1/2 cup margarine or butter
1 egg
2-1/2 cups all-purpose flour
1 teaspoon baking soda
1/4 teaspoon *each* nutmeg and cloves
1/2 teaspoon cinnamon
1/4 cup orange or pineapple juice
1 cup applesauce, unsweetened or diced
2 cups chopped candied fruit
1 cup *each* raisins and chopped walnuts

In large bowl cream sugar and margarine or butter; add egg; beat well. Mix flour with spices and soda; stir into creamed mixture alternately with applesauce and juice. Fold in fruits, raisins, and nuts. Pour into two greased, floured 7-1/2 x 3-1/2 x 2 inch loaf pans. Bake for 1 hour at 325 degrees or until tests done with toothpick. Remove from pans; cool. Lightly glaze tops with mixture of confectioners' sugar and enough fruit juice or water to spread thinly. When glaze is set, press halved candied cherries over the top. Wrap in foil; store in cool place or freeze until needed.

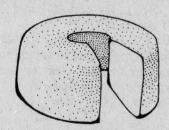

GRAPEFRUIT CHIFFON CAKE

2 cups all-purpose flour
1-1/2 cups sugar
3 teaspoons baking powder
1/2 teaspoon salt
1/2 cup oil
6 egg yolks
3 teaspoons grated grapefruit peel
2/3 cup grapefruit juice
6-7 egg whites
1/4 teaspoon cream of tartar

In a small mixer bowl stir together flour, sugar, baking powder, and salt. Make a well in center; in order add oil, egg yolks, peel, and juice. Beat smooth with an electric mixer. Wash beaters and in large bowl beat egg whites with the cream of tartar until stiff.

Gradually pour flour mixture (it will be thick) in a thin stream over surface and fold in gently. Bake in a 10-inch ungreased tube pan for 55 minutes at 350 degrees or until it tests done when lightly touched with the finger the cake springs back. Invert. Cool completely on cake cooling rack, loosen edges, and remove to cake plate. Glaze with the following:

2 cups sifted powdered sugar
3 teaspoons grapefruit peel, grated
1 teaspoon vanilla
2-3 tablespoons grapefruit juice

Mix all ingredients together using enough grapefruit juice to make it spread easily and drizzle down the sides when spread on top of cake.

Judy Smith, Indianapolis, IN

1 package yellow cake mix
1-6 ounce package instant vanilla pudding mix
1-1/4 cups cold milk
1-8 ounce package cream cheese
1-8 or 9 ounce container frozen whipped topping
1-20 ounce can crushed pineapple, well drained
1/2 cup chopped pecans
1/2 cup flaked coconut
1/2 cup Maraschino cherries, drained and chopped

Prepare cake according to directions on package. Pour into greased 10 x 15 jelly roll pan. Bake in preheated oven 350 degrees 15-20 minutes, or until done. Cool in pan.

Blend pudding mix with milk, beat in cream cheese (room temperature); then fold in frozen whipped topping. Spread on cooled cake. Sprinkle drained pineapple over pudding, then cherries, nuts, and coconut. Refrigerate until ready to cut. Can be made a day ahead. This not only makes a big beautiful cake but is very delicious. I've taken this to a lot of potlucks and someone always wants the recipe.

Roselyn Finan, Fort Wayne, IN

Cookies

CLASSIC

SAND COOKIES
Makes 4 dozen

1/2 pound (2 sticks) margarine, softened
3/4 cup sugar
1 teaspoon baking soda
1 teaspoon vinegar
1 teaspoon vanilla
1 1/2 cups flour
1/2 bag miniature chocolate chips

Beat margarine and sugar for 5 minutes. Dissolve soda in vinegar and add to margarine mixture. Add vanilla; beat in flour. Add chocolate chips.

Drop by teaspoonsful onto ungreased cookie sheets. Bake at 275 degrees for 30 minutes.

Donna Flick, Kalamazoo, Mich.

RICH DROP COOKIES

2 cups sifted flour
½ teaspoon baking soda
1½ teaspoons cream of tartar
1 cup white sugar
½ teaspoon salt
1 cup shortening
1 teaspoon vanilla
1 egg

Cream sugar and shortening. Add egg, vanilla and salt. Beat until smooth and fluffy. Sift flour, baking soda and cream of tartar. Add to creamed mixture. Roll into little balls; place on cookie sheet. Decorate with cherry half or colored sprinkles. Bake at 325 degrees for 10–15 minutes.

Rosie O'Connell, Greensburg, Pa.

MINT SWIRL BROWNIES

1 small package (3 ounces) cream cheese, softened
1/4 cup (1/2 stick) margarine, softened
3/4 cup sugar
2 eggs
2/3 cup flour
1/2 teaspoon baking powder
1/2 teaspoon salt
1/3 cup chopped nuts
3 tablespoons cocoa
1/2 teaspoon peppermint extract
Several drops of green food coloring
Chocolate Glaze:
1 tablespoon margarine, melted
1 cup confectioners' sugar, sifted
3 tablespoons cocoa
1/2 teaspoon vanilla
2 tablespoons boiling water

Cream together cream cheese, margarine and sugar; beat in eggs. Stir together flour, baking powder and salt; stir into creamed mixture.

Spoon half the batter into another bowl; stir in nuts and cocoa. Drop chocolate batter by tablespoonsful, checkerboard fashion, into a greased 9-inch square pan.

To remaining batter, add peppermint extract and green food coloring. Spoon green batter into spaces between chocolate batter. Swirl to marbleize, but do not overmix.

Bake in a preheated 350-degree oven for 15-20 minutes. While dough is baking, make *Glaze* by beating together all glaze ingredients until smooth. Remove brownies from oven and pour chocolate glaze over top. Cut at once into bars and cool.

Mrs. Sharon Crider, Evansville, Wis.

BUTTERSCOTCH WHISTLES

1 egg
⅛ teaspoon salt
2 tablespoons flour
½ cup brown sugar
¼ teaspoon vanilla
1 tablespoon chopped nuts

Beat egg; add sugar and salt. Beat thoroughly. Add nuts and flour. Drop mixture from teaspoon onto greased baking sheets. Bake in hot 400-degree oven until brown (1–2 minutes). Remove quickly with spatula. Roll over handle of spoon and cool.

Suzan L. Wiener, Spring Hill, Fla.

SUGAR COOKIES

1 cup confectioners' sugar
1 cup white sugar
1 cup butter (do not substitute margarine)
1 cup shortening
2 eggs
1½ teaspoons vanilla
1½ teaspoons salt
1½ teaspoons cream of tartar
1½ teaspoons soda
4¼ cups sifted flour

Blend first 4 ingredients until light and creamy. Add eggs and vanilla. Sift dry ingredients and add to creamed mixture; mix until well-blended. Form into balls. Put on greased cookie sheets. Flatten with glass dipped in sugar. Bake in 350-degree oven for 10 minutes.

Dorothy Pelster, Hastings, Neb.

LEMON DROP COOKIES

1/2 cup margarine or butter, softened
1-1/3 cups sugar
1/3 cup lemon juice from concentrate
1 (8-ounce) container sour cream
2-1/2 cups unsifted flour
1 teaspoon baking soda
1 teaspoon salt
1/4 teaspoon nutmeg
Lemon Icing (recipe follows)

Preheat oven to 350 degrees. In large mixer bowl, cream together butter and sugar. Blend in sour cream and lemon juice. Blend dry ingredients together and add to butter mixture. Mix well. Drop by rounded teaspoonfuls, 2 inches apart, on greased baking sheet. Bake 13-15 minutes, or until edges are lightly browned. Cool. Frost with Lemon Icing.

Lemon Icing: (Makes 1/2 cup)
1-1/2 cups confectioners' sugar
2 tablespoons water
1 teaspoon lemon juice from concentrate
1/8 teaspoon nutmeg

Combine all ingredients and mix well. Spread on cooled cookies.
Leota Baxter, Ingalls, Kans.

WRAP-AROUND CHERRY COOKIES

2 tablespoons white sugar
5 tablespoons confectioners' sugar
1/2 cup butter
1 cup all-purpose flour
Maraschino cherries

Mix together all ingredients, except cherries; wrap small amount of dough around well-drained maraschino cherries. Bake at 350 degrees for 12–15 minutes. Remove from pan; cool on rack. Use cherry juice to make confectioners' sugar icing or glaze.
Gwen Campbell, Sterling, Va.

APPLE-OATMEAL-HONEY GOODIES
Makes 5 dozen

1/2 cup shortening
1/2 cup brown sugar
1/2 cup honey
2 eggs, beaten
1 cup chopped apples
1/2 cup oatmeal (uncooked, quick)
1 3/4 cups sifted flour
1/2 teaspoon soda
1/2 teaspoon baking powder
1/4 teaspoon salt
2/3 teaspoon cinnamon
1/4 teaspoon cloves
1 1/2 cups chopped nuts
1 cup raisins

Cream shortening and brown sugar; gradually add honey, beating well. Add eggs and beat. Add chopped apples and oatmeal. Sift dry ingredients together and add. Stir in nuts and raisins. Drop by teaspoonfuls onto greased cookie sheet. Bake at 350 degrees for 10 minutes, or until done.
Brenda Peery, Tannersville, Va.

WALDORF SALAD COOKIES

2 3/4 cups flour
1/2 teaspoon baking soda
1/4 teaspoon salt
1 teaspoon cinnamon
1 1/2 cups brown sugar, packed
3/4 cup mayonnaise
2 large eggs
1 teaspoon vanilla
1 1/2 cups coarsely chopped apples
1 cup coarsely chopped nuts
1/4 cup finely chopped celery

In medium bow, stir together flour, baking soda, sslt and cinnamon. In a large bowl, beat together sugar, mayonnaise, eggs and vanilla until smooth. Add flour mixture and beat at low speed until smooth. Stir in apples, nuts and celery.

Drop by level tablespoonsful onto ungreased cookie sheets. Bake at 350 degrees 10-12 minutes, until lightly browned. Cool on racks completely before storing in tightly covered container.
Shirley Viscosi, Worcester, Mass.

LEMON SQUARES

1 cup sifted flour
1/4 cup confectioners' sugar
1/2 cup melted butter

Mix and press into 8-inch square pan; bake at 350 degrees for 20 minutes.

Then mix:
2 beaten eggs
3 generous tablespoons lemon juice
1 cup sugar
1/2 teaspoon baking powder
2 tablespoons flour

Pour on top of first mixture. Return to oven for 25 minutes. Cut into small squares (very rich) and sprinkle with confectioners' sugar while still hot.
Agnes Ward, Erie, Pa.

CHEWY CHOCOLATE COOKIES
Makes 4½ dozen

1¼ cups butter *or* margarine, softened
1¾–2 cups sugar
2 eggs
2 teaspoons vanilla
2 cups all-purpose flour
¾ cup unsweetened cocoa
1 teaspoon baking soda
Dash salt
1 cup chopped nuts, optional

Cream butter or margarine and sugar in large bowl. Add eggs and vanilla; blend well. Combine flour, cocoa, soda and salt; gradually blend into creamed mixture. Stir in nuts, if desired. Drop by teaspoonfuls onto ungreased cookie sheet. Bake at 350 degrees for 8–9 minutes. *Do not overbake.* Cookies will be soft. Cool on sheets until set, about 1 minute. Remove to wire rack to cool completely. Store in airtight container.
Marcella Swigert, Monroe City, Mo.

EASY NO-BAKE BROWNIES

Makes 2 dozen

1 cup finely chopped nuts
1 can sweetened condensed milk
2 (1-ounce) squares unsweetened chocolate
2 to 2-1/2 cups vanilla wafer crumbs (about 48-60 wafers)

In buttered 9-inch square pan, sprinkle 1/4 cup nuts. In saucepan, over low heat, melt chocolate with sweetened condensed milk. Cook and stir until mixture thickens, about 10 minutes. Remove from heat; stir in crumbs and 1/2 cup nuts. Spread evenly in prepared pan. Top with remaining 1/4 cup nuts. Chill 4 hours, or until firm. Cut into 24 squares. Store covered at room temperature.

Dawn Counsil, Williamsport, Pa.

DATE-NUT SQUARES

Makes 2 dozen

3 cups (1 pound) cut-up dates
1 cup water
½ cup *each* granulated sugar, chopped walnuts
¾ cup (1½ sticks) butter
1 cup firmly packed light brown sugar
1¼ cups all-purpose flour
¼ teaspoon salt
1¼ cups quick oats, uncooked

Combine dates, water and granulated sugar; boil 5 minutes, or until thickened. Cool slightly; add nuts; set aside. Preheat oven to 350 degrees. Cream butter. Gradually add brown sugar and continue beating until blended. Add flour, salt and oats. (Mixture will be crumbly.) Pack two-thirds of mixture evenly and firmly on bottom of buttered 13 x 9-inch baking pan; spread with date mixture. Sprinkle remaining crumb mixture over top; press down lightly. Bake 30 minutes. Cool in pan on wire rack. Cut into squares.

BROWN SUGAR CHEWS

1 egg
1 cup brown sugar, packed
1 teaspoon vanilla
½ cup flour
¼ teaspoon salt
¼ teaspoon soda
1 cup coarsely chopped walnuts

Stir together egg, brown sugar and vanilla. Add ½ cup flour sifted with salt and soda. Stir in nuts. Turn into a greased 8 x 8 x 2-inch baking pan and bake at 350 degrees for 18–20 minutes. Cool in pan and cut into squares.

Joy Shamway, Freeport, Ill.

CHICAGO CRUNCHY CHOCOLATE CHIP COOKIES

3-1/2 cups flour
3 teaspoons baking soda
1 teaspoon salt
1/2 cup butter
1/2 cup margarine
1 cup light brown sugar
1 cup granulated sugar
1 egg
1 tablespoon milk
2 teaspoons vanilla
1 cup vegetable oil
1 cup Special K cereal
1 cup quick-cook oats
1 (12-ounce) package semisweet chocolate chips

Mix flour, baking soda, and salt in a small bowl. Cream butter, margarine, and sugars. Add egg; beat well. Add milk, vanilla, and oil. Mix well. Add dry ingredients and mix well. Add Special K, oatmeal, and chocolate chips. Drop by teaspoonfuls on greased cookie sheets. Bake at 350 degrees for 12 minutes, or until lightly browned.

My family loves chocolate chip cookies and these are by far our favorite! I make a double batch and they don't last long.

Phyliss Dixon, Fairbanks, Alaska

CHERRY NUT COOKIES

Makes 4½ dozen

½ cup soft butter *or* margarine
1 cup light brown sugar, packed
1 egg, slightly beaten
1 teaspoon vanilla
2 cups all-purpose flour
½ teaspoon baking soda
¼ teaspoon salt
1 cup chopped walnuts
⅓ cup chopped maraschino cherries

Cream together the butter and sugar. Beat in egg and vanilla until smooth. Blend in flour, baking soda and salt. Stir in walnuts and cherries. Shape dough into a roll about 14 inches long. Wrap in foil or plastic wrap and refrigerate overnight. With a sharp knife, cut dough into ¼-inch slices. Place on ungreased cookie sheets. Bake at 375 degrees for about 10 minutes, or until just golden brown. Remove from cookie sheets while warm. Cool on rack. Store in airtight containers.

Make the dough for these cookies the day before baking, so it can firm up in the refrigerator for thin slicing. The chunks of cherries and nuts make it a good choice to serve during February.

Ella Evanicky, Fayetteville, Texas

POTATO CHIP COOKIES

Makes 2 dozen

1 cup margarine (2 sticks)
½ cup sugar
1 teaspoon vanilla
1 cup crushed potato chips
1 cup all-purpose flour

Preheat oven to 350 degrees. Mix margarine, sugar and vanilla together; blend well. Add potato chips and stir in flour. Form small balls from mixture and place on an ungreased cookie sheet. Press balls flat with the bottom of a glass that has been dipped in sugar. Bake 16–18 minutes, or until lightly browned.

Trenda Leigh, Richmond, Va.

HAWAIIAN BARS

3/4 cup margarine
1 1/2 cups flour
1/2 cup sugar
1/2 teaspoon salt
1 can pineapple pie filling
1 cup flaked coconut

Cut margarine into mixture of flour, sugar and salt until fine particles are formed. Reserve 2 tablespoons of crumb mixture and press remainder into bottom of a 13x9-inch pan. Bake in a preheated 375-degree oven for 15-20 minutes.

Spread pineapple pie filling over partly baked crust. Combine coconut with reserved crumbs and sprinkle over pineapple. Bake 25-30 minutes longer. Cool before cutting into bars.

Mrs. Sharon Crider, Evansville, Wis.

QUICK 'N' EASY COOKIES

1 stick (1/4 pound) margarine
1 cup molasses
1 cup sugar
2 eggs
4 cups flour
1 teaspoon baking soda
2 teaspoons cinnamon
2 teaspoons ginger
1/2 teaspoon ground cloves
1 teaspoon vanilla
3/4 canned milk
1 cup seedless raisins (optional)
1 cup nuts (optional)

Melt margarine and molasses together over low heat. In large mixer bowl, place sugar, eggs and vanilla. Beat at high speed until mixture is light and lemon-colored. Add melted margarine and molasses and beat hard again.

Sift together all dry ingredients. Alternately add flour mixture and milk to molasses batter. Beat until smooth. Stir in raisins and nuts by hand. Drop by teaspoonsful 2 inches apart onto lightly greased cookie sheets. Bake at 350 degrees, 10 minutes for small cookies, 12 minutes for larger cookies. Cool on rack and store in covered jar.

Pearle M. Goodwin, South Ryegate, Vt.

PECAN PIE SURPRISE BARS

1 package Pillsbury yellow cake mix
½ cup butter *or* margarine, melted
1 egg
1 cup chopped pecans

Grease bottom and sides of 13 x 9-inch baking pan. Reserve ⅔ cup dry cake mix for filling. In large mixing bowl, combine remaining dry cake mix, butter and 1 egg; mix until crumbly. Press into prepared pan. Bake at 350 degrees for 15–20 minutes until light golden brown. Meanwhile, prepare filling (recipe follows). Pour filling over partially baked crust; sprinkle with pecans. Return to oven, bake for 30–35 minutes until filling is set. Cool; cut into 36 bars.

Filling:
⅔ cup reserved cake mix
½ cup firmly packed brown sugar
1½ cups dark brown syrup
1 teaspoon vanilla
3 eggs

In large mixer bowl, combine all ingredients; beat at medium speed 1–2 minutes.

Mrs. Jerry Gibson, St. Ann, Mo.

GREAT GOOBER BARS

1 (5½-ounce) package instant chocolate pudding and pie filling
1⅓ cups buttermilk biscuit mix
⅓ cup sugar
1 cup milk
1 teaspoon vanilla extract
3 tablespoons vegetable oil
¾ cup salted peanuts, chopped

Combine pudding, biscuit mix and sugar. Add milk, vanilla and oil; mix well. Turn into a greased 8-inch square baking pan. Sprinkle peanuts on top. Bake at 350 degrees, 25–30 minutes; cut into bars.

Gwen Campbell, Sterling, Va.

ALMOND BARS

2 cups brown sugar
1 cup white sugar
¾ cup melted butter
¾ cup melted lard
4½ cups sifted flour
1 cup almonds, sliced
3 eggs, well-beaten
1 teaspoon soda
1 scant teaspoon salt

Cream butter and lard; add sugars and well-beaten eggs. Sift flour with soda and salt. Combine with creamed mixture; add almonds. Pack into bread pan. (I roll in waxed paper.) Chill in refrigerator 24 hours. Slice and bake until brown at 350 degrees. (I substitute margarine for both butter and lard.) This recipe has been passed down through the family for years.

J.P. Hart, Stoughton, Wis.

PUMPKIN SQUARES
Makes 12 servings

1 cup canned pumpkin
3 1/2 cups miniature marshmallows
1/2 teaspoon cinnamon
1/4 teaspoon ginger
1 cup crushed graham crackers (about 14 crackers)
1/4 cup (1/2 stick) margarine, melted
1 envelope whipped topping mix or 2 cups frozen prepared whipped topping

In large saucepan, melt marshmallow with pumpkin and spices over low heat, stirring until smooth. Cool about 15 minutes. Meanwhile, combine crushed graham crackers with melted margarine; reserve 1/4 cup for topping. Pat remaining crumbs firmly into the bottom of an 8-inch square baking dish.

If using dry whipped topping mix, prepare according to package directions. Fold prepared topping into cooled marshmallow mixture and spread over crust. Top with reserved crumbs and chill several hours or overnight.

Cut into squares to serve.

Mrs. Emily Dougherty, Montpelier, Ind.

CINNAMON SQUARES

Makes about 75 2-inch squares

1/2 cup margarine
3/4 cup sugar
1 egg yolk
2 teaspoons vanilla
2 cups flour
3 teaspoons cinnamon
1 egg white
Chocolate chips, chopped walnuts, or coconut

Cream margarine with sugar until fluffy; add egg yolk and vanilla; blend; add flour and cinnamon. Mix well. Divide dough between two greased 15x10x1-inch jelly roll pans. Flatten down with heels of hands in pans. Lightly beat the egg white; brush over batter, and mark batter into squares.

Place chocolate chips, nuts or coconut on top. Bake at 350 degrees 20-30 minutes.

Mrs. Bess Notkin, Chelsea, Mass.

BOBBIE'S APPLE CAKE BARS

Makes 12 bars

2 cups whole-wheat flour
1/4 cup toasted wheat germ
2 teaspoons baking soda
1 teaspoon cinnamon
1/2 teaspoon salt
1/2 teaspoon nutmeg
4 cups diced, peeled, tart cooking apples (4 large)
1 cup sugar
1 cup packed brown sugar
1/2 cup oil
1 cup chopped walnuts
2 eggs, beaten well
1 teaspoon vanilla

Stir together flour, wheat germ, soda, cinnamon, salt and nutmeg; set aside. In large bowl, combine apples, sugars, oil, walnuts, eggs and vanilla. Add flour mixture; stir gently with wooden spoon to blend well. Turn into a greased 9x13x2-inch pan.

Bake in a preheated oven at 350 degrees for 50 minutes until cake tests done (pulls away form sides of pan). Cool in pan on rack. If desired, sprinkle with confectioners' sugar. Cut into 12 bars.

Bobbie Mae Cooley, Bowen, Ill.

GINGERSNAPS

2 cups flour
1 tablespoon ground ginger
2 teaspoons baking soda
1 teaspoon cinnamon
½ teaspoon salt
¾ cup shortening
1 cup sugar
1 egg
¼ cup molasses

Measure flour, ginger, soda, cinnamon and salt; put aside. Cream shortening until soft. Gradually add sugar, creaming until light and fluffy. Beat in egg and molasses. Add dry ingredients over creamed mixture; blend well. Form teaspoonfuls of dough into small balls by rolling them lightly between palms of hands. Roll dough balls in granulated sugar to cover entire surface. Place 2 inches apart on ungreased cookie sheet. Bake at 350 degrees for 12–15 minutes until tops are crackly and cookies are brown.

A good, old-fashioned cookie!

Mrs. George Franks, Millerton, Pa.

CRANBERRY DROPS

About 1-1/2 dozen

1/2 cup butter
1 cup granulated sugar
3/4 cup brown sugar, packed
1/4 cup milk
2 tablespoons orange juice
1 egg
3 cups flour
1 teaspoon baking powder
1/2 teaspoon salt
1/4 teaspoon soda
1 cup chopped nuts
2-1/2 cups coarsely chopped cranberries

Preheat oven to 375 degrees. Cream butter and sugars together. Beat in milk, orange juice and egg. Measure flour before sifting. Stir together flour, baking powder, salt and soda. Blend well with sugar mixture. Stir in chopped nuts and cranberries. Drop dough by teaspoonfuls on greased baking sheet. Bake 10-15 minutes.

P. J. Leikness, Stoughton, Wis.

PEANUT BUTTER DROP COOKIES

1/2 cup sugar
2 tablespoons butter
1 egg
2 tablespoon milk
2 teaspoons baking powder
1/8 teaspoon salt
3/4 cup peanut butter
1 cup flour
1/2 cup nuts, chopped

Cream sugar and butter. Add egg and beat. Add milk and flour, sifted with salt and baking powder. Add peanut butter. Stir in nuts. Drop on greased baking sheet and bake 15 minutes in 400-degree oven.

Suzan L. Wiener, Spring Hill, Fla.

OLD FAMILY FAVORITE TOFFEE SQUARES

1 cup margarine *or* half margarine and half butter
1 cup brown sugar
1 egg yolk
1 teaspoon vanilla
2 cups flour
1 cup chocolate chips
¼ teaspoon Crisco
Ground walnuts

Cream shortening and sugar. Add egg yolk and vanilla; blend together. Add flour, mix together again. Spread this mixture onto a cookie sheet by pinching pieces of dough and pressing dough to cover the cookie sheet, working with your fingers. Bake 15 minutes at 325 degrees.

Melt chocolate chips. Add ¼ teaspoon Crisco to chocolate to keep it soft.

After dough is baked, spread with chocolate, while warm. Thinly spread chocolate with your fingers instead of a knife. While chocolate is still warm, sprinkle with ground walnuts. After chocolate is set, cut cookies into 1½-inch squares.

Luscious!!

Sally Simpson, Detroit, Mich.

Cooking
FOR TWO

LOUIS DRESSING
Serves 2

Good dressing to spoon over cooked fresh shrimp, crabmeat or chunks of canned salmon on a bed of lettuce.

1/4 cup mayonnaise
1 tablespoon sweet pickle relish
2 tablespoons chili sauce
1 teaspoon lemon juice
1/2 teaspoon horseradish
1/4 teaspoon salt
1 shake or grinding black pepper
1 green onion

In a small bowl combine all ingredients, except green onion. Snip in onion with scissors. Mix well. Cover; chill.

MEATBALL SANDWICHES
Serves 2

*Generous 1/2 pound lean ground beef
2 tablespoons chopped onion
1/4 teaspoon salt
Pinch pepper
Soy Barbecue Sauce (recipe follows)
2 pita bread rounds or buns

Combine beef, onion, salt, and pepper. Shape lightly into balls — I make small ones for sandwiches. Cook in a non-stick skillet over medium heat until brown, stirring as necessary. When fully cooked remove all drippings from skillet. Pour barbecue sauce over meatballs; stir to cook; cook on low a few minutes. These can be made ahead and reheated. Serve in warm pita or on toasted buns.

*Meat loaf mixture is a flavorful change for meatballs. It contains pork, so be sure to fully cook.

CHICKEN SALAD-FILLED JUMBO SHELLS
Serves 2

If you don't have cooked chicken on hand follow this work schedule: Cook 2 large chicken breast halves. In a saucepan, cover rinsed chicken with cold water; add 2 split garlic cloves and salt. Bring quickly to boiling; reduce heat; cover; simmer until fork tender, 30 to 40 minutes. Remove to a plate. Discard garlic.

Return chicken broth to boiling (add more water and salt, if necessary). Add pasta shells; cook until fork tender. Cool and drain as directed above. Meanwhile, cook bacon; chop celery; prepare dressing.

When chicken is cool enough to handle remove skin and bones; dice finely. Assemble according to following directions.

Filling:
1/3 cup mayonnaise
2 teaspoons water
1/3 cup celery, finely chopped
1 green onion
2 cups finely diced, cooked chicken
1/4 to 1/2 teaspoon salt (I like plenty of salt, so I use 1/2 teaspoon)
4 strips bacon, cooked until crisp and drained
6-8 jumbo shells, cooked and cooled
Chives for garnish, if available

Into a medium bowl measure mayonnaise and water. (The water prevents salad from being pasty.) Whisk until smooth. Stir in celery; snip in onion with scissors. Add chicken; sprinkle on salt; mix well. Crumble in bacon; mix.

Spoon chicken salad into pasta shells; sprinkle with chopped chives if using. Cover and refrigerate. To serve, arrange on a bed of lettuce.

SOFT PEACH ICE CREAM
Serves 2

Blender-quick and so refreshing.

1 large or 2 small peaches (*or* nectarines)
4 large scoops ice cream (vanilla, almond, butter pecan or whatever sounds good to you)
1/4 teaspoon almond flavoring

Chill 2 small-stemmed dessert or wine glasses.

Peel and pit peaches; slice into blender container. Place ice cream on top; dribble in almond flavoring. Let sit in refrigerator during meal. When ready to serve blend just long enough to combine thoroughly, scraping down as necessary. It's a very thick liquid. Pour into chilled glasses and serve immediately.

OVEN BARBECUED CHICKEN WINGS

Serves 2

4 tablespoons ketchup
2 tablespoons vinegar
2 tablespoons water
1 teaspoon Worcestershire sauce
1 teaspoon sugar
1/2 teaspoon salt
1/4 teaspoon dry mustard
1/4 teaspoon chili powder
1/8 teaspoon pepper or dash
   Tabasco sauce
8 chicken wings, tips removed

Measure all ingredients, except chicken wings, into medium size bowl; whisk until well blended. To do ahead, add chicken wings; toss well; cover and refrigerate up to 24 hours. For last-minute preparation, dip chicken wings in sauce to coat; place skin-side down on rack on pan prepared as directed in italics at beginning of this article. Bake at 425 degrees for 20 minutes. Brush with sauce; turn; brush other side; bake until brown and tender, about 30 minutes longer.

BEEF PAPRIKA

Serves 4

Freeze half for another meal.
1-1/2 pounds boneless round
   steak
1/4 cup flour
1 teaspoon salt
1/4 teaspoon black pepper
1 medium onion
1 clove garlic
4 tablespoons oil
1 cup beef broth (Swanson's works
   well)
3 drops Tabasco sauce
1 teaspoon paprika
1 tablespoon sour cream

Trim meat; cut into four serving-size pieces. Place meat on cutting board; pound with a mallet on both sides until about 3/8 inch thick. Measure flour, salt, and pepper onto a plate; mix with a fork; coat meat on both sides with flour; set aside.

Slice onion thinly; mince garlic. Heat 1 tablespoon oil in a 12-inch skillet. Cook onions and garlic until transparent. Remove from skillet. Add remaining 3 tablespoons oil to skillet; when hot add meat in single layer. Brown on both sides. Add onions, garlic, broth, Tabasco sauce, and paprika. Stir; bring to boiling; partially cover; cook on low heat until meat is tender, 10 to 15 minutes.

Remove half of meat and sauce to freeze. Stir sour cream into remaining sauce. Set over low heat until sauce is warm.

Serve with noodles. (I cook 2 cups dry noodles for us. Drain cooked noodles; return to warm pan; stir in a large spoonful of paprika sauce to flavor noodles and to prevent them from sticking together.)

For another meal thaw frozen beef in refrigerator. Reheat; stir in 1 tablespoon sour cream just before serving

SUMMER SPAGHETTI

Serves 2

1 large or 2 medium ripe tomatoes
1-1/2 tablespoons olive oil
1 small clove garlic, crushed
5 fresh basil leaves, slivered (or
   1/2 teaspoon crushed dried basil)
1 tablespoon minced parsley
Dash hot pepper sauce
Grinding or pinch black pepper
1/4 teaspoon salt
3 black olives, slivered (optional,
   but a real flavor boost)
2 to 3 ounces thin spaghetti

Peel tomato. Cut in half crosswise; remove and discard juicy seed sections (I use my thumb to scoop them out). Cut tomato into small chunks; set aside in strainer to drain.

In a small bowl combine oil, garlic, basil, parsley, hot sauce, pepper, salt, and olives if using. Add tomato chunks; mix well. Cover; set aside up to two hours on counter. Refrigerate for longer storage, but set out to warm to room temperature before serving.

Cook spaghetti according to package directions (I snap it in half before cooking). Quickly drain in a strainer; return to hot cooking pan; add tomato mixture; toss well. Serve immediately—with slotted spoon to drain, if necessary.

TOMATO-CHEESE BULGUR*

2 servings

A hearty Tex-Mex-flavored side dish to serve with beef or lamb patties, sausage links, roast pork, or lamb.

1-1/2 tablespoons margarine
1/2 onion, chopped
1 clove garlic, minced
1/4 green pepper, chopped
1/2 cup bulgur wheat
1/4 teaspoon dried basil
1/4 teaspoon chili powder
1/4 teaspoon salt
1/2 teaspoon sugar
1 cup tomato juice
1/2 cup shredded sharp Cheddar
   cheese

In medium skillet melt margarine on low heat. Add onion, garlic, and green pepper as you chop them. Cook until onion and green pepper are soft. Add bulgur. Cook one minute, stirring, on medium heat. Remove from heat. Measure in oregano, basil, chili powder, salt, and sugar, then stir in tomato juice. (If skillet is too hot when tomato juice is added, the dish will have a burned taste.) Over medium heat, stir to mix well. Bring to boiling; cover; reduce heat; simmer until all liquid is absorbed, about 20 minutes. Remove from heat; add cheese; stir until melted and serve.

BULGUR SALAD

2 servings

This do-ahead salad is an American version of Tabouli (or Tabbouleh). The mint leaves are optional, but an especially good addition if served with lamb.

1/3 cup bulgur wheat
Water
1 clove garlic
2 tablespoons olive oil
1 tablespoon lemon juice
1/2 teaspoon salt
Dash black pepper
2 sprigs parsley
1 green onion
4 mint leaves (optional)
1 large tomato

Measure bulgur into a small bowl; add hot tap water to cover. Split garlic clove; push down into bulgur; let stand about 20 minutes.

Meanwhile, in a medium bowl, whisk together oil, lemon juice, salt, and pepper. With scissors snip in parsley, green onion, and mint, if using. Chop tomato (on a plate to save juice); add tomato and juice to dressing.

Remove garlic from bulgur; drain in a strainer; press out excess water with back of spoon; add to tomato mixture. Mix well; cover; refrigerate several hours to overnight. (I usually make it in the morning for the evening meal.)

BULGUR PILAF

2 Servings

1 tablespoon butter
1 green onion
1/3 cup bulgur wheat
3/4 cup chicken or beef broth

In medium saucepan melt butter. With scissors snip in onion; cook until soft. Add bulgur; stir over medium heat about one minute. Remove from heat; stir in broth; bring to boiling over high heat; cover; reduce heat; simmer until all liquid is absorbed, 15 to 20 minutes. Taste for salt. Lighten with a fork. Sprinkle with chopped parsley, chives, or other fresh herb if desired. Try adding cooked (or leftover) peas just before serving.

If cooked ahead, add a little water to reheat.

PIEROGI ONE-DISH

12 potatoes, boiled and mashed
1 cup shredded cheddar cheese
1-1/2 cups butter (or margarine)
1 onion, minced
2 cups cooked noodles

Mash potatoes and mix in cheddar cheese. Sauté onions in margarine. Cook noodles and allow to cool. In a well-greased casserole, place a layer of noodles, potatoes, then onions. Repeat with second layer. Cover and bake at 325 degrees for 25 minutes.

FILLING

CHEESE 'N CHIVE

1/2 cup cottage cheese
3 eggs, beaten
1 teaspoon sugar
2 tablespoons chives

Combine all ingredients and mix well. Place by small teaspoonsful on pierogies and seal edges well.

FILLING

CABBAGE 'N BACON

1/2 head cabbage, chopped
1/2 pound bacon
1 small onion, minced

Steam cabbage and place in a meat grinder, cutting until very fine. Meanwhile, fry bacon and crumble. Add bacon and onion to cabbage and blend well.

FILLING

MUSHROOMS

1 cup mushrooms, chopped
2 tablespoons butter
2 egg yolks

Melt butter and sauté mushrooms. Remove from heat and add egg yolks for firmness. Mix well.

BLENDER PIEROGI DOUGH

2 cups cottage cheese
1 tablespoon butter
3 eggs, separated
1 teaspoon salt
1 teaspoon sugar
2-1/2 cups flour

In a blender, mix cottage cheese until smooth. Add egg yolks, salt, sugar and flour. Beat until light. Add egg whites and fold in. Knead on a floured board for about 15 minutes. Roll out as thin as possible and cut with biscuit cutter. Place filling in center of dough and fold. Moisten with water. Carefully place in boiling water until they rise to the top.

PIEROGI DOUGH

3 cups sifted flour
1 teaspoon salt
1/3 cup butter
2 eggs, beaten
3/4 cup warm water

Sift flour and salt together. Use a fork to work in butter (batter will be lumpy). Add eggs and water; stir until smooth. Place dough on well-floured board and knead until smooth, about 15 minutes. Set aside for 15 minutes.

Roll out dough as thin as possible. Cut dough with biscuit cutter. Spoon a small teaspoon of filling onto the center of each piece of pierogi dough.

Fold dough in half and pinch edges together by sealing with water. Carefully place in salted boiling water, cooking about 7 minutes, *or until they rise to the top*. Drain and serve with melted butter.

DESSERT PLUM SAUCE
Plenty for 2 sundaes

2 tablespoons sugar
1/2 teaspoon cornstarch
Pinch salt
2 large red plums
1/2 teaspoon lemon juice, if you have it
Few drops almond flavoring (optional)

In a small dry saucepan mix sugar, cornstarch, and salt until cornstarch disappears using a small whisk. Slice plums into saucepan. Stir gently over medium heat until boiling; reduce heat; simmer until sauce is thickened and clear, about 4 minutes. Stir in lemon juice and almond flavoring, if using. Set aside to cool completely. Serve over vanilla ice cream.

PINEAPPLE BUTTERMILK SHERBET

There is nothing more refreshing on a blistering hot day.

2 cups buttermilk
1/3 cup sugar
1 teaspoon vanilla
1 (8-ounce) can crushed pineapple, undrained (preferably in heavy syrup)

Measure buttermilk into a medium bowl. (I use a stainless steel bowl so that I can put it into the freezer.) Whisk in sugar and vanilla; stir in pineapple. Freeze until mushy. This takes about 2 hours. Whisk well; return bowl to freezer for about 2 hours, stirring now and then for a creamy sherbet.

Leftover sherbet will freeze solid—transfer to refrigerator to soften before serving.

LIME SORBET
Serves 2

A cool lime-flavored ice.

1/3 cup sugar
2/3 cup water
1 lime
Few grains salt

Place a one-quart freezer-safe bowl in freezer.

Combine sugar and water in a small saucepan. Stir over medium heat until sugar dissolves. When it comes to a boil, reduce heat and simmer for 6 minutes.

Roll lime on counter top to release juice; squeeze lime; add juice and salt to sweet syrup. Transfer to chilled bowl and freeze until mushy. It usually takes about 2 hours. Whisk thoroughly; freeze until barely firm. Serve in chilled dishes.

SHORTCAKE
(Two servings)

1/2 cup flour, spoon lightly into cup
3/4 teaspoon baking powder
1/8 teaspoon salt
1 tablespoons sugar
2 tablespoon shortening (I use half butter)
3 tablespoons milk

Preheat oven to 425-degrees. Measure flour, baking powder, salt and sugar into small bowl. Mix with pastry blender. Add shortening; cut in with pastry blender. When like fine crumbs, add milk; mix lightly with fork until it comes together (it will be a sticky ball). Drop into two mounds on small ungreased baking sheet. Use a fork to gently flatten and shape to a thick 3-inch biscuit. Sprinkle with sugar. Bake until beginning to brown, 10 to 12 minutes. Transfer to cooking rack. Split as soon as cool enough to handle, Serve warm or cold.

To assemble strawberry shortcake, spread bottom of shortcake with sweetened whipped cream; spoon on sliced, sweetened strawberries; cover with biscuit top, remaining whipped cream and berries.

SHORTCUT BREAD PUDDING WITH BOURBON SAUCE
Serves 2

Using cinnamon raisin bread is the shortcut. Expect a firm pudding because it is served with sauce.

1 tablespoon butter or margarine
2-1/2 slices cinnamon raisin bread
1 large egg
3/4 cup half-and-half or milk
1/4 cup sugar
1/8 teaspoon salt
1/2 teaspoon vanilla

Preheat oven to 350 degrees. Grease or spray a 1-quart casserole or souffle dish with pan release. Spread butter on one side of bread; cut into 1-inch squares. (1-1/2 cups loosely packed).

In a medium bowl, whisk egg to blend; whisk in half-and-half or milk, sugar, salt and vanilla. Add bread squares; stir until coated. (Let set a few minutes.) Pour into prepared dish. Set dish in pan containing 1/2 inch warm tap water. Bake until a rinsed knife inserted half way to center comes out clean, not milky, 35-40 minutes. Remove dish from hot water; cool at least 20 minutes before serving. Spoon into dessert dishes; pour on Bourbon Sauce.

Bourbon Sauce:
1/4 cup light brown sugar
1-1/2 teaspoons cornstarch
Few grains salt
1/3 cup water
1 to 2 tablespoons bourbon
1 tablespoon butter
1/4 teaspoon vanilla

Use brandy or dark rum instead of bourbon, if you prefer—one tablespoon for a mild-flavored sauce, two tablespoons for a powerful flavor.

In a small saucepan mix brown sugar, cornstarch, and salt. Stir in water; mix until smooth. With a rubber spatula stir over medium heat until boiling. Cook over low heat about 4 minutes, stirring often. Remove from heat; add bourbon; stir 1 minute over high heat (to evaporate the alcohol—empty calories); take off heat; stir in butter and vanilla. If made ahead, cover when cool and leave on counter. Serve sauce warm, or at room temperature, if dessert is hot.

SWEET MILK WAFFLES

An alternative mixing method — folding in beaten egg white — is also given. It makes a somewhat lighter waffle

3 tablespoons butter or margarine (see Note)
1 cup flour, lightly spooned into cup
2 teaspoons baking powder
1 teaspoon sugar
1/4 teaspoon salt
1 large egg
1 cup milk
1/4 teaspoon vanilla

Yield: 2 cups batter; two and one-half 10 by 6-inch waffles.

Spray waffle iron with Pam, release; preheat.

Melt butter in a custard cup in microwave oven or in small saucepan on stove; set aside.

Into pitcher or medium bowl measure flour, baking powder, sugar, and salt. Blend with mixer on lowest speed; set aside.

In a small bowl beat egg until light. On low speed beat in milk, vanilla, and melted butter. Add to dry ingredients; mix to blend well on low speed.

Pour over center three-fourths of preheated waffle iron. Cook until steam is no longer escaping around edge of waffle iron.

Note: If using 2% milk increase butter to 4 tablespoons.

Alternative mixing method: Melt butter. Separate egg putting white into a very clean small bowl and yolk into pitcher or medium bowl. Add milk to egg yolk. Measure flour, baking powder, sugar, and salt into small bowl; whisk to blend. Beat egg white until it will just hold stiff peaks. Transfer beater to yolk-milk mixture; beat until smooth. Add dry ingredients; beat smooth. With rubber spatula stir in melted butter, then fold in beaten egg white. This batter thickens a bit on standing, so refrigerate one hour before using if possible.

RICH BUTTERMILK WAFFLES

1/3 cup butter or margarine
1 cup flour, lightly spooned into cup
1/4 teaspoon salt
1/2 teaspoon soda
1 teaspoon baking powder
1 teaspoon sugar
2 eggs
1 cup buttermilk
1/4 teaspoon vanilla

Yield: 2-1/2 cups batter; three 10 by 6-inch waffles. Spray waffle iron with pan release; preheat.

Melt butter in a custard cup in microwave oven or in small saucepan on stove; set aside.

Measure flour, salt, soda, baking powder, and sugar into a small bowl. Blend with mixer on lowest speed; set aside.

In a pitcher or medium bowl beat eggs until light. On low speed add dry ingredients in three additions alternating with buttermilk in two additions. Blend in melted butter and vanilla.

Pour over center three-fourths of preheated waffle iron. Cook until steam is no longer escaping around edge of waffle iron.

DESSERT SOUFFLE
Two servings

Use one tablespoon dark rum, brandy or a liqueur instead of vanilla if desired.

2 large eggs
1-1/2 tablespoons butter
1-1/2 tablespoons flour
1/8 teaspoon salt
1/2 cup milk
1 teaspoon vanilla
1/4 cup sugar, divided

Separate eggs, whites into very clean medium mixing bowl, yolks into another medium bowl.

Grease or spray with pan release a one-quart straight-sided baking dish. Coat with sugar; set aside.

Preheat oven to 325 degrees.

In a small saucepan melt butter; whisk in flour and salt; cook, whisking, until boiling and bubbly. Whisk in milk; whisk over medium heat until smooth and thick. Remove from heat; whisk in vanilla or other flavoring; set aside to cool.

Beat egg whites just until peaks are soft (tips roll over) when beater is lifted. Gradually beat in half of sugar (2 tablespoons). Beat until stiff and glossy. Transfer beaters to yolks; tilt bowl so beaters are in yolks; beat about 1 minute; gradually beat in remaining sugar (2 tablespoons). On low speed beat in sauce. With a rubber spatula gently fold in egg whites. Pour into prepared dish. Bake until set—cake tester comes out dry— about 25 minutes. Immediately spoon into dessert dishes; pour on chocolate sauce.

ORANGE-FLAVORED APPLES
Serves 2

2 large cooking apples
1 tablespoon butter or margarine
1/4 cup brown sugar
1/4 cup orange juice
Pinch nutmeg

Peel; core and cut apples into eighths.

In medium-size skillet melt butter; swirl to coat bottom of skillet. Add apples. Sprinkle on sugar. Pour orange juice over apples. Cook on high heat until juice begins to boil. Stir; cover with lid ajar; reduce heat to low; cook until apples are barely tender, stirring now and then, about 8 minutes. Remove apples with slotted spoon to bowl. Add nutmeg to sauce; boil over high heat to reduce and thicken, about 1 minute; pour over apples.

Serve over vanilla ice cream, or plain, if you prefer a simple dessert.

Desserts
DELICIOUS

CRANBERRY DELIGHT
Serves 8

1 cup graham cracker crumbs
1/4 cup margarine, melted
1 cup cranberries
3/4 cup sugar
1/2 cup water
1/4 cup chopped nuts
2 tablespoons orange marmalade
   (optional)
1 (8 ounce) package cream cheese
1/3 cup confectioners' sugar
1 tablespoon milk
1 teaspoon vanilla
1 cup heavy cream, whipped

Combine graham cracker crumbs and margarine. Press into 8-inch square pan. In saucepan, combine cranberries, sugar and water. Simmer 20 minutes. Stir in nuts and marmalade. Chill in refrigerator; set aside.

Mix cream cheese, confectioners' sugar, milk and vanilla. Fold in whipped cream; spoon over crust. Top with cranberry mixture. Chill overnight.

Deborah M. Mucháy, Cleveland, Ohio

BETHEL GROVE'S ICE CREAM SOCIAL
Makes 1 gallon

1-3/4 cups sugar
6 eggs
1 (3-ounce) package instant vanilla
   pudding
1/2 cup light corn syrup
1 tablespoon real vanilla
1/4 teaspoon lemon extract
1 quart half-and-half

Beat all ingredients in the order listed until smooth. Pour into cylinder. Add milk to fill line or to 3 inches from top of container. Freeze in freezer (hand-cranked or electric).

ANGELIC PEACH TRIFLE
Makes 10 servings

1 (13-ounce) angel food cake
1 (16-ounce) can Lite sliced
   peaches, drained (reserve syrup)
1/4 teaspoon almond extract
1-1/2 cups cold skim milk
1 (4-serving-size) package sugar-
   free vanilla instant pudding and
   pie filling
1 envelope whipped topping mix (2-
   cup size)
1 (8-ounce) container low-fat peach
   yogurt
3 tablespoons natural sliced almonds

Cube cake and arrange 1/3 of the cubes in a 2-quart serving dish. Coarsely chop peaches. Measure 6 tablespoons reserved syrup. Add to peaches with almond extract. Pour milk into deep, narrow bowl. Add pudding and pie filling mix, along with whipped topping mix. Beat until thickened. Fold in yogurt.

Spoon 1/3 peach mixture over layer cake cubes in dish and 1/3 pudding mixture over peaches. Repeat layers, ending with pudding. Sprinkle top with almonds. Chill 4 hours, or overnight. (216 calories per serving)

Anna Y. Bodisch, Coplay, Pa.

GRAHAM CRACKER PUDDING

1 cup brown sugar
2 heaping tablespoons flour
1 teaspoon vanilla
2 cups milk
1 or 2 bananas

Cook sugar, flour, vanilla and milk until thick. Crush 10 graham crackers to very fine crumbs; stir into pudding, along with sliced bananas.

Nancy Mathias, Kokomo, Ind.

DELUXE FUDGY BROWNIES

4 squares unsweetened chocolate
½ cup butter *or* margarine
4 eggs
2 cups sugar
1 cup sifted flour
1 teaspoon vanilla
1 cup coarsely chopped nuts

Melt chocolate and butter together over hot water. Cool slightly. Beat eggs until foamy; gradually add sugar, beating thoroughly after each addition. Add chocolate mixture and blend. Stir in flour. Then add vanilla and nuts. Spread in greased 9 x 9 x 2-inch pan. Bake at 325 degrees for 40–50 minutes. Cool in pan, then cut into squares or bars. Will have crunchy top and bottom crust with a center almost like chocolate cream. Delicious served straight from the freezer.

Ruth Morris, Bradenton, Fla.

CRANBERRY CAKE DESSERT

1 cup sugar
2 cups flour
2 teaspoons baking powder
1/4 teaspoon salt
1 cup milk
3 tablespoons melted butter
2 cups whole cranberries (fresh or frozen)

Sift dry ingredients. Add milk and butter; mix. Add cranberries. Bake in greased 9x13-inch pan at 350 degrees for 30 minutes or until lightly browned. Serve with sauce.

Sauce:
1 cup sugar
1/2 cup butter or margarine
1/2 pint whipping cream

Bring ingredients to gentle boil for about 8 minutes. Spoon warm over cake.

Phyllis Lien, Stoughton, Wis.

DATE AND ALMOND BROWNIES
Makes 16–20 bars

⅔ cup flour
½ teaspoon baking powder
¼ teaspoon salt
¼ cup butter *or* margarine
2 squares baking chocolate
1 cup sugar
2 eggs, beaten
½ cup chopped almonds
½ cup chopped dates*
1 teaspoon vanilla extract

Preheat oven to 350 degrees. Grease an 8-inch square pan. Sift flour, baking powder and salt together. Melt butter and chocolate in top of double boiler. Add sugar to eggs; beat well. Add butter and chocolate; stir in flour and add almonds, dates and vanilla. Turn into pan. Bake 25 minutes. Cool in pan; cut into squares or bars. Decorate with dates or almonds, if desired.
*Chopped, uncooked prunes may be substituted for dates, if desired.

Mrs. A. Mayer, Richmond, Va.

FRUIT-COCKTAIL DESSERT
Serves 6

2 eggs
1 can fruit cocktail
1-1/2 cups sugar
2 cups flour
2 teaspoons baking soda
1 teaspoon vanilla
1/2 cup brown sugar
1 cup dry flaked coconut

Mix together eggs and fruit cocktail. Add sugar; mix well. Sift together flour and soda. Add egg mixture; mix. Add vanilla. Put into 9 x 13-inch baking pan. Sprinkle with brown sugar and coconut. Bake at 350 degrees for 30 minutes.

June Harding, Ferndale, Mich.

LIGHT 'N' LUSCIOUS CHILLED TORTE
Serves 5

½ cup fructose
2 tablespoons cornstarch
1⅓ cups skim milk
⅓ cup water
1 egg, well-beaten
1 teaspoon vanilla
1½ squares unsweetened chocolate, melted
1 (10-ounce) angel food loaf cake
1 tablespoon finely chopped nuts

In a saucepan combine fructose and cornstarch; mix to blend. Stir in skim milk and water. Cook, stirring constantly, until mixture begins to thicken. Stir small amount of hot mixture into egg; return egg mixture to pan. Continue cooking until mixture just comes to a boil and thickens. Stir in vanilla and chocolate. Cover surface with waxed paper; chill. Slice cake horizontally, making 3 layers. Fill and frost cake layers. Sprinkle nuts over top of cake. Chill several hours before serving. (150 calories per slice)

Gwen Campbell, Sterling, Va.

MANDARIN ORANGE DESSERT

Make any crumb crust you wish. I make this recipe with Ritz or Hi-Ho crackers.

Crust:
60 Ritz crackers, crushed (2 packages)
1/4 cup sugar
1/4 pound butter or margarine, melted

Mix and press in bottom of 9x13-inch pan.

Filling:
2 small boxes instant coconut pudding mix
2 cups cold milk
1 (8-ounce) Cool Whip
2 cans mandarin oranges, drained

Mix pudding with cold milk until stiff (I use egg beater for 2 minutes). Add Cool Whip. Stir in mandarin oranges; combine carefully. Chill 4–5 hours, or overnight before serving.

Ruth Daklin, St. Charles, Ill.

OLD-FASHIONED RICE PUDDING

2 cups rice
Cover rice with water
2 sticks margarine
1-1/2 cups sugar
1-1/2 cups raisins
2 teaspoons vanilla
4 eggs
4 cups milk (milk may be adjusted to your liking)

Cook rice until tender. Add margarine, sugar and raisins; stir; remove from heat. Mix together in a bowl, well-beaten eggs, milk and vanilla; stir well. Add to rice mixture and bake 30 minutes, covered, and 30 minutes, uncovered at 350 degrees. Do not let rice brown, but bake until fairly firm. Sprinkle cinnamon or nutmeg on individual servings when serving.

Georgia Jarman, Mt. Pleasant, Mich.

COBBLER TOPPING

2 cups flour
2 teaspoons baking powder
1/2 teaspoon salt
1 tablespoon sugar
1/4 cup (1/2 stick) butter
2/3 cup milk

Sift dry ingredients into a mixing bowl. Grate in butter, mixing well, rubbing between fingers.

Stir in milk gradually, until the dough holds its shape, adding another tablespoonful or two of milk, if necessary. Turn out onto a floured surface. Divide dough. Pat into 2 (9-inch) rounds or squares. Cut into wedges or squares. Use half to top the cobbler. Bake the other half separately. Rewarm the extras for breakfast.

This topping recipe also makes a good shortcake. Try it with frozen berries or with canned fruit and whipped cream.

APPLE COBBLER WITH HAZEL NUTS

7 tart apples
1/2 cup brown sugar, or to taste
1/3 to 1/2 cup shelled hazel nuts (filberts)
1 teaspoon cinnamon
1 tablespoon flour
Cobbler Topping (recipe follows)

Peel and slice apples. Mix them in a deep baking dish with nuts, sugar, cinnamon, and flour. Spoon biscuit-topping dough onto apples. Bake at 425 degrees for about 30 minutes, until topping is brown and apples are tender.

APPLE NUT TORTE

Serves 8–10

1-1/2 cups sugar
4 eggs, well-beaten
2/3 cup flour
1 teaspoon baking powder

1/2 teaspoon salt
2 cups peeled, chopped apples
1 cup chopped walnuts

Add sugar to eggs; beat until thick and light. Sift together flour, baking powder and salt; fold into egg mixture. Lightly stir in apples and nuts. Grease bottom of 13 x 9 x 2-inch pan. Pour in batter and bake in 350-degree oven for 40–45 minutes. Cool.

Shari Crider, Stoughton, Wis.

MINT BROWNIES

¾ cup plus 2 tablespoons sifted cake flour
1 cup sugar
7 tablespoons cocoa
½ teaspoon baking powder
¾ teaspoon salt
⅔ cup shortening
2 eggs
1 teaspoon vanilla
1 tablespoon light corn syrup
1 cup walnuts, coarsely chopped

In large bowl, beat all ingredients together at low speed, except walnuts; stir in walnuts with spoon. Pour battter into greased 8-inch square pan. Bake at 350 degrees about 40 minutes or until toothpick inserted near center comes out clean. Cool and frost.

Mint Frosting:

1 tablespoon shortening
1 tablespoon butter
2½ tablespoons scalded hot cream
2 cups powdered sugar
¼ teaspoon salt
½ teaspoon vanilla
¼ teaspoon peppermint extract
Green food coloring
1 ounce semisweet chocolate
1 teaspoon shortening

Melt 1 tablespoon shortening and 1 tablespoon butter in hot cream. Pour over powdered sugar and salt; stir well. Add vanilla and peppermint extract, beat until thick enough to spread. Add enough food coloring to tint a pastel mint green. Spread brownies with frosting. Melt chocolate and shortening together. Cool and drizzle over frosting in thin stream from teaspoon. Cut into squares.

Judy Haffner, Auke Bay, Alaska

CREAM CHEESE AND CHERRY DESSERT

Serves 18–20

Crust:
2 cups crushed pretzels
1 cup melted butter **or** margarine
¾ cup sugar

Filling:
1 (8-ounce) package cream cheese, softened
1 cup confectioners' sugar
1 (8-ounce) container whipped topping

Topping:
1 (30-ounce) can cherry pie filling

For crust: Combine ingredients and press into a 9 x 13-inch pan, reserving some for garnish.

For filling: Combine and beat cream cheese with confectioners' sugar. Add whipped topping to the cheese mixture, ½ cup at a time, mixing gently. Spread over crust.

Spread pie filling over top and sprinkle with reserved pretzel mixture. Refrigerate 2–3 hours.

Kit Rollins, Cedarburg, Wis.

APPLE BROWNIES

½ cup butter
¼ teaspoon salt
1 egg, beaten
1 cup sugar
3 medium apples, pared and diced **or** ½ cup applesauce
½ cup chopped walnuts
1 cup flour
½ teaspoon baking powder
½ teaspoon baking soda
½ teaspoon cinnamon

Preheat oven to 350 degrees. Cream together butter and salt, then add the egg and sugar; beat well. Stir in apples, nuts and dry ingredients. Blend well. Pour mixture into a greased and floured 8-inch square pan. Bake for 40 minutes. When cool, cut into squares.

Julie Cassat, Colorado Springs, Colo.

SWEET CHERRY FLAN
(10-inch)

1 cup all-purpose flour
1/2 teaspoon salt
1 (3 ounce) package cream cheese
1/4 cup butter or margarine
1/4 cup shortening
1 cup sour cream
1 cup milk
1 (3-3/4 ounce) package instant vanilla pudding mix
2 cups pitted fresh sweet cherries or 1 can (1 pound) sweet pitted cherries, drained
1 (8 ounce) jar red currant jelly
2 tablespoons lemon juice
1 tablespoon cornstarch

In medium bowl, sift together flour and salt. Cut in cream cheese, butter or margarine and shortening. Mix dough and chill several hours or overnight.

Preheat oven to 450 degrees. Roll out chilled dough to 1/8-inch thickness and line a 10-inch flan pan or pie plate. Prick bottom and sides with fork. Bake 12-15 minutes or until golden brown. Let cool.

In medium mixer bowl, combine sour cream and milk; beat until smooth. Add pudding mix; continue beating until blended and slightly thickened. Pour into baked pastry shell and chill until firm, about 1 hour. Arrange cherries on top of filling.

In small saucepan, combine jelly, lemon juice, and cornstarch. Cook over medium heat until thickened and clear. Cool slightly and pour over cherries.

Bobbie Mae Cooley, Bowen, Ill.

DOUBLE DELICIOUS FUDGIES
Serves 6-9

1 cup chocolate syrup
1 cup water
8 marshmallows, cut into quarters
1/2 cup chopped nuts
1 (18.25 ounce) package chocolate cake mix

Preheat oven to 350 degrees. Blend chocolate syrup and water together; pour into 8x8x2-inch pan. Sprinkle marshmallows and nuts over top of chocolate mixture. Prepare cake batter according to package directions. Pour half the batter over syrup, marshmallows and nut mixture. Bake 35-45 minutes. Cut into squares and serve warm, topped with whipped cream or ice cream.

NOTE: Remaining batter can be made into cupcakes or 1 layer cake.

Agnes Ward, Erie, Pa.

LINCOLN LOG
Serves 5

Cake:
5 eggs, separated
6 tablespoons sugar
½ cup all-purpose flour
½ teaspoon vanilla extract

Mocha Cream Filling and Frosting:
1 cup butter *or* margarine, softened
4½ tablespoons confectioners' sugar
2 tablespoons unsweetened cocoa
2 tablespoons strong, cooled coffee
2 cups whipping cream, whipped

Beat egg yolks with sugar; mix in flour and vanilla. Fold in stiffly beaten egg whites; spread mixture on a buttered waxed-paper–lined jelly roll pan. Bake at 350 degrees for 15 minutes; transfer to a dampened cloth dusted with confectioners' sugar. Roll cake in cloth; cool. Beat butter and confectioners' sugar; stir in cocoa and coffee. Unroll pastry; cover with a thin layer of mocha cream and whipped cream. Reroll cake (without cloth); cut off 2 ends diagonally; reserve. Cover cake and 2 slices with remaining mocha cream; place 1 slice on top of cake, the other slice on the side of cake (to resemble branches). With a fork, trace lines into the cream to simulate the bark.

Gwen Campbell, Sterling, Va.

FLUFFY CHIFFON DESSERT
Serves 4

1 cup hot water
1 cup cold water
1 (3-ounce) package fruit-flavored gelatin
½ cup non-fat dry milk

Prepare gelatin according to package directions. Chill until partially set. Using blender or mixer, whip non-fat dry milk in gelatin until fluffy. Serve immediately, or allow it to reset in refrigerator. (112 calories per serving)

Ann L. Garey, Columbus, Neb.

GELATIN RIBBON SQUARES
Serves 8

1 (3 ounce) package strawberry flavor gelatin
1 (3 ounce) package lemon flavored gelatin
1 (3-ounce) package lime flavored gelatin
3 cups boiling water
1 cup miniature marshmallows
2 medium bananas, diced
1/2 cup mayonnaise
1 (3 ounce) package cream cheese
1-1/2 cups halved seedless green grapes

Place 1 package gelatin in each of 3 bowls. Dissolve each gelatin using 1 cup of boiling water. Add 1/2 cup cold water to each. Chill strawberry gelatin until thick and syrupy. (Let remaining gelatin stand at room temperature). Fold marshmallows and bananas into strawberry gelatin. Pour into lightly-oiled 11x7x1-1/2-inch baking dish. Chill until set. Place mayonnaise and cream cheese in blender. Add lemon gelatin, blend until smooth, pour over strawberry layer. Chill until set. Chill lime gelatin until thick and syrupy. Fold in green grapes, pour over cream cheese layer. Chill until set. Cut into squares.

Melba Bellefeuille, Libertyville, Ill.

MARSHMALLOW POPS

1 (6 ounce) package semi-sweet chocolate morsels
1 teaspoon shortening
Regular sized marshmallows
Toothpicks

Melt chocolate and shortening in the top of a double boiler. Put a toothpick into each marshmallow. Dip marshmallows into the chocolate mixture, coating well.

Roll in colored coconut, sugar, candy "shot", crushed peppermint stick candy or peanut brittle, cookie crumbs or chopped nuts. These can also be decorated with colored gumdrops or colored frosting.

Banana, apple or orange chunks on toothpicks can be used instead of marshmallows.

Sue Hibbard, Rochester, NY

MIDNIGHT MINTS
Makes 36

Bottom layer:
1/2 cup margarine
5 tablespoons cocoa
1/4 cup sugar
1 egg, beaten
2 cups graham wafer crumbs
1/2 cup chopped nuts
1 cup coconut

Combine margarine, cocoa, and sugar in saucepan. Bring slowly to a boil. Stir in egg to thicken. Remove from heat; add crumbs, nuts, and coconut. Pack firmly into greased 9x9 inch pan.

Middle layer:
1/4 cup margarine
3 tablespoons milk
1 teaspoon peppermint extract
2 cups powdered sugar
Green food coloring

Combine all ingredients in bowl. Mix well, adding a few drops more liquid, if needed, for easy spreading. Tint a pretty green. Spread over first layer; chill until firm.

Top layer:
1 cup chocolate chips
2 tablespoons margarine

Melt chips and margarine in saucepan over low heat. Spread over chilled second layer. Chill and cut into squares. Keep stored in refrigerator. These squares are simply delicious and freeze well.

Gay Polier, Spillimacheen, B.C. Canada

MILLIONAIRE CANDY
Makes 4 dozen

1 package German sweet chocolate
1 package peanut butter chips
1 package butterscotch chips
1/4 bar paraffin
1 cup chopped pecans or 1 cup shredded coconut

Melt chocolate, peanut butter chips, butterscotch chips, and paraffin in top of double boiler. Add nuts; drop by spoonfuls on waxed paper; chill. When firm, may be packaged or served.

Sue Hibbard, Rochester, N.Y.

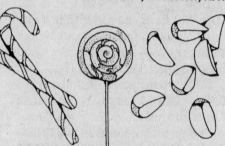

PEANUT BRITTLE
Makes 1-3/4 pounds

1-1/4 cups sugar
3/4 cup butter or margarine
1-1/2 teaspoons salt
1/4 cup Dr. Pepper
2 cups raw peanuts, shelled
1/2 teaspoon soda

Place all ingredients except soda into heavy saucepan. Boil, stirring often until temperature of 290 degrees is reached. Remove from heat; stir in soda. Pour into 15 x 10-inch pan. Cool and break into pieces.

Mrs. Bruce Fowler, Woodruff, SC

PEANUT BUTTER SWIRL CANDY

1 pound confectioners' sugar
1 stick margarine
2 tablespoons sweetened condensed milk
1 teaspoon vanilla flavoring
Peanut butter

Mix all ingredients (except peanut butter) together into a well-combined mixture and roll out on wax paper using some confectioners' sugar to keep from sticking. Spread peanut butter over dough and roll up in jelly roll fashion. Let sit 3 hours in refrigerator, then cut into 1/4 inch slices.

Peggy Fowler Revels, Woodruff, S.C.

PRALINES
Makes 20

2 cups sugar
1 teaspoon soda
1 cup buttermilk
1/8 teaspoon salt
2 tablespoons butter or margarine
2-1/2 cups (8 ounce package) pecan halves

In large (3-1/2 quart) heavy saucepan (Dutch oven) combine sugar, soda, buttermilk, and salt. Cook over high heat about 5 minutes (or to 210 degrees on candy thermometer); stir often; scrape bottom of pan. Mixture will foam up. Add butter or margarine and pecans. Over medium heat, continue cooking, stirring constantly and scraping bottom and sides of pan until candy reaches soft ball stage, (234 degrees on candy thermometer) about 6 minutes.

Remove from heat; cool slightly, about 2 minutes. Beat with spoon until thick and creamy. Drop from tablespoon onto sheet of aluminum foil or wax paper.

Check on pralines within a minute or so, should be hard enough to remove up. Do not leave on wax paper for too long as they could stick to countertop.

Jo Ann Harris, Dallas, Texas

PUDDING POPS

Serves 6

1 - 4 ounce package instant pudding mix (any flavor)
2 cups milk
6 paper cups
6 wooden sticks or plastic spoons

Pour cold milk into bowl. Add pudding mix. Beat slowly with hand rotary beater until mixture is well blended and creamy. Pour into 6 paper cups. Put a wooden stick or plastic spoon into each cup. Press a square of foil or waxed paper onto the top of the cup to cover. The handle or the stick will poke through the foil.

Freeze until firm, at least 5 hours. To serve, press firmly on the bottom of the cup to pop out.

Molly Baker, Killbuck, OH

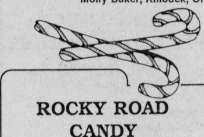

ROCKY ROAD CANDY

1 can sweetened condensed milk
1 (12 ounce) package chocolate chips
2 cups dry roasted peanuts (salted)
1 (10-1/2 ounce) bag mini marshmallows
2 tablespoons butter

On low heat melt together milk, chocolate chips, and butter. Pour into bowl with peanuts and marshmallows; blend well. Pour into 9 x 11 inch pan; refrigerate. Cut into squares and serve. If bottom of pan is covered with wax paper, candy is easier to remove.

Judy Fisk, Aberdeen, Wash.

SHAGGY DOGS

Makes 30

6 bars (1.45 ounces each) milk chocolate candy
1/3 cup milk

2-1/2 cups flaked coconut
1 (10 ounce) bag large marshmallows

In small saucepan, over low heat, melt chocolate. Stir in milk to make thin syrup. Put coconut in shallow dish. Using toothpicks, dip marshmallows into chocolate syrup, then roll in coconut. Allow to sit on wax paper.

Leona Teodori, Warren, Mich.

SWEDISH ROSETTES

(Makes 6 dozen)

1 egg
2 teaspoons sugar
1 cup milk
1 cup all-purpose flour
1/2 teaspoon salt
1 tablespoon lemon extract
Salad oil
Confectioners' sugar

Beat egg slightly; add sugar; add milk. Sift flour and salt. Stir into egg mixture; beat until smooth, about consistency of heavy cream. Add lemon extract. Put enough salad oil in a 1-quart saucepan to fill about 2/3 full. Heat to 400 degrees. Dip rosette forms into hot oil to heat them. Drain excess oil on paper towel. Dip heated forms into batter to not more than 3/4 of their depth. If only a thin layer of batter adheres to the forms, dip them again until a smooth layer adheres. Plunge batter coated forms into hot oil. Cook to desired brown-ness. With fork, ease rosettes off forms onto paper towels to drain. While still warm, dip into confectioners' sugar.

SWEETHEARTS

3/4 cup butter
1 egg yolk
1/2 cup sugar
1-1/2 cup flour

Pinch of salt
Raspberry jam

Cream butter; add sugar gradually, egg yolk, flour and salt. Knead together. Cool in refrigerator for 1 hour. Break off walnut-size pieces; roll in palm of hand; place on cookie sheet. Make indentation by pressing with the thumb. Fill hollow with jam. Bake in moderate 350 degree oven until a light brown. Remove from oven; sprinkle with confectioners' sugar.

Karen Shea Fedders, Dameron, MD

TURTLES

1 pound whole pecans (arranged in clusters of 3)
1 cup white syrup
1 can Eagle Brand condensed milk

Cook syrup and milk to 248 degrees. Stir to keep from scorching. Remove from heat. Put about 1 teaspoon mixture over each cluster of pecans. Place 1 small square of Hershey chocolate bar over each cluster. When melted, smooth out chocolate.

Note: May use melted milk chocolate chips with a little paraffin wax added, in place of chocolate bar squares. Very luscious and easy to make.

Janeen Winchell, Pleasant Hill, Ill.

VALENTINE HEART TARTS

Prepare your own recipe for pastry; roll very thin. Cut with 3-inch heart-shaped cookie cutter. Cut same amount again; cut hole in center. Prick all hearts with fork tines; bake at 350 degrees for 12 to 15 minutes. Cool. To assemble: spread strawberry jelly over uncut hearts. Place the cut-out pastry heart on the top; lightly dust with confectioners' sugar.

Mrs. Gwen Campbell, Sterling, VA

BLUEBERRY CREAM DESSERT

Serves 8

Crust:
1-1/4 cups graham cracker crumbs
1/4 cup sugar
6 tablespoons margarine, melted

Filling:
1/2 cup sugar
1 envelope unflavored gelatin
3/4 cup cold water
1 cup sour cream
1 cup blueberry yogurt
1 cup whipped topping
1 cup blueberries

In a small bowl combine crumbs, 1/4 cup sugar, and butter until crumbly. Reserve 1/4 cup crumbs for topping. Press remaining crumbs into bottom of an 8 x 8-inch dish. Bake at 375 degrees for 8-10 minutes until set. Cool. In a small saucepan mix 1/2 cup sugar, unflavored gelatin, and water. Heat mixture and stir until gelatin and sugar are dissolved. Set aside. In a small bowl, combine sour cream and yogurt. Blend into gelatin mixture. Chill until partially set. Fold whipped topping into yogurt mixture. Stir in blueberries. Spoon into crust. Sprinkle with reserved crumbs. Refrigerate until set, about 3 hours.

COCONUT DESSERT CRUST

1 stick butter
1 cup flour
2 tablespoons sugar
1/2 cup pecans

Mix flour, sugar, and butter. Add nuts and pat into 9x13-inch pan. Bake about 10 minutes at 350 degrees. Cool.

1st Layer:
1 package (8 ounce) cream cheese
1 cup powdered sugar
1 small Cool Whip

Mix all together.

2nd layer:
2 packages coconut cream instant pudding

Mix with 3 cups milk (like package says).

3rd layer:
Small container Cool Whip
1 small can coconut flakes, toasted

Place coconut flakes on top of Cool Whip or whipped cream.

Ruth Rueter, Madison, IN

ECLAIR DESSERT

2 (3 ounce) packages instant French vanilla pudding
3-1/2 cups milk
1 (12 ounce) container whipped topping
Graham crackers

Mix pudding and milk at low speed, 1-2 minutes. Fold in whipped topping. Layer graham crackers in bottom of 9x13-inch pan. Pour 1/2 of the pudding mixture over crackers. Layer graham crackers again. Pour remaining pudding mixture, and layer again with crackers.

Chocolate topping:
1-1/2 cups powdered sugar
1 teaspoon vanilla
2 envelopes Nestle Choco Bake (soften by kneading envelopes before opening)
1/4 cup milk

Mix above ingredients until well blended; pour over Eclair Dessert; smooth surface, and refrigerate.

Mary Spencer, Sandusky, Ohio

LEMON CAKE DESSERT

Serves 12

1 (3-ounce) package lemon flavored gelatin
1-1/2 cups sugar
3 cups packaged biscuit mix
4 eggs
3/4 cups salad oil
3/4 cup water
1-1/2 cups sifted powdered sugar
1/2 cup lemon juice

In large mixing bowl place gelatin, 1-1/2 cups sugar, biscuit mix, egg, salad oil, and water. Beat at slow speed until ingredients are combined, then beat at medium speed for 5 minutes. Pour into greased, floured 9-inch baking pan and bake at 350 degrees for 35-40 minutes or until cake tests done. Combine powdered sugar and lemon juice. Remove cake from oven; cool 5 minutes; then pierce cake all over with fork. Pour lemon mixture evenly over top. Cool and serve with whipped cream or ice cream.

Agnes Ward, Erie, PA

RHUBARB MERINGUE DESSERT

Serves 9

1/2 cup margarine, softened
1 cup flour
1 tablespoon sugar
3 eggs, separated
1 cup sugar
2 tablespoons flour
1/4 teaspoon salt
1/2 cup half and half or light cream
2-1/2 cups cut-up rhubarb
1/3 cup sugar
1 teaspoon vanilla
1/4 cup flaked coconut

Heat oven to 350 degrees. Mix margarine, 1 cup flour and 1 tablespoon sugar. Press into ungreased 9x9x2-inch baking pan. Bake 10 minutes at 350.

Mix egg yolks, 1 cup sugar, 2 tablespoons flour, salt and half and half. Stir in rhubarb. Pour over baked layer. Bake 45 minutes.

Beat egg whites until foamy. Beat in 1/3 cup sugar, 1 tablespoon at a time, continuing to beat egg whites until stiff and glossy. Do not underbeat. Beat in vanilla. Spread over rhubarb mixture; sprinkle with coconut. Bake until light brown, about 10 minutes.

A favorite for rhubarb lovers.

Marie Franks, Millerton, PA

CORN PUDDING

Mix together:
1 can creamed style corn
1 stick margarine (melted)
1 box corn bread mix
2 eggs (beaten)
1 (8 ounce) container sour cream

Pour into a casserole dish. Bake at 350 degrees for 45 minutes.

Diane Votaw, Decatur, Ind.

NOODLE PUDDING
Serves 6

8-ounces noodles, cooked
1/2 cup sour cream
1/4 cup granulated sugar
Pinch salt
2 eggs, beaten
1/2 cup creamed cottage cheese
1/2 teaspoon vanilla
Cinnamon to taste
1/4 cup raisins
Glaze:
1/4 cup oleo or butter
1/2 cup brown sugar
1/2 cup whole pecans

Rinse noodles in cold water; drain; add remaining ingredients, mix well. Pour into baking pan, Melt oleo; sprinkle with brown sugar. Press in pecans. Bake at 350 degrees for 1 hour or until done. Let cool 10 minutes,

Edna May Jenks, Chenango Forks, NY

CREAMY RICE PUDDING
(Use 3-quart pot)

1 quart milk
3/4 cup sugar
1/2 cup rice
Salt
1 egg
1 teaspoon cornstarch
1 teaspoon vanilla
1-1/2 cups milk

To milk, add sugar, pinch of salt and rice. Bring to boil; simmer slowly for 1 hour, stirring frequently. Beat egg with cornstarch and vanilla; add 1-1/2 cups milk and mix well. Add egg-milk mixture to rice mixture; stir constantly to prevent scorching. As soon as it thickens some, remove from heat and let stand 10 minutes. (The last addition of milk makes this creamy.)

Mrs. I. T. DeHart, Middletown, PA

GRANDMA'S RICE PUDDING

1/2 cup rice (not instant)
2 cups boiling water
3 cups milk
1/2 cup sugar
1/2 teaspoon salt
1 teaspoon vanilla
Cinnamon

Cook rice in water for about 20 minutes. Add milk and simmer for 20 more minutes. Add sugar and salt and continue simmering until creamy. Do not give up, it may take awhile. Remove from heat and add vanilla. Sprinkle cinnamon over top and serve either warm or at room temperature. Very delicious!

Bernice Streed, Waukegan, IL

QUICK GLORIOUS RICE PUDDING
Serves 6

1 cup pre-cooked quick rice
1 (3 ounce) package vanilla pudding mix (not instant)
1/4 cup raisins (optional)
3 cups milk
1 egg, beaten
1/4 cup sugar
1/4 teaspoon vanilla
Cinnamon sugar

Mix all of the ingredients except vanilla. Cook over medium heat, stirring constantly, until mixture comes to a boil. Remove from heat and cool slightly. Add vanilla. Spoon into individual dessert dishes and sprinkle cinnamon sugar on top. Chill and serve cold.

Hannah V. Ismiel, Chicago, IL

SUET PUDDING
Serves 10-12
About 90 years old

1 cup suet (pressed down and run through a coarse food chopper)
1 cup raisins
1 cup dark syrup
1 cup buttermilk
1/2 cup currants (optional)
2 even teaspoons soda
Pinch salt
Flour

Add flour enough to make stiff dough. Place into greased 2-quart baking dish and steam in steamer on top of stove for at least 1-1/2 hours or until done. Serve with lemon sauce or plain cream. Re-heat by re-steaming.
Lemon Sauce:
1 cup sugar
2 tablespoons cornstarch
Pinch of salt
2 cups cold water
2 tablespoons butter or margarine
1 teaspoon lemon extract

Mix sugar, cornstarch and salt in saucepan. Stir until cornstarch is blended. Add cold water gradually, stirring well. Place on stove and bring to boil, stirring constantly until mixture thickens. Add lemon extract and butter or margarine. Serve hot over pudding.

Mrs. Opal Hamer, St. Petersburg, FL

TOMATO PUDDING
Serves 4 to 6

10-ounce can tomato puree
1/2 cup boiling water
1/2 cup brown sugar
1/2 teaspoon salt
2 cups fresh bread, cut in 1" cubes
1/3 cup butter, melted

Add sugar and salt to puree. Add water; simmer 5 minutes. Add melted butter.

Place bread in greased casserole; cover with tomato butter. Cover, or if extra crispness is desired, bake uncovered at 350 degrees for 30 minutes.

Kit Rollins, Cedarburg, WI

SWEET POTATO PUDDING

4 cups grated raw sweet potatoes
1 cup molasses (or honey)
3/4 cup milk
1 teaspoon nutmeg
1/2 cup margarine, melted
1/2 teaspoon cloves
1/2 cup chopped nuts
1/2 teaspoon salt
2 eggs, well beaten

Mix all ingredients together, except eggs. Add eggs; stir until well blended. Pour into 1-1/2 quart baking dish sprayed with non-stick spray. Bake at 375 degrees for 50-60 minutes or until done (see testing note below).

Note: You may use 1/2 cup granulated sugar and 1/2 cup syrup in place of molasses or honey.

Testing custard for doneness: Insert tip of knife blade in pie/custard/pudding about halfway between edge and center of pie. If blade comes out clean, custard will be firm all the way through when it cools. If you insert knife in center, the filling should cling like a thick cream sauce.

BLUEBERRY TORTE

Crust:
1/4 pound margarine, plus 1 tablespoon
1 cup flour
2 tablespoons sugar

Combine and press into 9-inch square pan. Bake in preheated 375 degree oven about 20 minutes, or until browned.

Filling:
1 envelope Dream Whip, prepared according to package directions
1 (8 ounce) package cream cheese, softened
1 cup powdered sugar

1 can blueberry pie filling

Allow crust to cool. Meanwhile beat prepared Dream Whip with softened cream cheese and powdered sugar. Pour over cooled crust. Top with 1 can blueberry pie filling. Chill well.

Marie Popovich, Warren, MI

CHOCOLATE TORTE
Serves 20

1 (15-ounce) package Oreo cookies, crushed
1/3 cup melted butter
2 (3-ounce) packages instant chocolate pudding
1-1/2 cups milk
1 (9-ounce) carton Cool Whip
1 quart vanilla ice cream, softened

Mix together cookie crumbs and butter. Pat 2/3 of crumbs into a 9 x 13-inch pan. Reserve remaining 1/3 of crumbs for top. Beat together pudding and milk until very thick. Add the softened ice cream and beat together until well blended. Pour pudding mixture over the crumbs. Spread Cool Whip over the pudding mixture and top with remaining crumbs. Refrigerate overnight.

Ida Bloedow, Madison, WI

ELEGANT FINALE TORTE
Serves 12

2 cups sifted flour
2 teaspoons baking powder
1 teaspoon baking soda
1/4 teaspoon salt
1-1/2 teaspoons ground cinnamon
1/2 teaspoon ground cloves
1/8 teaspoon ground ginger
1/2 teaspoon pumpkin pie spice
2 cups firmly packed brown sugar
4 eggs
1 (1 pound) can pumpkin
1 cup finely ground graham crackers
1 cup vegetable oil
1 (6 ounce) package butterscotch morsels
1 cup chopped walnuts

Whipped cream:
1-1/2 cups heavy cream
1/2 teaspoon vanilla
2 tablespoons sugar

Into a large bowl, sift together first 8 ingredients and 2 cups sugar; set aside. In large bowl of mixer, beat eggs at high speed until foamy. Slowly mix in pumpkin, graham cracker crumbs, and oil. By hand, stir in butterscotch morsels and walnuts. Spread batter in 3 greased and waxed paper-lined, 9-inch round cake pans. Bake at 350 degrees for 25-30 minutes. Cool in pans; remove to racks. In chilled bowl beat cream, vanilla, and 2 tablespoons sugar at high speed until soft peaks form. Spread whipped cream on top of each cake layer. Stack layers, frosting-side up. Refrigerate 2-3 hours before serving.

Gwen Campbell, Sterling, Va.

STRAWBERRY REFRIGERATOR TORTE
Serves 8-12

3/4 pound "Nabisco Wafers"
3/4 cup butter
2 eggs, beaten
1 cup confectioners' sugar
1-1/2 cups whipping cream
1 quart fresh strawberries, quartered

Put "Nabiscos" thru a food chopper or crush to crumbs. Reserve 1/4 cup crumbs for topping. Stand additional whole "Nabiscos" wafers upright around and lay on bottom of torte pan. Press the crumbled "Nabiscos" in bottom of torte pan. Cream butter until light. Add eggs and sugar; beat well. Fold in whipped cream and strawberries. Pour into torte pan. Sprinkle with the remaining reserved crumbs. Chill in refrigerator 6-8 hours.

This is a very elegant dessert that could be served at a luncheon, surrounded with fresh whole strawberries for garnish.

Mrs. Edward Prinsen, Cedarburg, WI

APPLE DUMPLINGS

2 cups flour
2-1/2 teaspoons baking powder
1/2 teaspoon salt
1/2 cup shortening
1/4 cup milk
8 apples
8 tablespoons sugar
4 tablespoons butter
Cinnamon and sugar mixed

Sift flour, salt, and baking powder. Cut in shortening. Add milk and stir. Knead lightly on a floured board. Roll 1/8-inch thick. Divide dough into 8 parts. Peel and core apples. Place one apple on each section of dough. Fill hollow of apple with 1 tablespoon of sugar and 1 teaspoon of butter. Fold dough over apple, pressing edges together. Place in a shallow baking pan. Sprinkle with sugar-cinnamon mixture and dot with remaining butter. Bake at 400 degrees for 30-40 minutes. Serve with cream or half-and-half.

Joy B. Shamway, Freeport, Ill.

GOURMET ORANGE BAKED ALASKA
Serves 6

1 pint orange sherbet
3 large oranges
3 egg whites, stiffly beaten
1/4 teaspoon cream of tartar
1/4 cup plus 2 tablespoons sugar

Scoop sherbet into 6 balls; freeze at least 4 hours until very firm. Cut oranges crosswise in half; cut thin slice from bottom of each half. Cut around edges and membranes; remove fruit and membrane from orange shells. Line bottom of each shell with fruit; refrigerate. Beat egg whites

and cream of tartar. Beat in sugar, 1 tablespoon at a time; beat until stiff and glossy. Place orange shells on ungreased baking sheet; fill each with a frozen sherbet ball. Completely cover sherbet ball with meringue, sealing it to the edge of the shell. Bake at 400 degrees for 4-5 minutes, or until meringue is light golden brown. Serve immediately.

Gwen Campbell, Sterling, Va.

BLACK FOREST TRIFLE

1 (9-ounce) package chocolate cake mix
1/4 cup rum or brandy (optional)
1 can cherry pie filling
1 package instant chocolate pudding
1 medium Cool Whip

Bake cake as package directs. Cool and cut in cubes. Prepare pudding as package directs. Arrange one half cake cubes in glass bowl. Sprinkle 1 ounce rum or brandy. Layer one half of pudding, then one half of cherry pie filling; next, one half of Cool Whip. Repeat layering in order given.

Chill at least 3 hours before serving. Looks very pretty in a tall stemmed bowl.

Helen Harlos, Ethel, Miss.

PUMPKIN DESSERT

1-1/3 cups graham cracker crumbs
1/4 cup sugar
1/4 cup soft butter
60 marshmallows
2 cups pumpkin
1 teaspoon cinnamon
1/2 teaspoon ginger
1/2 teaspoon salt
2 packages whipped topping mix, prepared according to package directions
1 cup sweetened whipped cream
Toasted coconut

Mix graham cracker crumbs with sugar and soft butter. Press into a 9x13-inch pan. Bake at 375 degrees for 8 to 10 minutes. Let cool. Melt marshmallows. pumpkin, spices, and salt in a double boiler or other large pan. Fold in whipped topping and spread the mixture over graham cracker crust. Spread the whipped cream over top of pumpkin mixture. Top with toasted coconut. Chill in refrigerator before serving.

Mrs. James Williams, Brainerd, Minn.

OLD-FASHIONED BLUEBERRY BUCKLE
Serves 6

2 cups flour
3 teaspoons baking powder
1/2 cup margarine
1/2 cup sugar
1 egg, beaten
1/2 cup milk
1/2 teaspoon almond flavoring

Topping:
2 cups fresh or frozen blueberries
2 teaspoons lemon juice
1/4 cup sugar
1/3 cup flour
1/2 teaspoon cinnamon
1/4 cup margarine

Sift flour with baking powder. Set aside. In mixing bowl cream margarine and sugar. Add egg; beat until creamy. Combine milk and almond flavoring; add to creamed mixture alternately with flour; beat until smooth. Pour into buttered 9-inch square pan. Sprinkle lemon juice over blueberries and spread over batter. Mix sugar, flour, cinnamon and margarine thoroughly with fingers until crumbly. Spread over blueberries. Bake at 350 degrees for 45-50 minutes, or until it tests done. Serve warm or cold, with cream, if desired.

Fantastic
FRUITS

RHUBARB-PINE-APPLE COBBLER
Serves 8-9

1 cup granulated sugar
1 cup water
1 (20-ounce) can crushed pineapple, undrained
3 cups rhubarb, finely cut

Topping:
1 (9-ounce) package white or yellow Jiffy Cake Mix, prepared according to directions
1 (3-ounce) package strawberry gelatin

In a saucepan, combine the first 3 ingredients. Bring to a boil and boil 1 minute, stirring constantly. Set aside. Grease a 9x13-inch pan; put rhubarb on the bottom and pour sauce over all. Place in a 350-degree oven while making cake topping. For topping, prepare cake mix according to directions. Pour this evenly over rhubarb and sauce. Sprinkle dry gelatin over batter and cut in with knife. Return to the oven for 25 to 30 minutes, or until lightly browned.

SUMMER PEAR SUNDAE

2 1/2 cups fresh pears, pared and sliced
1 cup crushed pineapple
1 cup honey
2 1/2 tablespoons orange juice
2 1/2 tablespoons lemon juice
1 1/4 tablespoons pineapple juice

2 tablespoons cornstarch
3 tablespoons maraschino cherry juice
1/2 cup maraschino cherries, halved
Vanilla ice cream
1/2 cup whipping cream, whipped
2 tablespoons walnuts, finely chopped

Combine first 6 ingredients in a saucepan; bring to a boil. Blend cornstarch and cherry juice; stir into hot mixture. Cook 3 minutes, stirring constantly. Remove from heat. Add cherries; chill. Serve over vanilla ice cream. Garnish with whipped cream; sprinkle with walnuts.

Gwen Campbell, Sterling, Va.

EASY APPLE TARTS

4 cups peeled, sliced cooking apples
1/2 cup sugar
3 tablespoons flour
1 teaspoon cinnamon
1 teaspoon nutmeg
1 (8-ounce) can Quick Crescent Dinner Rolls

Topping:
1/2 cup brown sugar
1 teaspoon cinnamon
2 tablespoons margarine, melted

Combine first 5 ingredients. Separate dough into 4 triangles. Press 2 of these over bottom of pan. Spread apple mixture over dough and then place 2 remaining rectangles on top. Combine brown sugar and cinnamon; sprinkle over top; drizzle with margarine. Bake at 375 degrees for 30-40 minutes.

BAKED BANANAS AND COCONUT WITH CUSTARD

4 large, firm bananas
2 tablespoons butter
1/2 cup pineapple juice
1/4 cup packed brown sugar
1/8 teaspoon ground mace or nutmeg
1 cup flaked coconut

Heat oven to 400 degrees. Butter a baking dish about 10x6x2-inches. Peel bananas and cut in half lengthwise, then crosswise. Put bananas in prepared baking dish and dot each piece with some of the butter. Combine pineapple juice, brown sugar, and mace or nutmeg and pour over the bananas, then sprinkle coconut over all. Bake for about 12 minutes, or until coconut is browned and bananas are hot. Serve hot, topped with Custard Sauce.

Custard Sauce:
3/4 cup milk
2 egg yolks
2 tablespoons sugar
Pinch of salt
1/2 teaspoon vanilla extract

Scald milk in top of double boiler, over direct heat. Beat egg yolks; blend in sugar and salt, then gradually stir in milk. Pour back into the top of double boiler and set over simmering water. Cook, stirring, until mixture coats a metal spoon, about 10 minutes. Cool quickly and stir in vanilla. This is a delicious, light dessert.

Lillian Smith, Montreal, Quebec, Canada

STRAWBERRY SWIRL

2 (10-ounce) boxes frozen strawberries *or* 2 cups sliced fresh strawberries
2 tablespoons sugar
1 (3-ounce) package strawberry gelatin
1 cup water, boiling
34 large marshmallows (1/2 pound)
1/2 cup milk
1 cup whipping cream, whipped, *or* 1 package Dream Whip, whipped
Crumb Crust (recipe follows)

Sprinkle sugar over fresh strawberries; let stand 30 minutes. Dissolve gelatin in boiling water. Drain strawberries, reserving juice. Add water to juice to make 1 cup. Add to gelatin; chill until partially set, 1 hour and 15 minutes. Meanwhile, combine marshmallows and milk in double boiler; heat and stir until marshmallows melt. Cool thoroughly; fold in whipped cream. Add berries to gelatin, then fold in marshmallow mixture to marble. Pour into crumb crust. Chill until set. Cut into squares.

Crumb Crust:
Mix 1 cup graham cracker crumbs, 1 tablespoon sugar and 1/4 cup melted margarine. Press firmly into bottom of 9x9x2-inch baking dish. Chill.

This is nice to serve when you are having friends in for dessert and coffee.

Mrs. Albert H. Foley, Lemoyne, Pa.

RHUBARB CRUNCH

CRUST/TOPPING
1 cup flour
1 cup brown sugar
3/4 cup oatmeal
1/2 cup butter *or* margarine, melted
1 teaspoon cinnamon

Mix crust ingredients until crumbly. Press one-half of the mixture into a 9-inch pan. Cover with 4 cups sliced rhubarb.

1 cup sugar
1 cup water
2 tablespoons cornstarch
1 teaspoon vanilla

Cook over medium heat until thickened and clear. Pour over rhubarb. Crumble remainder of crust/topping mixture over top surface and bake at 350 degrees for 1 hour.

Phyliss Dixon, Fairbanks, Alaska

BLUEBERRY PUDDING
Serves 6

1 quart blueberries
2 cups water
1 cup sugar
1/8 teaspoon salt
Butter
8 slices white sandwich bread
Cool Whip

Stew blueberries in water with sugar and salt for 15 minutes. Butter bread slices. Place alternate layers of bread and blueberries in a deep, buttered baking dish. Bake at 350 degrees for 15–20 minutes. Cool and chill. Serve chilled with Cool Whip.

Joy B. Shamway, Freeport, Ill.

EASY FRUIT COBBLER

4 cups canned *or* fresh fruit
2 teaspoons butter
1 cup flour
1 teaspoon baking powder
1 cup sugar
1 cup sweet milk
1/8 teaspoon salt

Melt butter in baking dish (9x13-inch) allowing it to cover bottom; grease sides of dish well. Prepare a thin batter by stirring sugar and baking powder into flour. Beat in milk and salt. Pour batter into baking dish. Spread fruit over batter. (The batter will rise through the fruit and form a nice crust). Bake in a 350-degree oven for 25-30 minutes, or until light golden brown.

Dovie Lucy, McLoud, Okla.

BANANA TURNOVERS

4 cups flour
2 teaspoons salt
1⅓ cups shortening
⅓ cup cold water
4 bananas
8 tablespoons raisins
8 teaspoons sunflower seeds

Mix flour and salt together. Cut in shortening until mixture resembles coarse meal. Sprinkle with water and mix lightly with fork. Divide into 8 balls. Roll each ball out into an 8-inch square on floured board. Cut bananas into slices and put half on 1 half of the square. Add 1 tablespoon raisins and 1 teaspoon sunflower seeds. Fold dough over to make triangle. Seal edges. Bake at 400 degrees for 15–20 minutes on an ungreased cookie sheet. Remove from sheet and cool slightly.

Laura Hicks, Troy, Mont.

LIGHT—ENDING RAINBOW FRUIT BOWL

1 cantaloupe
1 pineapple
1 pint strawberries
1 pint blueberries
2 cups seedless green grapes
2 cups seedless red grapes
2 cups fresh orange sections, cut in half
1 cup sliced and cut peaches

Cut cantaloupe (rind and seeds removed) into bite-size pieces. Cut pineapple (rind and core removed) into bite-size pieces. Halve or quarter strawberries (depending on their size); add to cantaloupe along with blueberries, green and red grapes, fresh orange sections and cut peaches. Mix well, adding enough orange juice to moisten. Serve, topped with a generous dollop of sour cream.

Gwen Campbell, Sterling, Va.

PEACH COBBLER
Serves 8

3 cups sliced fresh peaches
2 tablespoons lemon juice '
2 tablespoons butter
4 teaspoons baking powder
1/3 cup butter
3/4 cup sugar
3 tablespoons flour
1/2 teaspoon salt
1 tablespoon sugar
1 egg, well-beaten
3/4 cup milk
2 cups flour

Put peaches in a greased baking dish. Mix together 1 tablespoon sugar and 3 tablespoons flour. Sprinkle over peaches. Sprinkle with lemon juice and dot with 2 tablespoons butter.

Topping:
Sift dry ingredients (2 cups flour, baking powder, salt and sugar); mix in 1/3 cup butter until mixture is like coarse crumbs. Add egg and milk; mix until just moistened.

Drop dough in mounds over peaches. Bake in 425-degree oven for 30 minutes.

Mrs. Olen Begly, West Salem, Ohio

SAUCY BANANA
Makes 1 serving

1 banana
1/2 cup orange juice
1 teaspoon butter
1 tablespoon brown sugar
Dash cinnamon
Frozen yogurt or ice cream

Peel and slice banana lengthwise with a table knife. Place banana in microwave bowl or shallow dish. Pour orange juice over banana and dot with butter and brown sugar. Shake a dash of cinnamon on top. Microwave on HIGH (100 percent) for 1 minute; turn and microwave another 30 seconds. May be served with frozen yogurt or vanilla ice cream.

Toaster-oven method: Assemble as above in a metal pan. Bake 12 minutes at 375 degrees.

Peggy Fowler Revels, Woodruff, S.C.

PEACH PECAN CROWN

1 package spice cake mix
1/4 cup melted margarine
2/3 cup packed brown sugar
1 1/2 cups pecan halves (any nuts)
1 pint heavy cream
1/3 cup confectioners' sugar
1/4 teaspoon nutmeg
6 peaches, peeled, sliced, sprinkled
    with brown sugar
1 1/2 tablespoons light corn syrup

Preheat oven to 350 degrees. Grease and flour a 9-inch layer cake pan and a 6-cup ring mold. Combine margarine, brown sugar and syrup; blend. Spoon 1/3 of this mixture into ring mold, the remainder into cake pan. Arrange nuts over mixture in both pans. Prepare cake mixture according to directions on package. Gently spoon enough of this batter on the nuts in the ring mold; fill half full. Pour remaining batter into layer-cake pan. Bake at 350 degrees for 30 minutes, or until tests done with toothpick. Invert round layer cake onto serving plate ... ring mold on a wire rack. Cool.

Cream confectioners' sugar and nutmeg together with heavy cream. Fold peaches into mixture and spread a layer of cream mixture over round layer. Place ring on top and fill center with remaining cream mixture. Chill several hours before serving. This can also be made with canned peaches that have been thoroughly drained.

ALOHA APPLE ROYALE

5   medium-size apples,
    peeled and thinly sliced
1/2 cup crushed pineapple
1/2 cup sugar
1/2 teaspoon cinnamon
1/4 teaspoon nutmeg
1/4 cup walnuts, chopped
1/2 cup shredded coconut
1/4 cup shortening
1/4 cup butter or marga-
    rine, softened

1/2 cup brown sugar, firmly
    packed
1   egg, beaten
3/4 cup all-purpose flour
1/2 teaspoon vanilla extract

Combine apple slices and crushed pineapple; spread into a 9-inch pie plate. Sprinkle with sugar and spices; top with walnuts and coconut. Cream together shortening and butter; add brown sugar; stir in egg. Add flour and vanilla; mix thoroughly. Spread batter on top of apple/pineapple mixture. Bake at 375 degrees for 35 minutes, or until top is crisp and golden.

Gwen Campbell, Sterling, Va.

CRANBERRY–PEAR CRISP
Serves 6

1   (12-ounce) package
    fresh or frozen cranber-
    ries, thawed
2   pears, cored and sliced
2   tablespoons flour
1   cup sugar
1   teaspoon ground
    cinnamon
1/2 cup brown sugar,
    packed
1/2 cup flour
1/3 cup butter or marga-
    rine, softened
3/4 cup old-fashioned oats,
    uncooked
3/4 cup chopped walnuts
    Whipped cream (op-
    tional)

Place cranberries and pear slices into an oblong 2-quart baking dish. Sprinkle with combined 2 tablespoons flour, sugar and cinnamon.

In medium size mixing bowl combine brown sugar and 1/2 cup flour. Cut in butter or margarine until mixture is crumbly. Add oats and walnuts. Mix well; sprinkle over fruit mixture. Bake in a preheated 350-degree oven for 30–35 minutes, or until juice is bubbly. Serve warm topped with whipped cream, if desired.

Quick, easy and delicious dessert!
Anna Y. Bodisch, Coplay, Pa.

Foreign & EXOTIC

EASY-AS-PIE SHORTCAKE
Serves 4

4 cake-type doughnuts (plain or sugar-dusted)
1 (10-ounce) package frozen strawberries (or berries of your choice)
Whipped topping

Split doughnuts lengthwise. Place 1 doughnut half in dessert dish. Top with whipped topping and 2–3 tablespoons of berries. Place other half of doughnut on top, and repeat layers. Top with whipped topping and berries.

SWEDISH POTATO SAUSAGE
Serves 12–14

2 pounds ground beef
1 pound ground pork
6 pounds potatoes, ground
2 medium onions, ground
1 cup milk, scalded
1 teaspoon black pepper
3 tablespoons salt
1 teaspoon allspice
2 teaspoons ginger

Mix all ingredients together. Pack into 2 greased angel food cake pans; cover with aluminum foil and steam in a 300-degree oven, over large pan of hot water, for 4–5 hours, using meat thermometer.

Kathy Somerville, Nashville, Ind.

RINDFLEISCH MIT APFELN (BEEF WITH APPLES)
Serves 4

4–6 tart apples, cored and sliced
3–4 tablespoons butter *or* bacon drippings
1 tablespoon sugar (or to taste)
1 cup beef gravy
Few drops lemon juice
Pinch cinnamon
¼ cup raisins *or* dried currants
4 large slices cooked beef (boiled or roasted)

Lightly fry apple slices in the drippings or butter until golden brown. Add sugar, beef gravy, lemon juice and cinnamon. Simmer over low heat until apples are soft. Add raisins or currants and the beef slices; cook just until meat is heated through.

Marguerite Seyse, Buffalo, N.Y.

DAD'S HUNGARIAN GOULASH
Serves 6

3 pounds lean beef stew meat
3-4 large onions, chopped
1/2 cup flour to coat meat
Salt to taste
Garlic powder to taste
Pepper to taste
Hungarian sweet paprika to taste
1 tablespoon caraway seeds
Dash soy sauce
Dash Worcestershire sauce
11 ounces of beef stock or consommé
2-3 tablespoons sour cream

In large skillet sauté chopped onions until golden brown in fat or oil on medium-high heat. Season stew meat with salt, pepper, garlic powder, paprika; roll meat in flour. Sauté in same pan with onions over medium-high heat. Add the beef stock with a dash of soy and Worcestershire sauce. Bring to boil and simmer, covered, for 2-1/2-3 hours until meat is fork tender. Add more beef stock, if necessary. Just before serving, stir in caraway seeds and sour cream.

Joan Ross, Amenia, Wyo.

RUSSIAN CREAM
Serves 6–8

3/4 cup sugar
1 envelope unflavored gelatin
1 1/4 cups cold water
1 teaspoon vanilla
1 cup sour cream
1 cup whipped cream *or* Cool Whip
1 (10-ounce) package frozen raspberries, thawed

Dissolve sugar and gelatin in water. Add sour cream and chill until thickened. Add vanilla and whipped cream; pour into 9x13-inch pan. Chill at least 3 hours. Cut into squares and serve topped with raspberries, undrained.

This recipe was given to my mother by the owner of a little restaurant in Vienna.

Jami Shimizo, Spokane, Wash.

CANTON ALMOND COOKIES
Makes 5 dozen

3 cups all-purpose flour
1 cup sugar
1/4 teaspoon salt
1/2 teaspoon baking soda
1 cup shortening, room temperature
1 egg, lightly beaten
1/4 teaspoon vanilla extract
1/2 teaspoon almond extract
1 cup almonds, blanched and split

Mix flour, sugar, salt, and baking soda. Add shortening; cut in until mixture resembles cornmeal. Add egg; vanilla extract, and almond extract. Mix until egg is absorbed and mixture is smooth. Shape into 3/4-inch balls; place on ungreased baking sheet. Flatten each cookie with a flour-dipped fork; press an almond half into the center. Bake at 350 degrees for 20 minutes or until a pale golden brown. Remove from baking sheet; cool on rack.

Gwen Campbell, Sterling, Va.

SWISS POTATO SOUP
Serves 8

1 large onion, chopped (1 cup)
3 tablespoons butter
3 large potatoes, cut up
1 teaspoon salt
1/4 teaspoon dry mustard
1/8 teaspoon white pepper
3 cups water
2 cups milk
8 ounces sliced Swiss cheese, cut up
2 tablespoons parsley, chopped

Sauté onion in butter until soft; stir in potatoes, salt, mustard, pepper, and water. Heat to boiling; cover. Simmer 30 minutes, or until potatoes are very soft; press through a fine sieve into large bowl; return to soup kettle. Stir in milk; heat slowly just to boiling. Stir in cheese until melted. Ladle into soup bowls or plates; sprinkle with parsley. You can chill several hours and serve cold, if you prefer.

Mrs. Merle Mishler, Hollsopple, ,Pa.

GRAMMA'S POTATO PANCAKES "KATOFEL PANNE KUCHEN" (GERMAN)

2 pounds peeled, raw potatoes
1 tablespoon salt
2 tablespoons flour
3 eggs, separated
1 cup milk or cream
Fat for frying (I use Crisco)

Grate raw potatoes into a bowl with cold water. Shortly before frying, squeeze through a clean cloth. Add salt, flour, egg yolks, and milk; beat egg whites until stiff and fold into potato mixture. Drop tablespoons of this mixture into hot fat in frying pan. Fry pancakes until crisp and golden. They should be served at once with pot roast or as a main dish with salad, vegetables, and fruit.
Note: 1/2 cup finely grated onion can be added to batter, before adding egg whites.

Agnes Ward, Erie, Pa.

CABBAGE ROLLS

12 cabbage leaves
1 pound lean ground beef
1/2 pound ground pork
1/2 cup rice, long grain
1 onion, chopped
2 eggs, beaten
1 teaspoon salt
1/2 teaspoon pepper
1 large onion, sliced

Sauce (Sweet-Sour):
1 can tomato soup, mixed with 1/4 cup water
1 (1-pound) can stewed tomatoes
1/3 cup lemon juice
1/8 teaspoon pepper
1/4 cup brown sugar

Add cabbage leaves to boiling water. Simmer 4 minutes until leaves are pliable. Remove and drain. Combine beef, pork, rice, onion, eggs, salt and pepper. Divide meat mixture into 12 balls and place in center of cabbage leaves. Fold sides over stuffing and fasten with toothpicks.

Preheat oven to 375 degrees. Place cabbage rolls in a greased 3-quart casserole. Add onion slices and pour sauce over rolls. Sprinkle with brown sugar and cover. Bake, covered, for 11/2–2 hours.

This may be served with a mushroom sauce, regular tomato sauce or sour cream, instead of the sweet-sour sauce. Reheated, they are even more delicious!

Betty L. Perkins, Hot Springs, Ark.

ITALIAN CHEESECAKE
Serves 6–8

Crust:
2 cups sifted flour
1/2 teaspoon salt
2/3 cup butter
2 tablespoons dry sherry
1 teaspoon water

Filling:
1-1/2 pounds ricotta cheese
1/3 cup toasted, chopped almonds
1 pound chopped citron
1 pound diced candied orange peel
1 pound diced candied cherries
1 teaspoon vanilla
4 eggs, slightly beaten
1/3 cup sugar

Sift flour and salt together. Cut in butter. Add sherry and water, stirring with a fork. Wrap dough in waxed paper and chill for 1 hour.

Mix the ricotta cheese, almonds, citron, orange peel, cherries and vanilla. Combine eggs and sugar, then add to cheese mixture, stirring until blended. Roll two-thirds of dough between 2 floured sheets of waxed paper in a circle to fit a 9-inch, loose-bottom cake pan or a 10-inch pie plate. Fit rolled dough in pan. Fill with cheese mixture. Roll remaining dough and cut into 1/2-inch strips. Arrange strips in a lattice pattern on top of filling. Crimp edges. Bake at 350 degrees for 45 minutes, or until lightly browned and crust is golden. Cool.

Leona Teodori, Warren, Mich.

RASPBERRY OATCAKE ROUNDS
Makes 18

½ cup hydrogenated shortening
1 cup oats *or* quick-cooking oats
1 cup all-purpose flour
⅓ cup granulated sugar
½ teaspoon baking soda
¼ teaspoon salt
2–3 tablespoons cold water
½ cup red raspberry jam
⅓ cup confectioners' sugar

Cut shortening into oats, flour, sugar, baking soda and salt until mixture resembles fine crumbs. Add cold water, 1 tablespoon at a time, until mixture forms a stiff dough. Roll until ½ inch thick on lightly floured surface. Cut 9 (2½-inch) rounds with a biscuit cutter and 9 (2½-inch) rounds with a doughnut cutter. Place on ungreased baking sheet. Bake in 375-degree oven until oatcakes start to brown, 12–15 minutes. Cool on wire rack. Spread raspberry jam on oatcakes cut with biscuit cutter; place oatcake cut with doughnut cutter on top. Fill center with raspberry jam. Dust top of oatcake with confectioners' sugar.

This recipe originated from Scotland. It is an old family recipe that was altered to be even more tasty and colorful by the addition of red raspberry jam and confectioners' sugar.

Tillie Minarik, Verdigre, Neb.

GREEK PASTITSIO BAKE
Serves 8

Pasta Layer:
2 cups cooked, drained elbow macaroni
2 eggs, beaten
1/3 cup grated Parmesan cheese
1 tablespoon butter, melted

In large bowl stir together above ingredients and spoon evenly into a 13x9-inch shallow baking dish.

Meat Layer:
1 pound ground beef, lean
1/2 cup onion, finely chopped
1 clove garlic, finely chopped
1 (8-ounce) can tomato sauce
1/8 teaspoon pepper
1/4 teaspoon ground allspice
1/4 teaspoon cinnamon
1/4 teaspoon nutmeg
2 teaspoons instant beef bouillon granules *or* 2 beef bouillon cubes

In large skillet, brown meat; pour off fat. Stir in onion and garlic; cook and stir until onion is tender. Add tomato sauce, spices, bouillon, and pepper. Mix well and simmer for 10 minutes. Spoon evenly over macaroni mixture.

Cream Sauce:
3 tablespoons butter or margarine
2 tablespoons flour
1 teaspoon chicken-flavored bouillon (instant) *or* 1 bouillon cube
1/8 teaspoon pepper
1/4 cup grated Parmesan cheese
2 cups milk

Melt butter or margarine; stir in flour, chicken bouillon, and pepper. Gradually stir in milk. Cook and stir over medium heat until slightly thickened. Remove from heat and stir in 1/4 cup grated Parmesan cheese. Spoon over the meat layer. Cover; bake at 325 degrees for 30 minutes, or until bubbly. Garnish with parsley. *Really tasty!*

Agnes Ward, Erie, Pa.

CAULIFLOWER ITALIANO
Serves 6

1 tablespoon chopped onion
1 small clove garlic, crushed
2 tablespoons low-calorie Italian salad dressing
3 cups small fresh cauliflowerets
2 tablespoons green pepper, chopped
1 cup cherry tomatoes, halved
1/2 teaspoon salt
1/8 teaspoon dried basil leaves, crushed

In an 8-inch skillet cook onion and garlic in salad dressing until tender; add cauliflowerets and 1/4 cup water. Cook, covered, over low heat for 10 minutes. Add green pepper; cook until cauliflower is tender, about 5 minutes. Stir in remaining ingredients; heat thoroughly. (35 calories per serving)

Charlotte Forney, Bellevue, Ohio

SHORTCUT CASSOULET
Serves 6

2 tablespoons oil
1 pound ground lamb
1 onion, chopped
4 cloves garlic, minced
6 cups white beans, cooked

3 cups sliced turnips
3 cups chicken stock
2 tablespoons rosemary
4 teaspoons oregano
2 tablespoons cornstarch
2 tablespoons cold water
4 scallions, thinly sliced

In a 10-inch Dutch oven or 5-quart heavy-bottom pan, heat oil and brown lamb with onions and garlic. Add cooked beans, turnips, stock, rosemary and oregano. Cover pan and simmer until turnips are tender. Dissolve cornstarch in cold water and add to the simmering mixture. Stir until thickened. Garnish with scallions before serving.

Leona Teodori, Warren, Mich.

ITALIAN BROCCOLI
Serves 4–6

1 bunch of broccoli
½ cup olive oil (any oil can be used)
2 tablespoons lemon juice
2 cloves garlic, crushed
¼ teaspoon oregano
Salt and pepper to taste

Cook broccoli in 1 inch of boiling water for 10–12 minutes, or until tender. Drain. Meanwhile, mix together remaining ingredients and pour over drained broccoli. Serve hot or cold.

Harriet Silverman, Plainview, N.Y.

DUTCH APPLE CAKE

3 cups flour
2 cups sugar
1 cup oil
2 teaspoons vanilla
3 teaspoons baking powder
1/2 cup orange juice
4 eggs

Mix all above ingredients together in bowl with electric mixer. Pour half of batter into greased and floured tube pan. Layer half of apple mixture into batter, and then spread on rest of batter. Pour rest of apple mixture on top. Bake in preheated 350 degree oven for 1 hour and 10 minutes until golden brown. Cool 1 hour in pan before removing.

Apple Mixture:
4 or 5 apples, thinly sliced
2 teaspoons cinnamon
5 tablespoons sugar

Toss together in bowl until apples are coated.

Mrs. Joseph E. Yokitis,
Sinking Spring, PA

PALACINKY (THIN PANCAKES)

2 eggs
Pinch of salt
3 tablespoons sugar
2 cups milk
2 cups flour
1/4 cup butter for pan
Jam

Beat together eggs, salt, sugar, milk, and flour until smooth. Heat a frying pan; brush with butter. Pour in a thin layer of batter and spread by tilting the pan. Pancakes must be very thin, almost transparent. Fry on both sides to a golden brown. Spread with jam, roll up, and dust with vanilla bean flavored powdered sugar.

Palacinky is the name for thin pancakes, usually served around the holidays—very similar to crepe suzettes.

BUCHE DE NOEL (FRENCH YULE LOG)
Serves 8

Spongecake:
4 eggs
2 egg yolks
3/4 cup granulated sugar
1 teaspoon vanilla
1 cup sifted all-purpose flour
1/2 teaspoon baking powder
3 tablespoons unsalted butter, melted
Confectioners' sugar
Raspberry preserves

Mocha Butter Cream Frosting:
1/4 cup butter or margarine
2 cups confectioners' sugar (divided)
1 teaspoon vanilla extract
1-1/2 tablespoons instant coffee powder
2 ounces bittersweet chocolate, melted
2 to 4 tablespoons heavy cream

To make cake, line greased jelly roll pan (15-1/2x10-1/2) with wax paper. Grease and dust lightly with flour. Set aside. In large bowl, put eggs, egg yolks, sugar, and vanilla. Beat at high speed for 8 minutes. Mixture will triple in volume and be creamy. Fold in sifted flour and baking powder gently with slotted spoon, lifting to aerate. Fold in melted butter. Do not over-fold. Pour batter into prepared pan. Bake at 350 degrees for 20-25 minutes. Remove from oven.

While cake is still in pan, cut off crisp edges. Invert pan on towel dusted with confectioners' sugar. Remove wax paper at once. Roll both cake and towel together. Cool on rack, seam side down. Unroll carefully and fill with preserves. Roll again. Frost.

To make frosting, blend butter, 1 cup confectioners' sugar. Add coffee, dissolved in vanilla. Add chocolate and heavy cream. Add remaining 1 cup confectioners' sugar until desired consistency.

ENCHILADAS

1 pound ground beef
1 onion, chopped
2 teaspoons salt
1/4 teaspoon pepper
2 teaspoons chili powder
1 dozen corn tortillas
2 cups sauce (recipe follows)
1-1/2 cups sharp grated cheese

Brown meat and onion; add seasonings. Dip each tortilla in warm oil. On each one, spoon 2 tablespoons sauce, a generous tablespoon of filling and a sprinkling of cheese; roll up and place close together in large pan. Pour remaining sauce and cheese over top. Bake at 350 degrees for 15-20 minutes.

Sauce:
1 (No. 2-1/2) can tomatoes
1 medium onion, chopped
2 teaspoons chili powder
1/8 teaspoon oregano
1 (6-ounce) can tomato paste
1 garlic clove, minced
1/2 teaspoon salt
1/4 teaspoon cayenne pepper

Combine above ingredients. Simmer about 1 hour until slightly thickened.
Jean Baker, Chula Vista, Calif.

SWEDISH TOAST

1 cup margarine
1-1/2 cups sugar
1 cup commercial sour cream
1/2 cup ground almonds
1/4 teaspoon salt
2 eggs
3-3/4 cups flour
1 teaspoon soda

Mix all ingredients and pour into two greased and floured loaf pans. Bake in 350-degree oven for 45 minutes. Cool. Slice and place slices on cookie sheet. Place in oven again for 13-15 minutes until lightly browned, or slice as you want and use your toaster. Then spread the toast with butter and eat. Delicious!

Sandra Young, Victoria, Texas

Holiday
SPECIALS

LECHERLE
About 70 2-inch cookies

3/4 cup honey
2 tablespoons orange juice
2 eggs
1 cup powdered sugar
3 cups flour
1/2 teaspoon salt
1 teaspoon baking soda
1/3 cup finely-chopped candied
   citron
2 teaspoons cinnamon
1 teaspoon ground cloves
Clear Glaze (recipe follows)

Put orange juice and honey into small saucepan and bring to boil. Remove from heat and set aside. Beat eggs, continue beating as you slowly add sugar. Stir in flour, salt and baking soda, mix well. Add citron, cinnamon, cloves, reserved honey and orange juice; mix until thoroughly combined. Cover dough, chill for 2 to 3 hours.

Preheat oven to 350 degrees. Place dough on lightly floured surface and sprinkle top of dough with a little flour. Roll to 1/4-inch thickness. Cut into circles, diamonds, squares or any shape you wish, and place about 1 inch apart on ungreased cookie sheets. Bake for 10-12 minutes or until slightly colored around the edges. Remove from oven and transfer cookies to racks to cool. While they are still warm, brush tops with Clear Glaze.

Store airtight for several days to mellow before using.

Clear Glaze:
1 cup powdered sugar
2 tablespoons water

Combine powdered sugar and water, and mix well to dissolve any sugar lumps, making a smooth, runny glaze. Brush or spoon on cookies while still warm.

Leona Teodori, Warren, Mich.

HOLIDAY CRANBERRY BREAD

2¼ cups flour
¾ cup sugar
1 tablespoon baking powder
½ teaspoon salt
1 cup milk
1 egg, beaten
3 tablespoons melted butter *or* margarine
1 teaspoon vanilla
1 cup chopped cranberries
½ cup chopped walnuts

Combine flour, sugar, baking powder and salt. Set aside. Combine milk, egg, butter and vanilla. Add milk mixture to flour mixture. Stir just until mixed. Stir in cranberries and walnuts. Turn into greased 9-inch round pan. Bake in 350-degree oven for 45–50 minutes, or until cake tester inserted in center comes out clean. Let cool in pans 10 minutes. Remove from pan and cool completely. Wrap lightly and store 1 day before serving.

HALLOWEEN PARTY DIP

½ cup pumpkin
½ cup orange marmalade
½ cup plain yogurt
¼ teaspoon cinnamon
⅛ teaspoon nutmeg
⅛ teaspoon cloves, ground
½ cup whipping cream, whipped
¼ cup pecans, coarsely chopped
   Banana chunks, apple slices, orange sections, strawberries for dipping

In a bowl combine pumpkin, marmalade, yogurt and spices; mix well. Fold whipped cream into pumpkin mixture; spoon into serving dish placed on a large platter; chill. Before serving, top with nuts; place "dippers" around party dip on platter.

Gwen Campbell, Sterling, Va.

MONSTER HASH

3 cups pumpkin seeds, washed
2 tablespoons margarine
1 teaspoon salt

Melt margarine in frying pan; add salt and pumpkin seeds. Sauté for 5 minutes, coating seeds well. Place on a cookie sheet and bake 20 minutes at 300 degrees.

MERRY MINT BROWNIES

3/4 cup plus 2 tablespoons sifted
  cake flour
1 cup sugar
7 tablespoons cocoa
1/2 teaspoon baking powder
3/4 teaspoon salt
2/3 cup shortening
2 eggs
1 teaspoon vanilla
1 tablespoon light corn syrup
1 cup walnuts, coarsely chopped

In large bowl, beat all ingredients together at low speed, except walnuts; stir in walnuts with spoon. Pour batter into greased 8-inch square pan. Bake at 350 degrees about 40 minutes or until toothpick inserted near center comes out clean. Cool and frost.

Mint Frosting:
1 tablespoon shortening
1 tablespoon butter
2-1/2 tablespoons scalded hot
  cream
2 cups powdered sugar
1/4 teaspoon salt
1/2 teaspoon vanilla
1/4 teaspoon peppermint extract
Green food coloring
1 ounce semi-sweet chocolate
1 teaspoon shortening

Melt 1 tablespoon shortening and 1 tablespoon butter in hot cream. Pour over powdered sugar and salt; stir well. Add vanilla and peppermint extract, beat until thick enough to spread. Add enough food coloring to tint a Christmas green. Spread brownies with frosting. Melt chocolate and shortening together. Cool and drizzle over frosting in thin stream from teaspoon. Cut into squares.

Judy Haffner, Auke Bay, Alaska

MEXICAN YULETIDE COOKIES

About 6-1/2 dozen

1 cup butter

3/4 cup powdered sugar
1 egg
1-1/2 teaspoons vanilla
1/8 teaspoon salt
2 cups sifted flour
1 cup uncooked oatmeal
1 cup chopped pecans
Powdered sugar for rolling

Cream butter; add sugar gradually; beat in egg and vanilla. Blend in salt, flour, oatmeal and pecans. Shape rounded teaspoonfuls of dough into balls. Place on ungreased cookie sheets. Bake at 325 degrees about 20 minutes. Roll in powdered sugar while warm.

P. J. Leikness, Stoughton, Wis.

CHRISTMAS CRANBERRY DATE SQUARES

Filling:
3 cups fresh cranberries
1 package pitted dates
2 cups water

Crust:
1 cup butter
1 teaspoon vanilla
1-1/2 cups brown sugar
2 cups flour
1/2 teaspoon baking soda
1/2 teaspoon salt
2 cups quick oatmeal

Glaze:
1-1/4 cups powdered sugar
1/2 teaspoon vanilla
2 tablespoons orange juice

Cream butter, adding sugar gradually. Blend in vanilla. Sift flour, soda and salt; add to creamed mixture. Stir in oatmeal. Pat slightly more than half of crust mixture in a buttered 10x15-inch jelly roll pan. Cook filling ingredients in water over medium heat until cranberries pop, stirring constantly. Cool. Spread filling over crust. Sprinkle rest of crust mixture over top. Bake in preheated oven at 350 degrees for 25-30 minutes. Cool in pan on wire rack. Beat glaze ingredients until smooth. When bars are cool, drizzle with glaze. Cut into bars.

Mrs. Carmen J. Bickert, Dubuque, Iowa

CHRISTMAS EGGNOG BREAD

This is delicious for a Christmas brunch.

3 cups flour
¾ cup sugar
1 tablespoon baking
   powder
1 teaspoon salt
½ teaspoon nutmeg
1½ cups Borden's eggnog
1 egg, beaten
¼ cup margarine, softened
1 cup white raisins
½ cup red cherries
½ cup green cherries
¾ cup chopped nuts
   (pecans)

In a large bowl put together the dry ingredients. In separate bowl, mix eggnog, egg and softened margarine; add to dry ingredients. Add nuts and fruit. Bake for 60 minutes at 350 degrees in a greased 9x5 inch loaf pan. Let stand 10 minutes and place onto rack; cool.

Esther M. Garback, Gloversville, N.Y.

PATRIOTIC BISCUITS

2 cups sifted flour
2 tablespoons sugar
3 teaspoons baking powder
1/2 teaspoon salt
1/2 cup butter
1 egg, beaten
1/2 cup milk

Sift together flour, sugar, baking powder and salt. Cut in butter with a pastry blender. Add egg and milk. Blend thoroughly. Knead the dough on a lightly floured surface until smooth. Roll to 1/2-inch thickness and cut with biscuit cutter. Place on a greased baking sheet and brush with melted butter. Bake at 450 degrees for about 7 minutes.

CHRISTMAS WREATH
Makes 1 wreath

2-1/4 to 2-3/4 cups flour
1 package active dry yeast
3/4 cup milk
3 tablespoons sugar
3 tablespoons butter or margarine
1/4 teaspoon salt
1 egg
Milk
Pecan halves

In large mixer bowl, combine 1 cup flour and yeast. Heat milk, sugar, butter or margarine and salt just to warm (115-120 degrees) and butter starts to melt, stirring constantly. Add to flour mixture, add egg. Beat on low speed with electric mixer for one-half minute, scraping bowl constantly. Beat for 3 minutes at high speed. Stir in as much remaining flour as you can mix in with a spoon. Turn onto lightly floured surface; knead in enough remaining flour to make moderately-soft dough that is smooth and elastic (3-5 minutes total). Place in lightly-greased bowl, turn once to grease surface. Cover, let rise until double, about 1 hour.

Punch dough down, divide into 3 portions, shape into balls, cover and let rest 10 minutes. Roll each ball to 20-inch rope. Grease outside of a 6-ounce custard cup and invert the dish in the center of greased baking sheet. Starting at center, braid ropes loosely to ends. Wrap braid around custard cup, stretching as necessary to join ends, pinch to seal. Cover, let rise until nearly double, about 30 minutes. Brush carefully with milk, tuck pecan halves in braid. Bake at 375 degrees for 20 minutes. Cool bread on wire rack. Loosen braid from custard cup with narrow spatula, remove cup. If desired, wrap and freeze bread until needed. To thaw, let stand at room temperature.

Leona Teodori, Warren, Mich.

IRISH BROWN SODA BREAD

2 cups stone-ground whole-wheat or barley flour
1 cup unbleached white flour
3/4 teaspoon salt
3/4 teaspoon soda
1-1/4 cups buttermilk **or** whole milk soured with 1 tablespoon lemon juice or vinegar
1-1/2 tablespoons vegetable oil **or** melted butter

Preheat oven to 425 degrees. Sift dry ingredients into a big bowl or just stir with clean hands. You'll need them floured for the kneading step. Combine buttermilk or milk mixture and melted butter or oil in a measuring cup and stir into dry ingredients.

Knead dough a few moments until it sticks together nicely in a ball. Place on a greased and floured, or non-stick, baking sheet or in a 10-inch pie pan, and pat the ball into a flat circle 1-1/2 inches high.

Dip a knife into flour and score the giant biscuit with a cross 3/4 inch deep. Bake at 425 degrees for 15 minutes, then at 350 degrees for 15 more minutes. Thump the loaf. If it sounds hollow, it's done. Turn it out onto a rack to cool to lukewarm before serving.

If the crust seems too hard, wrap the bread for a few minutes in a cloth wrung out of warm water. To serve, remove the damp cloth and wrap the bread in a clean, dry cloth and place in a basket.

At the table, each person breaks off his farl (fourth) with his hands. The only knife to touch the bread is the one with the butter on it. Treated so kindly, the warm bread tastes better.

Soda bread goes well with butter and jam and a glass of milk for a snack. It's glorious with an Irish stew, or a seafood chowder, or with Red Flannel Hash that is baked along with the bread. An apple cobbler for dessert shares the oven.

HOLIDAY MERINGUE COOKIES
Makes 3 dozen

2 egg whites
Dash salt
1/8 teaspoon cream of tartar
3/4 cup sugar
1/2 teaspoon vanilla
1 cup miniature chocolate chips
1 cup chopped walnuts
Crushed peppermint candy (3–4 tablespoons)

Beat egg whites in small mixer bowl at high speed until foamy. Add cream of tartar and salt; beat to form soft peaks. Add sugar, 1 tablespoon at a time, beating after each addition. Meringue should be stiff and shiny. Fold in vanilla, chocolate chips and nuts. Drop by teaspoonfuls onto lightly greased cookie sheets, leaving about 1½-inch space between cookies. Sprinkle with candy. Bake 40 minutes at 250 degrees. Cool on wire racks. Store in airtight container.

Deanna Nilvar, Temple, Texas

HARVEST POPCORN
Makes 2½ quarts

2 quarts freshly popped popcorn, unsalted
2 (1½-ounce) cans potato sticks
1 cup salted mixed nuts
½ cup unsalted butter, melted
1 teaspoon lemon-pepper seasoning
1 teaspoon dried whole dill weed
1 teaspoon Worcestershire sauce
½ teaspoon garlic powder
½ teaspoon onion powder

Combine popcorn, potato sticks and nuts in a 15 x 10 x 1-inch jelly roll pan. Combine remaining ingredients; pour over popcorn mixture, stirring until evenly coated. Bake at 350 degrees, for 6–8 minutes, stirring mixture once.

Sharon Case, Chicago, Ill.

CHRISTMAS STOLLEN

3/4 cup warm water
1 package active dry yeast
1/2 cup sugar
1/2 teaspoon salt
3 eggs
1 egg yolk (save egg white)
1/2 cup margarine
3-1/2 cups unsifted flour
1/2 cup chopped blanched almonds
1/4 cup chopped citron
1/4 cup chopped candied cherries
1/4 cup golden raisins
1 tablespoon grated lemon rind
2 tablespoons margarine
1 tablespoon water

Measure warm water into large warm mixing bowl. Sprinkle in yeast; stir to dissolve. Add sugar, salt, 3 whole eggs, egg yolk, 1/2 cup margarine, and half the flour. Beat 10 minutes at medium speed of electric mixer. Blend in remaining flour, almonds, fruits and lemon peel. Cover, let rise in warm place until double in size, about 1 hour and 30 minutes. Stir down batter by beating 25 strokes. Cover tightly and refrigerate overnight.

Turn dough onto well-floured board, divide in half. Press each half into 10x7-inch oval. Spread ovals with 2 tablespoons margarine. Fold each oval in two, lengthwise; firmly pressing folded edges only. Place on greased baking sheets, brush with slightly-beaten egg white, blended with 1 tablespoon water. Let rise in warm place until doubled, about 1 hour. Bake at 375 degrees for 15-20 minutes or until done. Frost with powdered sugar glaze and decorate with blanched almonds, citron and candied cherries.

Judy Haffner, Auke Bay, Alaska

PUMPKIN GINGERBREAD

Serves 8–12

½ cup butter *or* margarine, softened
½ cup sugar
½ cup molasses
1 egg
1½ cups all-purpose flour
¾ teaspoon baking soda
¾ teaspoon ground ginger
¾ teaspoon cinnamon
1 cup canned pumpkin
1 (4-serving size) package *instant* vanilla pudding mix
½ cup milk
½ of a 4½-ounce carton frozen whipped dessert topping, thawed
Pecan halves

Cream together butter *or* margarine and sugar. Beat in molasses and egg. Stir together flour, soda, spices and ¼ teaspoon salt. Add to creamed mixture alternately with ½ cup water (batter may appear curdled). Pour into a greased 9 x 9 x 2-inch baking pan. Bake at 350 degrees for 30–35 minutes. Cool. Stir together pumpkin, pudding mix and milk. Fold in whipped topping. Chill. To serve, cut gingerbread into squares and top with some of the pumpkin mixture. Garnish with pecans.

Diantha Susan Hibbard, Rochester, N.Y.

CHOCOLATE SNOWBALLS

3/4 cup margarine
1/2 cup sugar
2 teaspoons vanilla
1 beaten egg
2 cups flour
1/2 teaspoon salt
1 cup chopped nuts
1 small package (6 ounces) chocolate chips
Confectioners' sugar

Combine all ingredients except confectioners' sugar, mixing well. Shape into 1-inch balls. Place on ungreased cookie sheets. Bake in a preheated 350-degree oven for 15-20 minutes. Cool slightly, then roll in confectioners' sugar. Cool completely and store in a covered tin.

Mrs. Sharon Crider, Evansville, Wis.

FESTIVE CRANBERRY CHEESECAKE

Serves 12

1 cup graham cracker crumbs
3 tablespoons sugar
3 tablespoons margarine, melted
3 (8-ounce) packages cream cheese, softened
¾ cup sugar
2 tablespoons flour
2 teaspoons vanilla
3 eggs
1 cup sour cream

Combine crumbs, sugar and margarine. Press onto bottom of 9-inch springform pan. Bake at 325 degrees for 10 minutes.

Combine cream cheese, sugar, flour and vanilla, mixing at medium speed on electric mixer until well-blended. Add eggs, 1 at a time, mixing well after each addition. Blend in sour cream. Pour over crust. Bake at 325 degrees for 55 minutes. Loosen cake from rim of pan. Cool before removing rim of pan. Chill. Spoon relish over cheesecake. Garnish with whipped cream and orange peel, if desired.

COCONUT SNOWDROPS

2 cups confectioners' sugar
1 cup unsweetened cocoa
2/3 cup sweetened condensed milk
2 teaspoons vanilla extract
3 cups flaked coconut

In medium bowl, combine sugar and cocoa. Add sweetened condensed milk and vanilla. Stir until well-blended. Mixture will be very stiff. Stir in 1 cup coconut. Shape into 1-inch balls and roll in remaining 2 cups coconut. Place in an airtight container and refrigerate.

Leona Teodori, Warren, Mich.

PAINTED COOKIES
About 5 dozen

1 cup butter or margarine
1 cup sugar
2 eggs
1/4 cup milk
2 teaspoons vanilla
4 cups all-purpose flour
1 teaspoon baking powder
3/4 teaspoon baking soda
Egg yolk paint (recipe follows)

Cream butter, gradually add sugar, beating until light and fluffy. Add eggs, one at a time, beating after each addition. Add milk and vanilla, mix well. Combine flour, baking powder and soda, add to creamed mixture, stirring until blended. Shape dough into 2 balls, wrap each in waxed paper and chill 4 hours. Work with half of dough at a time, store remainder in refrigerator. Roll dough to 1/8-inch thickness on floured waxed paper, cut with 2-1/2 to 3-inch cookie cutter, and transfer to lightly-greased cookie sheets. Paint assorted designs on cookies using small art brush and egg yolk paint. Bake at 375 degrees for 6-8 minutes, cool on racks.

Egg Yolk Paint:
1 egg yolk, beaten
1/4 teaspoon water
Paste or liquid food coloring

Combine egg yolk and water, stir well. Divide mixture evenly into 2 custard cups, tint as desired with food coloring. Keep paint covered until ready to use. If paint thickens, add a few drops of water, and stir well.

NOTE: Prepare one recipe egg yolk paint for every 2 colors of paint desired. Makes 1-1/2 tablespoons.

Leona Teodori, Warren, Mich.

ALMOND HOLLY LEAVES
Makes 12 dozen

1 pound butter, softened
1 cup sifted confectioners' sugar
2 eggs, beaten

4 cups all-purpose flour
1 cup almonds, toasted and finely chopped

Cream butter; gradually add confectioners' sugar, beating well. Add eggs; beat well. Stir in flour and almonds. Roll dough to 1/4-inch thickness on a floured surface with a floured rolling pin. Cut into holly-leaf shapes with 1½-inch cookie cutter. Place cookies on ungreased cookie sheets, and bake in 350-degree oven for 10 minutes, or until edges are golden. Cool on wire racks.

Leona Teodori, Warren, Mich.

IRISH PORK CHOP CASSEROLE

4 pork chops
1 pound apples
½ cup brown sugar
  Water
4 carrots, chopped
1 onion, cut into small circles
¼ teaspoon sage

Put chops into greased baking dish. Place apples and brown sugar on top of chops. Add a little water, if necessary. Bake at 300 degrees for 2½ hours. With 1 hour of baking time remaining add carrots and onions. Return to oven to continue with baking time. If a thick sauce is necessary, it can be thickened when cooked. Sage can be added before cooking, if desired.

FIREWORKS LEMONADE

1 cup sugar
1 cup hot water
Juice of 7 lemons
1 1/2 lemons, thinly sliced
1 quart cold water
2 cups crushed ice

In a large pitcher combine the sugar and hot water. Add lemon juice, lemon, water and ice. Enjoy!

CHRISTMAS EVE PARTY CANAPÉS
Makes 35

1 cup Swiss cheese, shredded
1 cup mayonnaise
1 (3-ounce) package cream cheese, softened
½ cup sour cream
2 tablespoons mustard
1 tablespoon fresh lemon juice
1 (6-ounce) package frozen crabmeat, thawed and drained
  Assorted bite-size breads

Combine Swiss cheese, mayonnaise, cream cheese, mustard, sour cream and lemon juice. Gently fold crabmeat into cheese mixture. Spread generously on bread squares. Place squares on baking sheet. Place into preheated broiler and broil until lightly browned; serve immediately.

Gwen Campbell, Sterling, Va.

GOBLINS' JELLY DOUGHNUTS

1 cup milk
⅓ cup shortening
⅓ cup sugar
½ teaspoon salt
2 packages yeast
¼ cup warm water
3 eggs, beaten
4 teaspoons vanilla
6 cups sifted flour

Scald milk. Add shortening, sugar and salt; set aside to cool. Dissolve yeast in water and add to milk mixture. Mix in eggs, vanilla and half of flour. Beat until smooth, adding more flour slowly. Knead about 7 minutes. Let rise until double in bulk. Punch down and divide into 4 parts. Roll out dough and cut into doughnuts. Let rise until double in bulk. Deep-fry until lightly browned and drain. When doughnuts are slightly cooled garnish with your favorite jelly.

EASTER BONNET COOKIES

You may use commercial, plain round cookies or make the following recipe, using a scalloped, circle cookie cutter.

Rolled Cookies:
- 3½ cups all-purpose flour
- 1 teaspoon baking powder
- ½ teaspoon salt
- 1 cup shortening
- 1½ cups sugar
- 2 eggs, well-beaten
- 1½ teaspoons vanilla

Sift flour, baking powder and salt together. Cream shortening; add sugar gradually; beat until light. Add beaten eggs; blend well; add vanilla. Combine dry ingredients with creamed mixture. Chill. Roll out dough thin; cut with cookie cutter. Grease baking sheet. Bake at 400 degrees for 6–10 minutes. When cool, frost with yellow icing. Use tines of small fork to draw lines around edge of cookies. This simulates the appearance of a straw hat.

Frosting:
- 2 cups confectioners' sugar
- 2 tablespoons hot water *or* milk
- 1 teaspoon vanilla *or* almond flavoring

While frosting is still moist, place a colored marshmallow in center of cookie. May add colored-sugar flowers. Dip underside of flowers in frosting and place on marshmallow crown or straw brim of hat. Sugar flowers can usually be found in a supermarket section where colored sugars and cake decorating icings are displayed.

Dorothy Stranix, Victoria, B.C., Canada

CHRISTMAS ORANGE BREAD

Makes 1 loaf

- ½ cup shortening
- ¾ cup granulated sugar
- 3 eggs
- ½ cup mashed bananas
- ½ cup orange juice
- 2½ cups sifted flour
- 4 teaspoons baking powder
- ¾ teaspoon salt
- 1½ cups mixed candied fruit
- ¼ cup raisins
- ¾ cup chopped nuts

Cream shortening; add sugar and beat until light and fluffy. Add eggs, 1 at a time, beating well after each addition. Combine bananas and orange juice; add to creamed mixture alternately with sifted dry ingredients mixed with fruits and nuts. Pack into greased and waxed-paper–lined loaf pan, 9 x 5 x 3-inch. Bake in a 350-degree oven for 1 hour, or until done. Cool about 20 minutes before turning out onto rack.

Jennie Lien, Stoughton, Wis.

GREEN & WHITE PUDDING SQUARES
Serves 8

- 2 cups grated coconut
- 4 cups boiling water
- 2 cups hot milk
- 6 tablespoons cornstarch
- 1/4 teaspoon salt
- 6 tablespoons sugar

Pour boiling water over coconut in a large bowl. Steep 10 minutes. Process in blender, half at a time, and strain.

Add hot milk to the coconut pulp. Blend 5 seconds. Strain.

Measure 4 cups of liquid. Heat to just boiling.

Combine salt, sugar, and cornstarch. Stir in a little liquid to make a paste. Slowly add to the hot liquid and stir-cook until thick. Pour half the pudding into a shallow buttered pan or platter. Stir 6 drops green food coloring and 1/4 teaspoon mint extract into the remaining pudding.

When the white pudding has set, pour the green pudding on top of it. Chill until completely set. Cut into squares. Serve on small plates.

COLONIAL FRIED CHICKEN

- 3 pounds fryer chicken parts
- 1 cup salad dressing
- 3 tablespoons flour
- 1 teaspoon paprika
- 1/4 teaspoon thyme
- 1 teaspoon salt
- 1/2 teaspoon pepper
- 3 tablespoons oil

Rinse chicken in cool water and pat dry. Pour salad dressing over chicken in a shallow dish, coating each piece. Then mix flour, paprika, thyme, salt and pepper together. Dip chicken into flour mixture. Heat oil and lightly brown chicken in a frying pan for about 3 minutes on each side.

Then place chicken in the shallow dish and cover with foil. Bake for 1 hour at 350 degrees; remove foil and bake an additional 10 minutes at 400 degrees.

IRISH LAMB STEW
Serves 4

- 8 medium-size potatoes
- 2 large onions
- 2 pounds lamb stew meat, bone-in if available

- 2 stalks celery
- 1/3 teaspoon dried thyme leaves
- 1 teaspoon salt, or to taste
- 1/4 teaspoon black pepper, or to taste
- Water to cover

Thinly peel all the potatoes. Slice 4 of them, thinly. In a heavy Dutch oven, layer sliced potatoes, 1 sliced onion, and the lamb. Sprinkle generously with the salt, pepper, and thyme. Add the other sliced onion and the 4 whole potatoes. Pour in the water and bring to boiling. Reduce heat and cover. Simmer 2-1/2 hours, or until the sliced potatoes have melted into the broth, or bake at 350 degrees for 2-1/2 hours.

GALA EGGNOG CAKE

2 cups flour
1-1/2 cups sugar
1 tablespoon baking powder
1 teaspoon salt
1/4 teaspoon nutmeg
3 eggs
1 teaspoon vanilla
1 cup eggnog
1/2 cup soft butter

Grease and flour bottoms of two 9-inch round pans or two 8-inch square pans. Combine all ingredients in large mixing bowl. Blend well on low speed of electric mixer. Then beat 1 minute at low speed. Pour into pans. Bake at 350 degrees for 25-30 minutes or until cake springs back when lightly touched in the middle. Cool; fill and frost.

Eggnog Frosting:
1/4 cup flour
1/4 teaspoon salt
1 cup eggnog
2/3 cup butter
1 cup sugar
1 teaspoon vanilla

Combine flour, salt and eggnog in a small saucepan. Cook over low heat, stirring constantly until very thick. Cool. Cream butter, gradually add sugar; cream well. Add flour mixture, beat until light and fluffy, blend in vanilla.

Joy Shamway, Freeport, Ill.

JINGLE-JAM MERINGUES

Makes 3 dozen

⅔ cup margarine
2 egg yolks, unbeaten
1 teaspoon vanilla
2 teaspoons baking powder
½ cup thick raspberry jam
1 cup sugar
2 tablespoons milk
2½ cups flour, sifted
⅛ teaspoon salt

Meringue Frosting:
2 egg whites
½ cup plus 2 tablespoons sugar

⅔ cup chopped pecans *or* walnuts

Cream together margarine and sugar until light and fluffy. Beat in egg yolks, milk and vanilla. Sift flour, baking powder and salt together and stir into creamed mixture; mix thoroughly. Make balls of heaping teaspoonfuls of mixture. Place on greased baking sheet. Flatten balls to ¼-inch thickness; top each with ½ teaspoon jam. Beat egg whites until stiff, adding sugar gradually; fold in nuts. Spread meringue on cookies, completely covering the jam. Bake at 350 degrees for 15 minutes.

These cookies are a little different and very delicious. Any flavor jam can be used. Instead of the jam, you might like to use peanut butter and jam or jelly mixed for Goobers.

Shirley Anne Crist, Marion, Ind.

CANDY CANE ANGEL CAKE

10 egg whites
1 teaspoon cream of tartar
1-1/4 cups white sugar
1 cup sifted white flour
1/2 teaspoon peppermint extract
1/2 cup finely-crushed peppermint candy canes
1/2 cup finely-chopped walnuts

Beat egg whites and cream of tartar together in large bowl until frothy, and peaks will just hold without tipping over. All other ingredients are mixed by hand until blended. Fold all into egg whites using a rubber spatula and folding over and over until all ingredients are evenly distributed. Gently spoon into ungreased 10-inch tube pan and place in preheated 375 degree oven. Bake for 20 minutes. Reduce heat to 275 degrees and finish baking 15-20 minutes. Remove from oven and invert pan; let cake cool to room temperature. With thin knife work all around edges of cake to remove it from pan. Serve with very lightly-sweetened whipped cream with a garnish of maraschino cherry.

Pearle M. Goodwin, South Ryegate, Vt.

BROWN SUGAR CHRISTMAS CUT-OUT COOKIES

1 pound (2 cups) butter
1 cup brown sugar
1 cup white sugar
1 teaspoon vanilla
2 eggs
1 teaspoon soda
1/2 teaspoon salt
6 cups flour

Cream butter with sugars until well blended; mix in vanilla, eggs, soda and salt. Blend in flour until dough is stiff. Chill dough about 1 hour or store in refrigerator until ready to use. Roll out about 1/4 of the dough at a time and cut into desired shapes. Place on lightly greased cookie sheets and bake in 375 degree oven for 10-12 minutes or until lightly browned around edges. Decorate with powdered sugar icing.

Barbara Beauregard - Smith, Northfield, S. A., Australia

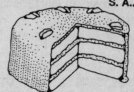

SNOWBALLS

Makes 4 dozen mini-donuts

3-1/2 cups all-purpose flour
1-1/2 cups sugar
1 cup milk
2 eggs
2 teaspoons vanilla
Dash salt
Salad oil
Confectioners' sugar

In large bowl, combine all ingredients except oil and confectioners' sugar, stirring until mixture forms sticky dough.

In deep skillet, heat 1-inch oil to 375 degrees. Drop batter by teaspoonfuls a few at a time, into hot oil. Fry 1 minute or until browned. Drain on paper toweling. Roll in confectioners' sugar.

Bobbie Mae Cooley, Bowen, Ill.

SNOWY WHITE FRUIT CAKE

1 (8 ounce) package cream cheese
1/3 cup shortening
1-3/4 cups sugar
6 egg whites
3 cups sifted flour
4 teaspoons baking powder
3/4 teaspoon salt
3/4 cup milk
1/2 cup water
1 teaspoon vanilla
2 cups candied fruit
1/2 cup candied cherries
1/2 cup chopped nuts
1/2 cup flour

Cream shortening and cream cheese together. Add sugar and cream well. Add egg whites, 2 at a time, beat well after each addition. Sift dry ingredients together. Combine milk, water and flavoring. Add sifted dry ingredients to creamed mixture alternately with liquid. Add 1/2 cup flour to nuts and candied fruit, then fold into cake batter. Bake in two well-greased loaf pans at 275 degrees for one hour.

Mrs. H. W. Walker, Richmond, Va.

MEXICAN YULETIDE COOKIES
Makes 6½ dozen

1 cup butter
¾ cup confectioners' sugar
1 egg
1½ teaspoons vanilla
⅛ teaspoon salt
2 cups flour
1 cup uncooked oatmeal
1 cup chopped pecans
Confectioners' sugar for rolling

Cream butter; add sugar gradually; beat in egg and vanilla. Blend in salt, flour, oatmeal and pecans. Shape rounded teaspoonfuls of dough into balls. Place on ungreased cookie sheets. Bake at 325 degrees for 20 minutes. Roll in confectioners' sugar while warm.

P.J. Leikness, Stoughton, Wis.

POOR MAN'S FRUIT CAKE

4 cups flour
1 teaspoon baking powder
1 teaspoon salt
1 teaspoon ground cloves
1 teaspoon nutmeg
1 teaspoon allspice
1 teaspoon cinnamon
2 teaspoons baking soda
1 cup shortening
2 cups sugar
2 cups raisins
2 cups hot water
1 cup coarsely-cut nut meats (your choice)

Sift together flour, baking powder and salt. Mix in cloves, nutmeg, allspice and cinnamon. Cream sugar and shortening. Add raisins to hot water and bring to boil; cool. Add soda in a little water. Add sugar mixture; mix well. Add dry ingredients, mix well. Add nut meats; mix well. Bake in 13x10-inch cake pan at 350 degrees until done, about 45-50 minutes.

Joy Shamway, Freeport, Ill.

CRANBERRY MINCEMEAT PIE

Pastry for 2-crust (9-inch) pie
2 cups prepared mincemeat
1 can (16 ounces) whole-berry cranberry sauce
1 cup coarsely chopped pecans
2 tablespoons grated orange rind
1 teaspoon tapioca
2 teaspoons rum or rum extract (optional)

Line pie plate with prepared bottom crust. Mix mincemeat, cranberry sauce, pecans, orange rind, tapioca and rum; pour mixture into pie shell and cover with top crust. Seal edges and slash top as a vent. Bake in a 400-degree oven 30-35 minutes, or until brown. Cool before cutting.

CHRISTMAS CAKE
Serves 20

2 cups flour
3 cups sugar
2 teaspoons baking soda
2 eggs, beaten
2 cups crushed pineapple
1/2 cup butter or margarine
1 small can evaporated milk
1 can coconut
1 teaspoon vanilla
1 cup chopped nuts

Sift flour, 2 cups sugar and soda together into bowl; stir in eggs and pineapple. Mix thoroughly; turn batter into cake pan 9x13x2-inches. Bake at 350 degrees for 30 minutes.

Meanwhile, combine remaining ingredients except coconut, vanilla, and nuts in saucepan and cook over low heat until butter melts, then cook for 2 minutes. Remove from heat and stir in coconut, vanilla and nuts; spread over hot cake.

Agnes Ward, Erie, Pa.

CHOCOLATE STARS
Makes 8 dozen

1½ cups sifted flour
1½ cups unblanched almonds, grated
1 teaspoon grated lemon peel
1 cup butter
1½ cups sugar
2 egg yolks
4 (1-ounce) squares unsweetened chocolate, melted and cooled

Mix flour, nuts and rind. Cream butter; add sugar gradually; cream until fluffy. Add egg yolks and chocolate; mix well. Add flour mixture gradually; mix. Roll ⅛ inch thick on floured board and cut with floured 2¾-inch star-shaped cutter. Bake on ungreased cookie sheets in preheated, 350-degree oven for 8 minutes.

Kit Rollins, Cedarburg, Wis.

PUMPKIN BREAD ROLL

Makes 4 1-pound coffee can breads

1 can pumpkin
4 eggs
1 cup oil
2/3 cup water
3 teaspoons cinnamon
3-1/4 cups flour
3 cups sugar
2 teaspoons baking soda
1 cup chopped walnuts
4 (1 pound) coffee cans
Powdered sugar

Grease and flour coffee cans generously. In mixer bowl, combine all ingredients, except powdered sugar, until well blended. Distribute equally in coffee cans. Bake at 350 degrees for 60 minutes or until top tests done. Remove from cans to rack, cool on sides, turning occasionally to keep round. Set upright and sprinkle with powdered sugar. Freezes well.

Agnes Russell, Concord, N.H.

CORN BREAD STUFFING

1 (10-ounce) package corn bread mix
½ cup butter
1 cup chopped onion
1 cup diced celery
2 eggs, beaten
¼ cup chopped parsley
½ teaspoon poultry seasoning
¼ teaspoon black pepper

Mix and bake corn bread mix according to package directions. Cool and cut into ½-inch cubes. In a large skillet cook onion and celery in ¼ cup melted butter over medium heat, stirring occasionally for about 10 minutes. Stir in parsley, poultry seasoning and pepper. Combine with corn bread and ¼ cup butter in a large bowl. Mix well. This stuffing may be prepared one day in advance and kept refrigerated. Do not fill turkey until ready to roast.

Sarah M. Burkett, Centralia, Ill.

SANTA'S WHISKERS

Makes 5 dozen

1 cup butter *or* margarine, softened
1 cup sugar
2 tablespoons milk
1 teaspoon vanilla *or* rum flavoring
2½ cups flour
¾ cup finely chopped red or green candied cherries
½ cup finely chopped pecans
¾ cup flaked coconut

In mixing bowl, cream butter or margarine and sugar; blend in milk and vanilla or rum flavoring. Stir in flour, chopped candied cherries and chopped pecans. Form dough into 2 (8-inch) rolls. Roll in flaked coconut to coat outside. Wrap in waxed paper or clear plastic wrap; chill thoroughly.

Cut into ¼-inch slices. Place on ungreased cookie sheet and bake in 375-degree oven until edges are golden, about 12 minutes.

Kit Rollins, Cedarburg, Wis.

MINCEMEAT COOKIES

2 cups shortening
5 eggs
1 teaspoon salt
6½ cups flour
3 cups mincemeat
3 cups brown sugar
2 teaspoons soda
3 tablespoons hot water
1 cup nuts

Cream shortening. Add brown sugar and mix until well-blended. Add eggs and beat thoroughly. Mix salt and soda with the flour. Add water to first mixture. Add mincemeat and flour mixture alternately to first mixture. Add nuts. Mix thoroughly. Drop with a spoon onto greased baking sheet and bake 10 minutes in a moderately hot 375-degree oven.

These cookies don't last long in my house as they are really extra-delicious!

Suzan L. Wiener, Spring Hill, Fla.

WILD RICE STUFFING

2 cups precooked wild rice
½ cup finely chopped onion
½ cup finely chopped celery
½ cup finely chopped mushrooms
2 tablespoons butter
1 teaspoon lemon juice
1 teaspoon tarragon
½ teaspoon thyme
1 egg, beaten
Salt and pepper to taste

Precook washed rice for 10 minutes and drain. In a skillet, melt butter; cook chopped onion and celery until tender, but not brown. Add wild rice. Add mushrooms, lemon juice, tarragon and thyme. Add beaten egg, salt and pepper. Mix well, and stuff your bird.

Lucy Andrews, Sequim, Wash.

CRANBERRY COOKIES

Makes 2 dozen

½ cup butter *or* margarine
1 cup sugar
¾ cup brown sugar, packed
¼ cup milk
2 tablespoons orange juice
1 egg
3 cups sifted flour
1 teaspoon baking powder
¼ teaspoon soda
½ teaspoon salt
1 cup chopped nuts
2½ cups (12-ounce package) fresh cranberries, chopped

Preheat oven to 375 degrees. Cream butter and sugars together; beat in milk, orange juice and egg. Sift together flour, baking powder, soda and salt. Combine with creamed mixture; blend well. Stir in cranberries and chopped nuts. Drop by teaspoonfuls on greased cookie sheet. Bake at 375 degrees for 10–15 minutes.

Edna Askins, Greenville, Texas

Ice Cream
TREATS

MAPLE ICE CREAM
Makes 1 gallon

6 tablespoons flour
1-1/2 cups brown sugar
2/3 cup white sugar
1/2 and 1/8 teaspoon salt
3 eggs, separated
2-1/2 quarts milk
1 can evaporated milk
1 teaspoon maple flavoring
1/2 teaspoon vanilla flavoring

Mix flour, sugars, salt, egg yolks, and 1-1/2 cups of the milk. Bring 1-1/2 quarts of the milk to a boil; add flour mixture to milk and boil 5 minutes; remove from heat and cool. Add stiffly beaten egg whites, remainder of milk, vanilla, maple, and evaporated milk; freeze.

To freeze: Use a 4-quart hand-crank or electric ice-cream maker. Pour maple mixture into freezer container; insert dasher and cover with lid. Place in bucket; attach the hand crank or motor.

Fill bucket half full with ice. Sprinkle on about 1 cup salt (rock). Continue adding layers of ice and salt in a 4-to-1 proportion to 1 inch below can lid. (As ice melts, add more ice and salt up to this level.) Begin cranking. (For electric ice-cream maker, follow manufacturer's direction.) It takes about 20-25 minutes to freeze.

To serve, remve crank or motor. Drain off water. Wipe off lid before removing. Remove dasher. Serve immediately for best texture. Makes about 1 gallon or 8 (8 ounce) servings.

Mrs. Olen Begly, West Salem, Ohio

DOUBLE BERRY FROST
Serves 5–6

1 pint (2 cups) strawberry ice cream
1 (10-ounce) package frozen strawberries
2 cups milk

Place all ingredients in blender container. Cover; blend until smooth and frothy, about 1 minute. Pour into cups.

Peggy Fowler Revels, Woodruff, S.C.

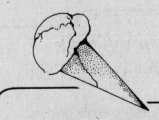

MOM'S BLUE-RIBBON ICE CREAM
Makes 1 gallon

2-1/2 cups sugar
4-6 eggs
1/8 teaspoon salt
1 tablespoon flour
1-1/2 tablespoons vanilla
1/2 teaspoon lemon flavoring
1 quart cream

Beat sugar and eggs until very thick. Mix all remaining ingredients with the creamed sugar and eggs. Pour mixture into chilled gallon freezer cylinder. Pour in milk to reach fill line or 3 inches from top. Freeze by hand-crank or electric freezer until firm or very hard to crank.

LIME MILK SHERBET
Makes 1-1/2 pints

3/4 cup sugar
3/4 cup water
2 cups evaporated milk
1/2 teaspoon vanilla
1/4 - 3/8 cup lime juice

Boil sugar and water to a thin syrup. Cool and put into ice-cream can with the milk. Add vanilla and lime juice. Freeze with 1-to-8 salt-ice mixture. Note: Ice used in the freezing mixture should be finely cracked. For cracking, a heavy sack and a wooden mallet are very useful.

Marcella Swigert, Monroe City, Mo.

PINK BANANA BLIZZARD
Makes 6 cups

1 (6-ounce) can frozen red punch concentrate, undiluted
2 bananas, cut into chunks
2 cups milk
1 pint vanilla ice cream

In electric blender container, combine half of all ingredients. Cover; blend until smooth and frothy, 15 to 20 seconds. Pour into tall glasses. Repeat with remaining ingredients. Serve immediately with straws.

Leota Baxter, Ingalls, Kan.

ORANGE-PINEAPPLE ICE CREAM
Makes 1 gallon

1 (6-ounce) package orange-pineapple gelatin
2 cups boiling water
4 eggs
1-1/2 cups sugar
2 tablespoons flour
1/4 teaspoon salt
2 cups half-and-half
1 (20-ounce) can crushed chilled pineapple, undrained
1 (14-ounce) can sweetened condensed milk, chilled
1 (8-ounce) carton non-dairy frozen whipped topping, thawed
1 (12-ounce) can frozen orange-pineapple concentrate, thawed and undiluted

Dissolve gelatin in boiling water; let cool to room temperature. Set aside. Beat eggs in large bowl on medium speed of electric mixer until frothy. Add sugar, flour, salt, and half-and-half, mixing to blend. Place mixture in heavy saucepan over medium heat, stirring constantly until mixture coats back of a spoon (soft custard), about 10 minutes. (Mixture may also be cooked in a microwave.) Cool; stir in gelatin mixture, pineapple, condensed milk, whipped topping, and concentrate. Chill ingredients thoroughly (overnight is best). Pour into freezer can of a 1-gallon ice cream maker. Freeze according to manufacturer's directions. Allow ice cream flavors to ripen at least 1 hour before serving.
Marcella Swigert, Monroe City, Mo.

PEANUT BUTTER SHAKE
Makes 4 cups

2 cups milk
1 pint vanilla ice cream
1/4 cup creamy peanut butter

Combine all ingredients in container of electric blender; process until smooth. Serve at once.
Bertha Fowler, Woodruff, S.C.

ICE–CREAM TREAT
Serves 12

32 chocolate chip cookies
1/4 cup margarine, melted
1 cup chocolate fudge topping
2 quarts ice cream, any flavor
Prepared whipped topping for garnish
Strawberries for garnish

Finely roll or crush 20 cookies. Combine cookie crumbs and margarine. Press onto bottom of pie plate. Stand remaining cookies around edge of pie plate. Spread 3/4 cup fudge topping over prepared crust. Freeze about 15 minutes. Meanwhile, soften 1 quart ice cream. Spread softened ice cream over fudge layer. Freeze for about 30 minutes. Scoop remaining ice cream into balls. Arrange over ice-cream layer. Freeze until firm for about 4 hours, or overnight. Garnish with whipped topping, remaining fudge topping and strawberries.
Suzan L. Wiener, Spring Hill, Fla.

ICED TEA A LA MODE
Serves 3

2 cups double-strength cold tea
1 pint vanilla ice cream

Blend tea and ice cream until smooth and pour into a tall glass.

ICED TEA SODA
Serves 8

4 cups double-strength cold tea
1/2 cup light corn syrup
1 pint vanilla ice cream
Carbonated water

Blend tea and corn syrup. Fill a tall glass half-full with mixture. Add a scoop of ice cream, then fill the glass to the top with carbonated water.

PINEAPPLE BUTTERMILK SHERBET
Serves 6

2 cups buttermilk
1 cup sugar
1 (9-ounce) can crushed pineapple
1 egg white, stiffly beaten
1 teaspoon vanilla
1/2 teaspoon unflavored gelatin
2 teaspoons cold water

Drain pineapple. Combine buttermilk, sugar, pineapple, and vanilla. Add gelatin which has been soaked in cold water and dissolved over hot water. Fold in egg white.

To freeze in churn-type freezer: Pour into freezer can and freeze according to directions with freezer.

Great as a dessert following a dinner and super with brownies!
Anne S. Moffett, APO, N.Y.

LEMON VELVET ICE CREAM
Serves 6

2 cups (1 pint) heavy cream or half-and-half
3/4 cup granulated sugar
1/2 cup frozen lemonade concentrate, thawed

Stir heavy cream and sugar in an 8-inch square metal baking pan until sugar is dissolved. Stir in lemon juice until blended. Freeze about 3 hours until firm. Remove from freezer and let stand at room temperature, 5 minutes before serving.
Diantha Susan Hibbard, Rochester, N.Y.

CITRUS ICED TEA A LA MODE
Serves 5

3 cups double-strength cold tea
1/2 cup chilled orange juice
1 pint vanilla ice cream

Blend ingredients until smooth and pour into a tall glass.

Kids

IN THE KITCHEN

PEACH 'N PINEAPPLE SHAKE

- 1 pint vanilla ice cream, softened
- ¾ cup drained, chilled, canned, sliced peaches
- ¾ cup chilled unsweetened pineapple juice
- 1 cup cold milk
- ½ teaspoon vanilla extract
  Fresh mint, if desired

Place ice cream, peaches and pineapple juice in blender and cover. Blend on high speed until smooth. Add milk and vanilla. Blend well again. Serve at once in chilled, tall glasses garnished with fresh mint.

Veronica Gengler, Saukville, Wis.

JUICY FRUIT SHAKE

Serves 4

- 1½ cups sweetened pineapple juice
- 2½ cups milk

In blender, blend chilled sweetened pineapple, apricot and strawberry or raspberry juice and milk. Serve over ice.

Leah Seymour, Columbia Cross Roads, Pa.

FRUIT MILK SHAKE

Serves 4

A delicious new way to serve fruit!

- 3 cups ripe fresh fruit in season *or* canned fruit in light syrup *or* natural juice
- ½ cup non-fat dry milk
- 1 cup water or drained juice from can
- 8 ice cubes

Peel fruit if necessary. Cut fruit into pieces; mash through a strainer or in a food mill. Crush ice cubes (one way is to place them in a heavy plastic bag and use a rolling pin or hammer). Blend fruit, milk powder and liquid with a beater. Add crushed ice and blend again.

Mary Linger, Jacksonville, Fla.

COTTONTAIL MILK SHAKE

Serves 1

- 1 banana
- 1 egg
- 1 cup cold milk
- 1 tablespoon honey
- 1 tablespoon peanut butter

Put all ingredients in blender and blend on high speed for 30 seconds. Pour into glass and serve.

Mrs. Floyd Morrison, Omaha, Ga.

ELEPHANT'S JUG

- 1 cup milk
- ¼ cup peanut butter (either crunchy *or* smooth)
- 1 ripe banana
- 2 teaspoons sugar
- 4 ice cubes

Combine all ingredients, except ice cubes, in blender and blend until smooth. Add ice and blend just until ice is crushed.

Pour into 2 glasses and serve immediately.

This makes a good snack for children after school or a quick breakfast when time is short.

Monica W. Cox, Cleveland, Miss.

ORANGE JULIUS

Serves 2

- ⅓ cup frozen orange juice concentrate
- ½ cup milk
- ½ cup water
- ¼ cup sugar (*or* less, depending on taste)
- ½ teaspoon vanilla
  Ice cubes—5 or 6

Combine all ingredients in blender container; cover and blend until smooth, on lowest speed of blender. Serve immediately.

Richard Ferschweiler, Paisley, Ore.

LEMON REFRIGERATOR PUDDING
Serves 10

1 (21-ounce) can lemon pie filling
2 (11-ounce) cans mandarin oranges, drained
½ cup flaked coconut
2 cups miniature marshmallows
1 cup dairy sour cream
Cocktail cherries

Combine all ingredients, except cocktail cherries. Chill in refrigerator until needed; then serve decorated with cherries.

Marie D. Robinson, Largo, Fla.

SHERBET DESSERT

1 teaspoon vanilla
1 pint whipping cream *or* Dream Whip
18 soft coconut macaroons, crumbled
½ cup nuts
1 quart lime sherbet
1 quart raspberry sherbet

Combine vanilla and whipping cream or Dream Whip. Beat on high speed with electric mixer until creamy and fluffy. Mix macaroons and nuts in whipping cream. Take half the mixture and spread in pan. Spoon lime sherbet and raspberry sherbet over this, then top with remaining cream mixture. Place in freezer. Makes enough for one 9 x 13-inch pan or two 8 x 8-inch pans.

Mrs. Andrew L. Asaro, El Cajon, Calif.

PUDDING TORTONI
Serves 8

1 (4-serving size) package coconut cream pudding and pie filling, not instant
1¼ cups milk
⅓ cup sugar
½ teaspoon almond *or* rum extract

2 cups whipped cream *or* prepared Dream Whip topping
¼ cup coconut, toasted

Combine pudding mix, milk and sugar in a saucepan; cook as directed on package. Cover surface with waxed paper; chill. Beat until creamy. Add almond extract; then fold in whipped cream. Pour into individual soufflé cups. Sprinkle with toasted coconut. Freeze until firm, about 3 hours. Remove from freezer 15 minutes before serving.

Agnes E. Verska, Upper Marlboro, Md.

WAFFLE SUNDAES

2 frozen blueberry waffles (jumbo size), toasted
2 scoops strawberry *or* vanilla ice cream
Banana slices
Strawberry preserves
Whipped topping

For each serving, top 1 waffle with 1 scoop ice cream. Arrange banana slices around ice cream. Spoon preserves over ice cream. Garnish with whipped topping. Serve immediately.

Quick and easy to fix.

Mrs. Bruce Fowler, Woodruff, S.C.

CHOCOLATE MARSHMALLOW CUPS

3 cups miniature marshmallows
1 (12-ounce) package semisweet chocolate bits
1 cup crunchy peanut butter
1 stick butter
24 (1¾-inch) paper-lined muffin cups *or* 48 miniature muffin papers

Place 4 marshmallows in each cup. Combine chocolate bits, peanut butter and butter in a 2-quart saucepan. Cook over low heat, stirring often, until mixture is melted and smooth; remove from heat. Spoon chocolate mixture over marshmallows, using 3 or 4 table-

spoons for each cup. Cover and refrigerate. Store in refrigerator.

Jane Weimann, Woodstock, Conn.

STRAWBERRY YOGURT PIE

1 graham cracker pie shell
1 (8-ounce) carton strawberry yogurt
1 (8-ounce) carton Cool Whip
1 (10-ounce) package frozen strawberries (thawed)

Combine yogurt, Cool Whip and thawed strawberries; pour into pie shell. Freeze. Before serving, thaw pie for about 30 minutes. Garnish with additional Cool Whip and strawberries.

Jodie McCoy, Tulsa, Okla.

ICE-CREAM DELIGHT
Serves 2–3

1 (3-ounce) package gelatin, any flavor
1 cup boiling water
1 pint vanilla ice cream
Lime juice, if available

Dissolve gelatin in boiling water. Add softened ice cream and stir well. Add a squeeze of lime juice, if desired. Mix lightly and well. Pour into dessert dishes and refrigerate until set.

Miss Bald, Montserrat, West Indies

ANGEL FOOD CAKE WITH FLUFFY FROSTING

1 (already prepared) angel food cake
1 envelope Dream Whip
1 (4-serving) package any flavor instant pudding
1½ cups cold milk

Combine Dream Whip, pudding mix and cold milk. Beat at high speed to soft peaks (4–6 minutes). Frost angel food cake. Store in refrigerator.

Mary Lou C. Hendrickson, Deer River, Minn.

PAPER CUP FROZEN SALAD

2 cups sour cream
2 tablespoons lemon juice
⅛ teaspoon salt
½ cup sugar
1 (8-ounce) can crushed, drained pineapple
1 banana, diced
4 drops red food coloring
¼ cup chopped nuts
1 (1-pound) can pitted bing cherries, drained

Combine sour cream, lemon juice, sugar, salt and red food coloring. Add fruit and nuts. Put in paper cups and freeze. Muffin tins can be used.

Barbara G. Swain, England, Ark.

SCRUMPTIOUS SALAD MOLD

1 (30-ounce) can fruit cocktail, drained
1 (9-ounce) carton whipped topping
1 (1-pound) container cottage cheese
1 (3-ounce) package gelatin, any flavor
½ cup chopped nuts

Drain fruit cocktail. Fold together whipped topping, cottage cheese and dry gelatin. Fold in fruit cocktail and nuts.

This is a delicious salad—no effort to make.

Amelia Gydus, Trumbull, Conn.

SUMMER FRUIT SALAD

Serves 4

Change the fruit depending on the season.

½ cup cubed melon or watermelon

½ cup fresh or canned pineapple in natural juice or light syrup
1 cup diced fruit: pears, apples, peaches, etc.
¼ cup orange juice

Cut up fruit. Combine fruits and orange juice. Stir. Chill 1 hour or more. *Variation:* When in season, try seedless grape halves or other fruits as a change.

Mary Hale, Tulsa, Okla.

BEST DEVILED EGGS

6 hard-cooked eggs
¼ cup mayonnaise or salad dressing
2 tablespoons finely chopped onion
1 tablespoon finely chopped green olives
1 teaspoon vinegar
1 teaspoon prepared mustard
Dash of salt and pepper
Paprika

Slice eggs in half lengthwise and remove yolks. Mash yolks with mayonnaise or salad dressing. Add the remaining ingredients and stir all together well. Stuff egg white with yolk mixture. Sprinkle paprika lightly on top.

Jodie McCoy, Tulsa, Okla.

PISTACHIO DESSERT

1 medium-size can crushed pineapple (do not drain)
1 (3½-ounce) box pistachio instant pudding
1 large container Cool Whip

Empty can of pineapple into bowl. Sprinkle pudding mix over the pineapple, and stir by hand until mixture thickens. Add the Cool Whip and stir until all is blended. Spread in flat container to chill. For a shortcut, chill for 15 minutes in freezer. Serve with Ritz crackers.

Bea Nagy, Natrona Heights, Pa.

ORANGE DELIGHT

1 package orange gelatin
½ pint vanilla ice cream
½ pint whipped cream

Prepare gelatin according to package directions. When gelatin is partially set, add ice cream and beat well. Stir in whipped cream and allow to set again. Put in sherbet glasses to serve and top with whipped cream and chopped nuts.

Ellen A. Johnson, Payette, Idaho

SCALLOPED APPLES

4 medium (1–1¼ pounds) tart apples, peeled, cored and sliced
½ cup sugar
¼ teaspoon cinnamon
¼ teaspoon cloves
½ cup butter or margarine
2 cups fresh bread crumbs (4 slices bread)

Toss apples with sugar and spices. In skillet, melt butter; add crumbs and toss lightly, stirring. In greased 8-inch square baking pan, layer half the apples, then half the crumbs. Top with layers of remaining apples and crumbs. Bake in preheated 350-degree oven for 45 minutes, or until tender. Serve warm as a side dish with pork or ham, or as a dessert topped with vanilla ice cream.

Eleanor Swift, Commack, N.Y.

RICE AND CHERRY SUPREME

1 cup whipping cream
½ cup sugar
3 cups cold cooked rice
½ teaspoon vanilla
1 can cherry pie filling

Beat cream and sugar together. Gently fold in rice, vanilla and cherry pie filling.

Sharon M. Crider, Evansville, Wis.

EASY MARSHMALLOW FUDGE

⅔ cup evaporated milk
1½ cups sugar
½ teaspoon salt
32 marshmallows (½ pound)
1 (12-ounce) package sem-isweet chocolate chips
1 teaspoon vanilla extract
½ teaspoon peppermint extract

Combine evaporated milk, sugar, salt and marshmallows in a saucepan. Cook over low heat, stirring constantly, until marshmallows melt. Blend in chocolate chips; stir until smooth. Add both extracts. Pour into buttered 8-inch square pan. Chill. Cut into squares.

Patty Ross, Trenton, Ohio

BANANA PEANUT BUTTER SALAD

6 bananas
⅓ cup peanut butter
4 red apples, diced, unpeeled
⅓ cup chopped nuts
½ teaspoon salt
¼ cup lemon juice
Mayonnaise
Lettuce leaves

Cut bananas lengthwise. Spread with peanut butter. Place on lettuce. Toss together the apples, nuts, salt and lemon juice. Sprinkle over bananas, accompanied by mayonnaise.

Margaret Lewis, Dubuque, Iowa

RICH-N-COOL SALAD

1 large package lemon gelatin
1 large container Cool Whip
1 (8-ounce) package cream cheese

Make gelatin according to directions on package. Soften cream cheese. Just before gelatin sets, add Cool Whip and cream cheese. Beat with hand mixer until smooth. Chill and serve.

Mrs. John Pyle, Burbank, Ill.

TUNA-APPLE SALAD
Serves 4

Try as a crunchy salad or in a sandwich.

1 (6½ - or 7-ounce) can tuna (packed in water)
1 unpeeled, diced apple
1 stalk celery, chopped
2 tablespoons mayonnaise
1 tablespoon lemon juice
Lettuce, as desired

Rinse and drain tuna. Mix tuna and other ingredients, except lettuce, in bowl. Use immediately or chill 1–2 hours. Serve on a bed of lettuce leaves. *Variations:* Oil-packed instead of water-packed tuna may be used. Pour oil from tuna can; rinse tuna with cold water, and drain well.

Jane Martin, Van Wert, Ohio

5-CUP SALAD

1 cup mandarin oranges, drained
1 cup shredded coconut
1 cup miniature marshmallows
1 cup crushed pineapple, drained
1 cup sour cream

Combine all of the ingredients in a bowl and chill until serving time.

This may be used as a fruit salad or as a dessert.

Martha Short, Bloomington, Ind.

EASY FRUIT SALAD

1 large can pineapple, reserve juice
1 can mandarin oranges, drained
3 bananas, sliced
1 package instant coconut pudding

Mix pudding with pineapple juice; add mandarin oranges and bananas. Stir. Ready to serve.

Nene Jordon, Rome, Ga.

EGG AND BAKED BEAN SALAD
Serves 4–5

2½ cups (No. 2 can) baked beans, well-drained
4 hard-cooked eggs, chopped
½ cup sliced celery
¼ cup chopped parsley
½ cup finely chopped onion
1 tablespoon mayonnaise
1 teaspoon prepared mustard
Prepared horseradish (1–2 teaspoons, or as desired)
½ teaspoon salt
⅛ teaspoon pepper
Several leaves lettuce
3 slices bacon, cooked and crumbled

Combine beans, eggs, celery, parsley and onion in a bowl. Blend mayonnaise with the seasonings. Stir into bean and egg mixture. Chill at least 1 hour. Serve in bowls lined with crisp lettuce. Garnish with crumbled bacon.

Esther Baumler, Decorah, Iowa

GREEN BEAN SALAD

2 cups chopped green beans
½ cup chopped green pepper
¼ cup radishes, chopped
½ medium onion, diced
½ medium pickle, diced
Salt and pepper to taste
Creamy Italian dressing, enough to hold salad together

Chop vegetables together and mix well. Add dressing. Chill and serve.

B.J. Nall, New Mexico

APPLESAUCE DELIGHT
Serves 6

1 (3-ounce) package red gelatin
1 cup boiling water
1½ cups applesauce (15 ounces)

Dissolve gelatin in water; blend in applesauce. Pour into mold or serving dish and chill until firm. Makes 2½ cups.

Mrs. Charles Coburn, Chicago, Ill.

CANDY CHEESE GEMS

8 ounces cream cheese, softened
7 ounces flaked coconut
1 (3-ounce) package lemon-flavored gelatin
1 tablespoon sugar
1 cup chopped pecans

Combine first 4 ingredients. Chill until firm. Roll into 1-inch balls. Coat balls with chopped nuts. Chill until firm.

Bonnie Broton, Dodge Center, Minn.

RICE KRISPIE DATE BALLS
(No-Bake)

1 cup margarine
1½ cups sugar
2 tablespoons milk
2 cups chopped dates
1 teaspoon salt
1 cup chopped nuts
2 teaspoons vanilla
4½ cups Rice Krispies
Coconut

Mix first 5 ingredients and bring to a boil. Boil for 2 minutes. Add next 3 ingredients. Shape into balls and roll in coconut.

Mrs. Beryl Becker, Cressona, Pa.

FRUIT-FLAVORED SYRUP
Makes 1 pint

1 envelope unsweetened Kool-Aid, any flavor
½ cup water
1¾ cups light corn syrup

In a tightly covered jar, shake Kool-Aid and water. Add corn syrup and shake until thoroughly blended. Keep covered and store in refrigerator. Children will love this on pancakes.

Mrs. S.R. Burt, Imlay, Nev.

PEANUT BUTTER CRUNCH

1½ sticks margarine
2 cups peanut butter
1 (1-pound) box confectioners' sugar
3 cups crushed Rice Krispies

Melt margarine and peanut butter together. Add confectioners' sugar and cereal. Mix with hands and shape into 1-inch balls. Refrigerate 1 hour.
Dip:
1 (12-ounce) package chocolate chips
½ cake of paraffin (make sure Mom supervises!)

Melt together in double boiler. Remove from heat and dip in balls. Refrigerate 1 hour.

Terry Hasty, Mackinaw, Ill.

CHOCO-PEANUT BUTTER BALLS
Makes 4 dozen

¾ cup margarine
1½ cups peanut butter
1 pound confectioners' sugar

Melt margarine and peanut butter in a saucepan on low heat. Stir well and remove from heat. Add confectioners' sugar and beat until well-blended. Roll mixture into small balls. Refrigerate on waxed paper for at least 30 minutes.

Chocolate Covering:
½ bar of paraffin wax
1 (12-ounce) package chocolate bits

Melt wax and chocolate bits in a double boiler. Dip shaped peanut butter balls into chocolate. Place on waxed paper and let chocolate become hardened. Store in refrigerator or a cool place.

Ruth Pratt, Greensburg, Pa.

LAYER FUDGE

12 ounces butterscotch-flavor pieces
1 (15-ounce) can sweetened condensed milk
2 teaspoons vanilla
2 cups miniature marshmallows
1 cup chopped pecans
12 ounces semisweet chocolate pieces

Line a 10 x 6 x 2-inch loaf pan with foil; butter foil. Melt butterscotch pieces; remove from heat. Stir in ⅔ cup sweetened condensed milk and 1 teaspoon vanilla. Spread in pan; sprinkle evenly with marshmallows and pecans, pressing lightly into candy layer. Melt chocolate pieces; remove from heat, stir in remaining milk and vanilla. Spread evenly over marshmallow layer. Chill 3 hours, or until firm. Lift candy out by lifting foil out; peel off. Cut in 1-inch squares. Makes about 3 pounds.

Mrs. Phil Hamilton, Tucson, Ariz.

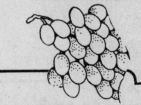

FRUIT AND JUICE GELATIN
Serves 4

A low-sugar salad or dessert for all the family.

1 tablespoon unflavored gelatin
2 cups unsweetened fruit juice (do not use fresh or frozen pineapple juice; it will not gel)
1 cup sliced fruit such as peaches, pears, apples, bananas, berries, etc.

Mix together ¼ cup juice and gelatin in a bowl. Measure another ¼ cup juice; boil it, then add hot juice to the above mixture and stir until gelatin is dissolved. Add remaining juice and stir. Put in refrigerator to set. After the gelatin begins to set a little, add the sliced fruit and return gelatin to refrigerator until firm.

Sally Simpson, Detroit, Mich.

CHOCOLATE YUMMIES

Tube of saltine crackers
2 sticks butter
1 cup brown sugar
12 ounces chocolate chips

Grease a jelly roll pan. Single layer saltines on the bottom of pan and set aside. Melt butter and mix in brown sugar; bring to a boil, stirring constantly, for 3 minutes. Remove from burner and pour evenly over crackers. Bake at 350 degrees for 7 minutes on middle rack of oven. Remove from oven and pour chocolate chips over hot topping; spread evenly to make thin coating. Refrigerate. Break up into chunks or separate the crackers.

Easy candy for the children to make. Freezes well.

Jane and Shirley Weimann, Woodstock, Conn.

CHOCOLATE CARAMEL TURTLES

1 (1-pound) package caramels
2 tablespoons water
¾ pound salted cashews
1 (6-ounce) package semisweet chocolate pieces

Heat caramels and water in top part of double boiler over boiling water, about 5 minutes. Stir occasionally until evenly melted. Grease baking sheet. Arrange 36 groups of 4 cashews each, about 2 inches apart on sheet. Drop melted caramels by teaspoonfuls on each group of nuts. Let turtles cool 15 minutes. Melt chocolate pieces over hot water, not boiling water. Drop by teaspoonful on top of each caramel turtle; spread chocolate if necessary with spatula. Set in cool, dry place until firm. All children love to make and eat these.

Beverly Brannon, Vidor, Texas

MARSHMALLOW WALNUT FUDGE

½ pound butter (2 sticks)
8 squares (8 ounces) un-
   sweetened chocolate
1 cup coarsely chopped walnuts
1 pound sifted confectioners'
   sugar
1 teaspoon vanilla extract
32 marshmallows

Combine butter and chocolate in saucepan. Melt over low heat. Pour into large bowl. Add nuts, sugar and vanilla. Knead until well-blended. Pat into greased 8 x 8-inch pan. Cut marshmallows in half crosswise. Place cut side down at 1-inch intervals so marshmallows will be in center of each piece. Chill several hours. Cut between the marshmallows in 1-inch squares.

Heather Williams, Dayton, Ohio

RAISIN CANDY

1½ cups seeded raisins, chopped
½ cup coconut
½ cup chopped nuts
¼ cup confectioners' sugar

Combine all ingredients. Roll into balls.

Ann Albritton, Salem, Ore.

GRAND GRAHAM CRACKERS

2 tablespoons butter *or* margarine
½ teaspoon vanilla
⅛ teaspoon salt
1 cup confectioners' sugar
   Half-and-half (3–4 tablespoons)
   Graham crackers

Melt butter or margarine; add remaining ingredients and blend until spreading consistency. If necessary, thin with additional half-and-half. Spread mixture between graham crackers.

Alice McNamara, Eucha, Okla.

NO-COOK COCONUT CANDY

1 (6-ounce) can frozen orange
   juice, unsweetened
1 (12-ounce) box vanilla wafers,
   crushed
1 (1-pound) box confectioners'
   sugar
½ cup melted margarine
1 cup chopped nuts
1 cup coconut
   Additional coconut for garnish

Thaw orange juice until slushy. Combine all ingredients in a large bowl and mix thoroughly. Mixture will be stiff. Sprinkle a layer of coconut into a 9 x 13-inch pan. Pour in candy and press down evenly with your hands. Be sure to cover the entire layer of coconut. Sprinkle more coconut over the top and press down gently. Cut into bars of the desired size and refrigerate.

Jodie McCoy, Tulsa, Okla.

NOODLE DROP CANDY

1 (12-ounce) package chocolate
   chips
1 small can chow mein noodles
1 (12-ounce) package butterscotch chips
1 small can peanuts

Melt chips in double boiler. Add noodles and peanuts. Drop on waxed paper by spoonfuls. Let cool and then enjoy.

Cheryl Brooks, San Jose, Calif.

CARAMEL NUGGETS

36 caramels
4 tablespoons milk
1 cup Rice Krispies
1 cup coconut
1 cup chopped nuts

Melt caramels and milk in top of double boiler. Add Rice Krispies, coconut and nuts. Mix well; form into 1-inch balls. Roll in confectioners' sugar.

Brent Habiger, Spearville, Kan.

STUFFED FRANKS

Serves 4

Mashed potato buds
2 tablespoons grated onion
2 tablespoons chopped parsley
1 teaspoon prepared mustard
8 frankfurters

Prepare mashed potato buds as directed on package. Mix potatoes, onion, parsley and mustard. Cut the franks lengthwise, being careful not to cut completely through. Flatten frank and spread with potato mixture. Set oven control at broil; broil franks 5 inches from heat for 5–8 minutes, or until potatoes are brown.

Cary L. Woods, Bellevue, Mich.

GRILLED TURKEY SANDWICH

Makes 8 sandwiches

8 slices bread
1 (4½-ounce) can deviled ham
Slices cooked turkey (8–12)
1 (8-ounce) package American cheese (8 slices)

Toast bread under broiler on 1 side. Turn over and spread untoasted side with deviled ham. Cover with turkey and top with cheese slice. Broil until cheese is browned and bubbly. Serve hot.

Mrs. Henry Wettach, Springwater, N.Y.

HAMBURGER

Place one ¼-pound hamburger patty on microwave roasting rack. Cover with waxed paper. Microwave at HIGH 1 minute. Turn over; cover. Microwave 30 seconds to 1½ minutes, or until meat is no longer pink. Let stand 1–2 minutes.

For 2 patties, microwave first side 1½ minutes; turn. Microwave second side 1–2½ minutes.

Mary Hale, Tulsa, Okla.

PIZZA BURGERS

¼ cup onion, chopped
1 pound ground beef
1 can tomato soup (regular size)
⅛ cup shredded cheese (long-horn may be used)
½ teaspoon oregano
Pepper
Buns (8–10)

Brown onion and ground beef. Add remaining ingredients and simmer 30 minutes. Fill buns with meat mixture and serve with tossed salad.

Mrs. James Schwan, Aberdeen, S.D.

PINK POPCORN BALLS

7 cups popped corn
3 cups miniature marshmallows
2 tablespoons butter
¼ teaspoon salt
Few drops red food coloring

Place popped corn in large buttered bowl. In bottom of double boiler, heat about 1 inch of water to boiling. Combine butter, marshmallows and salt in top of double boiler, over hot water. Stir until melted together. Stir in food coloring to desired shade. Pour over popcorn. Stir gently to coat.

Grease hands with butter and quickly shape popcorn into 10 medium-size balls.

Sharon Crider, Evansville, Wis.

WHITE CHOCOLATE CLUSTERS

3 pounds white chocolate
6 cups Rice Krispies
1 pound Spanish peanuts

Melt chocolate in top of double boiler and combine with Rice Krispies and nuts. Drop by tablespoonfuls onto a cookie sheet and refrigerate.

Mrs. William Wiedenhoeft, Sullivan, Wis.

PEANUT BUTTER FUDGE

2 cups creamy *or* chunky peanut butter
2 sticks (½ pound) margarine
1 pound confectioners' sugar

Melt peanut butter and margarine together. Stir in confectioners' sugar and mix well. Pour into greased 9 x 13-inch pan. Chill. Cut in squares.

Jean Ginnetty, Weymouth, Mass.

PEANUT BUTTER GRAHAMS

Makes 3 dozen

1 cup peanut butter, smooth *or* chunky
1 cup raisins
1 cup quick-cooking oatmeal
3 tablespoons butter *or* margarine
½ cup chopped nuts
¼ cup brown sugar or honey
½ cup graham cracker crumbs
½ cup graham cracker crumbs, reserved to roll balls in

Combine all ingredients and roll into 1-inch balls. Roll balls in graham cracker crumbs. Refrigerate.

Jeanette Schneider, Oceanside, Calif.

BONBONS

Easy enough for a young child. They love to work the dough.

½ cup butter
2½ cups confectioners' sugar
1 teaspoon vanilla
½ cup nuts, if desired

Mix thoroughly with a fork. Add nuts last. Roll into small balls. If desired, cover with melted chocolate.

Ryan Sykes, Monmouth, Ill.

DEVILED CHEESE
Serves 6

Children like to make this for after-school snacks or after the game.

1½ cups (6 ounces) grated cheese
1 teaspoon dry mustard
½ teaspoon salt
⅛ teaspoon cayenne
2 tablespoons melted butter
1 teaspoon vinegar
Toast

Blend cheese, mustard, salt, cayenne and butter; gradually stir in vinegar. Spread on hot toast; bake in hot oven at 400 degrees for about 5 minutes. Serve with hot chocolate.

Elsie Swanson, Ellsworth, Maine

CLUB SANDWICH

3 slices bread (for each sandwich)
Ham
Mustard
Swiss cheese
Mayonnaise
Lettuce
Turkey
Tomatoes
Bacon, cooked crisp

Toast 3 slices of bread for each sandwich. Between 2 slices, place layers of ham (can use boiled), mustard, Swiss cheese, mayonnaise and lettuce. Top with turkey, mayonnaise, lettuce, tomato, bacon (3 or 4 slices per sandwich) and third slice of bread. Hold together with frilled toothpicks. Cut diagonally in quarters and stand on plate with points upward.

Mrs. Charles L. Savy, Secane, Pa.

CRAZY CRUST PIZZA

1 cup flour
3 eggs
⅔ cup milk
½ pound ground beef
½ cup onions

Pizza sauce
Cheese
Pepperoni
Mushrooms
Peppers
Onion

Mix flour, eggs and milk. Beat 2–3 minutes. Brown ground beef and onions. Grease baking sheet; pour flour mixture onto sheet. Add meat and onions. Bake 25 minutes in 425-degree oven. Take out of oven; add sauce, cheese and rest of ingredients. Bake 10 additional minutes.

Lorraine Ritchey, Mars, Pa.

JIFFY JOES
Makes 6 sandwiches

1 pound ground beef
½ cup chopped green pepper
½ cup Kraft barbecue sauce
1 (8-ounce) jar Cheez Whiz pasteurized process cheese spread
6 hamburger buns, split

Crumble meat into 1-quart casserole; stir in peppers. Microwave on HIGH for 5–6 minutes, or until meat loses pink color when stirred; drain. Add barbecue sauce to meat mixture; mix lightly. Microwave Cheez Whiz according to label directions; stir into meat mixture. Microwave 2 minutes, or until thoroughly heated. Fill buns with meat mixture. A saucy, super sandwich.

Heather Williams, Dayton, Ohio

SUNBEAMS

1 cup non-fat dry milk powder
½ cup honey
½ cup peanut butter
½ cup granola-type cereal, crushed

Mix dry milk, honey and peanut butter together; chill. Form into balls the size of marbles. Roll in crushed cereal.

These are easy to make, good and nutritious.

Kimberly Slavin, Fort Calhoun, Neb.

CONEY ISLAND DOGS
Serves 5–6

1 (15-ounce) can chili with beans
1 package hot dogs
8 hot-dog buns, split
½ cup grated cheese

Place chili in glass bowl. Microwave 2 minutes on HIGH power. Stir. Microwave another minute, or until hot and bubbly. Set aside. Place hot dogs on open buns on a paper plate. Microwave 1½–2 minutes, or until warm. Spoon chili over hot dogs. Sprinkle cheese on top.

Shirley Jones, Indianapolis, Ind.

BEEF BACON CHEESEBURGERS
Makes 6–8 patties

2½ pounds ground beef
2 onions, chopped
2 tablespoons A-1 Sauce
1 pound bacon
Cheese slices (6–8)

In a large bowl, mix together ground beef, onions and A-1 Sauce. Fry bacon until done. Remove from pan and place on paper towel and set aside. Cook hamburgers until done. Place a slice of cheese on hamburger and bacon, as desired. Continue to cook hamburgers until cheese melts.

Christina Cooper, New Castle, Ind.

HOT DOGS

Place hot dog in a split hot-dog bun. Wrap loosely in paper towel to prevent the bun from becoming soggy. Place hot dog in the microwave. Follow the chart below for the plain hot dog or any of the other hot-dog recipes.

1 hot dog	30–45 seconds
2 hot dogs	45–50 seconds
3 hot dogs	1–1½ minutes
4 hot dogs	1½–2 minutes
5 hot dogs	2–2½ minutes

Defrost hot dog first, if frozen.

Mary Hale, Tulsa, Okla.

CORNFLAKES CRUNCHIES

1 cup dark corn syrup
1 cup sugar
1 teaspoon vanilla
2 cups peanut butter
5 cups cornflakes

Bring syrup, sugar and vanilla to a boil in small saucepan. Remove from heat. Add peanut butter and stir until mixture is smooth. Pour over cornflakes in large bowl. Mix well. Drop by spoonfuls onto waxed paper. Chill. Store in tightly covered container.

Marla Weech, Hoisington, Kan.

BACON-WRAPPED HOT DOGS

Hot dogs
Yellow cheese
Breakfast bacon
Prepared mustard
Worcestershire sauce

Cook hot dogs in boiling water about 8 minutes. Drain water off and let cool. When hot dogs are cold, slice lengthwise almost through in the center. Now put a piece of cheese in each hot dog and a little prepared mustard. Wrap breakfast bacon around each hot dog. Put hot dogs in casserole and sprinkle Worcestershire sauce over all. Cover casserole with foil and bake until bacon is cooked. If not brown enough, take foil off and cook a little longer.

Eunice Roscher, Waco, Texas

HOT DOG ON A STICK
Serves 1

Insert wooden ice-cream stick in hot dog lengthwise 1½–2 inches. Microwave on paper plate 30–45 seconds on HIGH power. Serve with mustard, ketchup or relish.

Mary Hale, Tulsa, Okla.

MINI-BURGERS

1 (10-count) can biscuits
1 pound ground beef *or* pork (make into 10 small patties)
3 slices cheese (cut each slice into 4 pieces)
Tomato slices
Lettuce
Pickles
Salad dressing

Bake biscuits as directed on can; remove from oven and cool. Fry patties until done. Remove from pan and place a slice of cheese on each. Break each biscuit apart and spread with salad dressing. Stack like a hamburger to each child's taste with tomato slices, lettuce and pickle. These are just the right size for children's hands. Serve them with carrot sticks, radishes and celery.

Mella Smith, Blossom, Texas

PIZZA HOT DOGS

4 hot-dog buns
4 hot dogs
12 slices mozzarella cheese
Pizza sauce
Parmesan cheese, grated

Split hot-dog buns and hot dogs lengthwise. Place layer of cheese on buns. Add hot-dog slices to each bun. Top with pizza sauce. Sprinkle with Parmesan cheese. Place on broiler pan. Broil until brown and bubbly.

Betty Klopfenstein, Waterman, Ill.

CHEESY HOT DOG
Serves 1

Slash hot dog lengthwise, but not completely through. Place in bun. Fill hot dog center with ¼-inch slice of cheese. Microwave on HIGH power on paper plate or towel 30–45 seconds.

Mary Hale, Tulsa, Okla.

HURRY-UP TACOS
Serves 8

1 pound ground beef
½ cup chopped onion
1 (8-ounce) jar Cheez Whiz pasteurized process cheese spread
Shredded lettuce
Chopped tomato
Pitted ripe olive slices
8 taco shells

Crumble meat into 1-quart casserole; stir in onions. Microwave on HIGH 5–6 minutes, or until meat loses pink color when stirred; drain. Microwave Cheez Whiz according to label directions. Wrap taco shells in paper towels. Microwave 1 minute, rearranging shells after 30 seconds. Fill shells with meat mixture. Top with remaining ingredients.

Mary Linger, Jacksonville, Fla

SPEEDY MACARONI AND CHEESE
Serves 3–4

1 cup uncooked macaroni
2 tablespoons flour
1 tablespoon instant minced onion
1 teaspoon salt
Dash Tabasco sauce
1 cup milk
1 cup water
2 tablespoons margarine
1 cup shredded cheddar cheese

In 2-quart glass casserole combine macaroni, flour, onion, salt and Tabasco sauce. Stir in milk and water. Dot with margarine and cover. Microwave on HIGH for 5 minutes, then on SIMMER (MEDIUM) for an additional 10 minutes, or until macaroni is almost tender. Stir about 3 times during cooking. Stir in cheese. Let stand 5 minutes before serving.

Mary Bell, Cincinnati, Ohio

CHOCOLATE FLUFF AND STUFF

¾ cup water
2 envelopes unflavored gelatin
⅔ cup sugar
¼ cup cocoa
½ cup milk
½ teaspoon vanilla
2 cups frozen whipped dessert topping, thawed

Place water in 1-cup measure; cover. Microwave on HIGH, 2–2½ minutes, or until boiling. Add gelatin; stir to dissolve. Set aside.

In small bowl combine sugar and cocoa. Slowly blend in milk, stirring to dissolve sugar and cocoa. Stir in vanilla. Blend in dissolved gelatin. Skim off any foam. Pour ½ cup of chocolate-gelatin mixture into small bowl. Blend in whipped topping. Pour remaining gelatin mixture into an 8 x 8-inch baking dish. Spoon chocolate-whipped topping mixture over and spread evenly with spatula.

Refrigerate until firm, about 1 hour. Cut into 16 squares.

Shirley Jones, Indianapolis, Ind.

CRUNCHOLA MIX

4 cups cereal (Cheerios, Corn Chex, etc., *or* any combination)
1 cup peanuts *or* mixed nuts
1 cup pretzel sticks, the smallest size
1 cup seasoned croutons
½ cup salad oil *or* 6 tablespoons melted butter
2 teaspoons Worcestershire sauce
¼ teaspoon garlic powder

In a large shallow pan coat crunch ingredients with the combined oil and seasonings. Heat in oven at 250 degrees for about 45 minutes, stirring every 15 minutes. Spread on absorbent paper to cool.

Fran Sievers, Atlanta, Ga.

MAGIC MARSHMALLOW PUFFS

1 can crescent refrigerator rolls
Several large marshmallows
¼ cup melted butter
¼ cup sugar
1 teaspoon cinnamon

Separate rolls into triangles. Dip 1 marshmallow at a time into the melted butter. Then roll marshmallow in a mixture of sugar and cinnamon. Wrap the dough triangle around marshmallow; completely cover it and squeeze edges of dough tightly to seal. Dip into melted butter again and place buttered side down in muffin tin. Place muffin tin on sheet of foil (to prevent gooey drippings in the oven) and bake in a 375-degree oven for 10–12 minutes, or until golden brown. As they bake, the marshmallows melt and leave a hollow puff in the center. Immediately remove from the muffin cups when done and, if desired, drizzle with a glaze made of confectioners' sugar and water.

Carol Wallace, Hastings, Mich.

SPICY SNACKIN' CORN
Makes 4 cups

4 cups popped popcorn
¼ teaspoon instant minced garlic
1 tablespoon imitation bacon bits
½ cup sliced almonds
¼ teaspoon lemon pepper
4 slices processed cheese

Spoon popcorn, garlic, bacon and almonds into 8-inch round glass cake dish. Sprinkle with pepper. Mix well. Lay cheese slices on top of mixture. Bake at 350 degrees until cheese melts, 5–10 minutes. Blend well with spoon. Cool. Break up into pieces.

Jean Fulgham, Eureka, Calif.

GRAHAM CRACKER SNACKS

Graham crackers
½ cup margarine
½ cup butter
½ cup sugar
Almonds *or* pecans, sliced

Line jelly roll pan with graham crackers, with sides touching. (Keebler's are best since they don't get soggy.)

Melt together margarine, butter and sugar. Bring to boil; boil for 2 minutes. Pour over graham crackers. Sprinkle with sliced almonds *or* pecans.

Bake at 350 degrees for 10 minutes. Remove from pan while still warm. Place on cooling racks.

Marilyn Holmer, Belvidere, Ill.

PIZZA DOG
Serves 1

Slash hot dog lengthwise, but not completely through. Place in bun. Spread center of hot dog with pizza sauce, ketchup or tomato sauce. Sprinkle with Italian seasoning and mozzarella cheese. Microwave on HIGH power on paper plate or towel 30–45 seconds.

May Hale, Tulsa, Okla.

CRISPY PIZZA POTATO SKINS
Makes 16 wedges

4 baking potatoes
1 cup spicy pizza sauce
¼ cup grated Parmesan cheese
1 cup shredded mozzarella cheese

Bake potatoes as usual. Cut each potato into wedge-shaped quarters. Scrape out most of the pulp (save potato to make patties).

Brush or spread pizza sauce over each wedge. Sprinkle with Parmesan cheese, then with mozzarella cheese. Bake 8–10 minutes in 450-degree oven, or until cheese melts. Serve very hot.

Winter Eve Gore, Aztec, N.M.

Micro- MAGIC

MISSISSIPPI MUD CAKE
Serves 16

Cake:
1 cup butter *or* margarine
2 cups granulated sugar
1/2 cup unsweetened cocoa powder
4 large eggs
2 teaspoons vanilla extract
1-1/2 cups all-purpose flour
1/4 cup walnut pieces, chopped
    coarsely
1/4 teaspoon salt
1/2 cup miniature marshmallows

Frosting:
1/2 cup butter *or* margarine
1/3 cup milk
1/4 cup unsweetened cocoa powder
1/2 teaspoon vanilla extract
1 (16-ounce) box confectioners' sugar

To make cake, put butter in large mixing bowl. Microwave on HIGH for 1–1-1/2 minutes until melted. Stir in sugar and cocoa powder. Add eggs and vanilla; beat vigorously until well-blended. Stir in flour, walnuts and salt. Let batter rest 10 minutes. Pour into an 11-3/4 x 7-1/2-inch baking dish. Place on a plastic trivet or inverted saucer in microwave oven. Microwave on MEDIUM for 9 minutes, rotating dish 1/2 turn after 3 minutes. Shield the corners of the dish with small triangles of foil (don't let triangles touch each other or sides of oven). Microwave on HIGH for 3–5 minutes, rotating dish 1/2 turn once, until top is mostly dry with a few moist spots and pick inserted near center comes out clean. Sprinkle marshmallows evenly over top of cake. Let stand about 5 minutes until marshmallows are slightly melted.

Meanwhile to make frosting, put butter in a large bowl. Microwave on HIGH for 30–60 seconds until melted. Stir in milk, cocoa powder and vanilla. Add sugar and beat vigorously until smooth. Spread evenly over marshmallows (cake will be warm). Let stand on flat, heatproof surface for 30 minutes until slightly warm, or cool completely and serve at room temperature.

Karen Waido, Mendota, Ill.

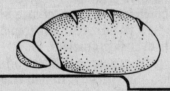

BREAKFAST RING
Serves 4

1/2 cup brown sugar
1 teaspoon cinnamon
1/4 cup maple syrup
1/2 cup chopped nuts
1 package (8- *or* 10-count size)
    refrigerator biscuits

Put nuts in bottom of small microwave bundt pan. Mix together cinnamon and brown sugar. Dip each biscuit in maple syrup and then in sugar mixture. Arrange in pan sideways. Microwave at power level 4, MEDIUM, for 9 minutes.

Sue Thomas, Casa Grande, Ariz.

CHOCOLATE SHEET CAKE

1 cup margarine
1/2 cup unsweetened cocoa
2 cups granulated sugar
4 eggs
1 teaspoon baking powder
1/4 teaspoon salt
1-1/2 cups flour
2 teaspoons vanilla
1/2 cup pecan pieces
1-1/4 cups miniature marshmallows

Place margarine in a 2-quart casserole. Microwave on HIGH for 1-1/2–2 minutes. Beat in cocoa with wooden spoon with sugar; then add eggs. Blend in baking powder, salt and flour; stir in vanilla and pecans. Spread batter in a 2-quart dish. Microwave on MEDIUM-HIGH (70 percent) for 11–12 minutes. Rotate, if necessary, every 3 minutes. Leave cake in pan; layer the marshmallows over hot cake. Cover with plastic wrap; let stand 5 minutes. Uncover; spread over top of cake; let cool.

Frosting:
2 tablespoons margarine
2 tablespoons unsweetened cocoa
2 tablespoons milk
2 cups confectioners' sugar
1 teaspoon vanilla

Place margarine in a 4-cup measure; microwave on HIGH for 30–40 seconds. Stir in cocoa, then milk; blend in sugar and vanilla. Spread on top of sheet cake.

APPLESAUCE BARS

¼ cup margarine
¾ cup brown sugar, packed
¾ cup sweetened applesauce
1 cup flour
½ teaspoon baking soda
½ teaspoon cinnamon
⅛ teaspoon nutmeg
⅛ teaspoon cloves
½ cup chopped nuts
¼ cup raisins
2 tablespoons confectioners' sugar

Microwave margarine on HIGH for 30 seconds; blend in brown sugar; beat in applesauce. Stir in flour, soda, cinnamon, nutmeg and cloves. Mix in nuts and raisins. Spread in an 8-inch baking dish, greased on bottom only. Microwave on HIGH for 6–7 minutes, uncovered. Cool and sprinkle with confectioners' sugar.

PUMPKIN CUSTARD
Serves 6

1 (16-ounce) can pumpkin
2 eggs, beaten
1 cup evaporated skimmed milk
1/3 cup packed brown sugar
1/4 cup granulated sugar
1-1/2 teaspoons ground cinnamon
1/2 teaspoon salt
1/4 teaspoon ground ginger
1/4 teaspoon ground nutmeg
Whipped topping

In medium mixing bowl, combine all ingredients, except whipped topping. Blend with whisk. Divide evenly among 6 (6-ounce) custard cups. Arrange in circular pattern in microwave oven. Microwave at 50 percent, MEDIUM, for 18–23 minutes, or until centers are soft-set, rearranging and rotating cups 2 or 3 times. Serve warm or cool. Garnish with dollop of whipped topping.

Sharon M. Crider, Stoughton, Wis.

FIESTA ROLL-UP
Serves 4

1 strip ham, 1-1/2-inches wide and 6 inches long
1/4 cup butter *or* margarine
1/2 cup green pepper, chopped
1 medium onion, chopped
5 eggs, beaten
1/4 cup water
2 tablespoons chopped pimiento

Place ham in an 8 x 8 x 2-inch baking dish. Cover. Microwave on HIGH (100 percent) for 3–4 minutes, or until heated through. Cover with aluminum foil and let stand while cooking eggs and vegetables.

Place butter, green pepper and onion in an 11-3/4 x 7-1/2 x 1-3/4-inch baking dish. Microwave on HIGH (100 percent) for 3–4 minutes, or until vegetables are tender. Stir together eggs and water. Pour over vegetables. Sprinkle with pimiento. Cover with plastic wrap. Microwave on HIGH (100 percent) for 8–10 minutes, or until set, but glossy on top. Turn dish 4 times during cooking. Remove plastic wrap. Loosen bottom and edges of omelette with a rubber spatula. Cover dish with waxed paper. Place cookie sheet over waxed paper. Flip omelette out onto cookie sheet. Place the ham on small end of omelette. Roll ham inside omelette in jelly-roll fashion. Place seam side down on serving dish. Set parsley around edge of dish. Place sliced olives on top of the "egg roll-up." Serve immediately.

Marie Fusaro, Manasquan, N.J.

PEANUT BUTTER BLONDIES
Makes 1 dozen

1/2 cup sifted cake flour (not self-rising)
1/4 teaspoon baking powder
1/8 teaspoon coarse (kosher) salt
1/4 cup (1/2 stick) unsalted butter
1/2 cup creamy peanut butter

1/2 cup firmly packed light brown sugar
2 eggs
1 teaspoon vanilla
1/3 cup unsalted peanuts, coarsely chopped (1-3/4 ounces)

Sift together flour, baking powder and salt onto sheet of waxed paper. Set aside. Place butter and peanut butter in a microwave-safe, 4-cup glass measure. Cover tightly with microwave-safe plastic wrap. Microwave at full power (100 percent) or HIGH for 2 minutes. Carefully pierce plastic wrap with tip of small knife to release steam. Uncover glass measure carefully. Stir in sugar and eggs, 1 at a time. Stir in vanilla, flour mixture and peanuts. Spread mixture in microwave-safe 9-1/2 x 6 x 2-inch dish. Microwave, uncovered, at full power (100 percent) or HIGH for 3–3-1/2 minutes, or until set. Center bottom may be slightly fudgey. If you prefer blondies more done, cook 1 minute longer. Cool on rack before cutting.

Leona Teodori, Warren, Mich.

APPLE CRISP AND BRAN

5 cups sliced baking apples
1 tablespoon water
¼ cup margarine
⅓ cup brown sugar, packed
⅓ cup quick-cooking oats
½ cup oat bran
1 teaspoon vanilla
¼ teaspoon nutmeg
1 teaspoon cinnamon
1 cup non-fat yogurt

Combine apples and water in an 8-inch round baking dish. Set aside. Microwave margarine on HIGH in an uncovered bowl for 20–30 seconds. Blend in brown sugar; mix in rolled oats, bran, cinnamon, nutmeg and vanilla until crumbly. Sprinkle over apples. Microwave on HIGH, uncovered, for 9–10 minutes. Serve warm or cold, topped with non-fat yogurt.

CHICKEN AND DUMPLINGS
Serves 4–6

1 (3-pound) broiler-fryer, cut up
3 small onions, quartered
4 medium carrots, cut in 1-inch pieces, then halved
2 stalks celery, diced
4 sprigs parsley
1 (13-3/4-ounce) can chicken broth
2 bay leaves
2 teaspoons salt
1/4 teaspoon thyme
1–2 cloves garlic, cut in half
1/4 teaspoon poultry seasoning
1/8 teaspoon pepper
2 cups water
4 tablespoons cornstarch
1/3 cup water

Dumplings:
1 cup biscuit baking mix
1/3 cup milk
1/4 teaspoon poultry seasoning

Place chicken, vegetables and parsley in 4-quart casserole. Mix together the broth, bay leaves, salt, thyme, garlic, poultry seasoning and pepper. Pour over chicken. Cover and cook on HIGH power for 20–25 minutes, or until vegetables are tender. Remove chicken. Add the 2 cups water; cover and microwave on HIGH power for 5 minutes longer.

Mix cornstarch and water; add to vegetable mixture; blend well. Microwave, uncovered, 5 minutes on HIGH power, or until thickened. Return chicken to casserole.

To make dumplings, mix together biscuit mix, milk and seasoning until moistened. Spoon mixture over casserole by the tablespoon. Microwave, *covered,* on HIGH power for 5–6-1/2 minutes, or until dumplings are done.
Tip: For a low-fat dish, skin the chicken before cooking.
Yvonne Schilling, Wauwatosa, Wis.

GOURMET STUFFED YAMS
Serves 4

4 medium-size yams
1/4 cup apple juice *or* cider
1/2 cup chopped apple (do not peel)
1/4 cup chopped pecans
1/4 teaspoon cinnamon
Thin apple wedge for garnish

Microwave yams on HIGH for 10–13 minutes, or until tender. Cut a thin, horizontal slice from top of each yam with sharp knife. Scoop out pulp, leaving 1/4-inch shell. Heat apple juice or cider in microwave for 30 seconds, or until hot. Mash and whip pulp with juice. Stir in apples, nuts and cinnamon. Pile into shells. Garnish with apple wedge to serve.

Hint: For more servings add 2 tablespoons chopped apple, 1 tablespoon chopped pecans, 1 tablespoon juice or cider and a dash of cinnamon for each additional yam.

Delicious with any kind of poultry, roast pork or ham! For the health-conscious cook, there is no salt, butter or sugar in this recipe!
Mary E. Finley, Jonesville, Mich.

CINNAMON APPLES
Serves 6

6 large apples
3/4 cup raisins
1/2 cup brown sugar
1 tablespoon butter
1 teaspoon ground cinnamon
1/2 teaspoon ground nutmeg
1/2 cup water
1 cup half-and-half

Core apples. Cut a strip of peel around the top of each apple. Place apples in a round, 2-quart microwave casserole or microwave ring mold. Fill apples with raisins. In a 1-quart microwave bowl, place brown sugar, butter, cinnamon, nutmeg and 1/2 cup water. Cover and microwave on HIGH for 1 minute, 30 seconds. Sugar should be melted, and mixture very hot. Pour hot sugar mixture over and around apples. Cover and microwave on HIGH for 12 minutes. Turn dish 1/4 turn every 3 minutes. Apples will be very tender. Put apples into individual serving dishes. Serve with half-and-half.
June Harding, Royal Oak, Mich.

BAKED APPLES
Serves 4

2 large baking apples, cored and cut in half
2 tablespoons margarine
1/2 cup dark corn syrup
Cinnamon
Red hot cinnamon candies

Slice apples in half and core. Set half-apples in a shallow 1-1/2-quart microwave-proof baking dish. Place 1/4 tablespoon margarine in center of each apple half. Spoon 1 tablespoon corn syrup into each half. Sprinkle with cinnamon.

Put 1 or 2 red hot cinnamon candies in center of each apple half (adds color and flavor).

Cover with plastic wrap. Microwave on HIGH for 4 minutes, turning apples and spooning syrup over them after 2 minutes. When cooking time is up, let stand 2 minutes before serving.
Flo Burtnett, Gage, Okla.

HOT HAM SALAD
Single serving

2 slices (1 ounce each) sliced, chopped ham, cut into 1/2-inch pieces
1/4 cup herb-seasoned croutons
1/4 cup thinly sliced celery
1/4 cup frozen green peas, thawed
1/4 cup mayonnaise
1/4 teaspoon instant minced onion
Dash of pepper
1 tablespoon shredded cheddar cheese

Mix all ingredients, except cheese. Spoon lightly into 14-ounce shallow casserole. Sprinkle with cheese. Cover loosely and microwave on MEDIUM-HIGH (70 percent) for 2-1/2–3-1/2 minutes, or until hot and bubbly.
Barbara Nowakowski, North Tonawanda, N.Y.

MICRO-GOOD BEEF STROGANOFF
Serves 2

1 pound round steak, trimmed
4 tablespoons butter
1 (3-ounce) can mushrooms with liquid
1 package dry onion soup mix
1 tablespoon steak sauce
1/4 teaspoon garlic powder
1 cup sour cream

Cut meat diagonally across the grain into thin strips. In 1-1/2-quart casserole dish microwave in butter 3 minutes on HIGH. Add mushrooms and liquid to equal 1 cup; stir in soup mix; heat to boiling. Add steak sauce and garlic powder; cook on MEDIUM 3 minutes; stir in sour cream. Serve on thin or broad egg noodles.

Gwen Campbell, Sterling, Va.

TINY PEAS AND LETTUCE AU VIN
Serves 4

2 (15-ounce) cans tiny peas, drained
8 whole white pearl onions
8 Boston lettuce leaves, coarsely shredded
1/2 teaspoon sugar
1/4 teaspoon salt
3 tablespoons butter
3 tablespoons chicken broth
1 tablespoon cornstarch
2 tablespoons dry white wine

Place first 7 ingredients in a 1-1/2-quart microwave casserole. Cover; cook 8 minutes on HIGH. Combine cornstarch and white wine; stir into casserole gently; cook 2 minutes on HIGH.

Gwen Campbell, Sterling, Va.

TEN-MINUTE MEAT LOAF
Serves 4-6

1 pound ground beef
1 egg
1/2 cup bread crumbs
1/4 cup milk

2 tablespoons onion soup mix
2 tablespoons ketchup
2 tablespoons soy sauce
1/2 cup shredded Swiss cheese

Combine all ingredients and shape in round or oval loaf. Place in microwave-safe dish; cover with waxed paper and microwave on HIGH for 10 minutes, turning dish after 5 minutes of cooking. Drain and cover with foil. Let stand 10 minutes before slicing.

Microwaves vary. Test for doneness.

Marian B. Hamilton, Ypsilanti, Mich.

TANGY MUSTARD CAULIFLOWER
Serves 6-8

1 medium head cauliflower, broken into florets
1/2 cup mayonnaise *or* salad dressing
1/4 teaspoon instant minced onion
1 teaspoon prepared mustard
1/2 cup shredded cheddar cheese

Place cauliflower in 1-1/2-quart casserole with cover. Add 2 tablespoons water. Cook, covered, on HIGH 7-8 minutes, or until just about tender. Combine mayonnaise, onion and mustard, mixing well. Place cooked cauliflower in serving dish. Spread mayonnaise mixture over cauliflower. Sprinkle with cheese. Cook, uncovered, on HIGH for 1 minute to heat topping and melt cheese.

Mary Ann Donlan, Waterloo, Iowa

SIMPLY ELEGANT TOMATOES
Serves 4

4 fully ripe medium tomatoes
1/4 cup chopped onions
1/4 cup chopped green pepper
1/3 cup grated Parmesan cheese
1/2 teaspoon oregano
1/2 teaspoon garlic powder
1/8 teaspoon pepper
1 tablespoon parsley flakes

Wash and core tomatoes; scoop out pulp and put into a bowl. Add remaining ingredients and mix. Place back into tomatoes and microwave on HIGH for 6-7 minutes.

Mrs. Merle Mishler, Hollsopple, Pa.

CREAMY GINGERED SCALLOPS
1 serving

1 tablespoon chopped green onion (with tops)
1-1/2 teaspoons margarine
1-1/2 teaspoons flour
1/4 cup half-and-half
1 tablespoon dry white wine
1/4 teaspoon grated gingerroot
1/8 teaspoon salt
3 ounces bay *or* seal scallops, cut into 1/2-inch pieces (about 1/3 cup)
1 (2-1/2-ounce) jar whole mushrooms, drained

Place onion and margarine in 2-cup measure. Microwave, uncovered, on HIGH about 30 seconds, or until margarine is melted. Mix in flour. Stir in half-and-half, wine, gingerroot and salt.

MICROWAVE POTATOES
Serves 4

5 large potatoes, peeled and diced
1/4 cup margarine
1/4 cup minced onion
1/2 teaspoon garlic powder
1/2 teaspoon black pepper
1/4 cup Parmesan cheese

Place all ingredients, except cheese, into a 3-quart microwave-safe dish with lid. Microwave, covered, on HIGH for 10 minutes. Stir; add cheese; stir again. Cover, microwave on HIGH for 10 minutes. Stir again just before serving.

Christine Sweet, Green, N.Y.

PEANUT BUTTER ROCKY ROAD

1 (6-ounce) package semisweet chocolate chips
1 (6-ounce) package butterscotch chips
1/2 cup peanut butter
3 cups miniature marshmallows
1/2 cup salted peanuts

Place chocolate chips, butterscotch chips and peanut butter in 2-quart bowl. Microwave, uncovered, on HIGH (100 percent) until softened, 2–2-1/2 minutes. Stir until melted and smooth. Mix in marshmallows and peanuts until evenly coated. Spread in buttered square 8 x 8 x 2-inch baking pan. Refrigerate until firm, at least 1 hour. Cut into squares.

Shari Crider, Stoughton, Wis.

ATLANTIC CITY TAFFY
Makes 1 pound

2 cups dark corn syrup
1/4 cup strong black coffee
2 squares unsweetened baking chocolate
1/4 teaspoon salt
1 tablespoon butter *or* margarine
1 teaspoon vanilla

In a 2-quart glass measure combine first 4 ingredients. Cook on HIGH for 12–18 minutes. Add butter and vanilla; pour into 8-inch square baking dish; cool enough to "pull." Grease hands; pull taffy until elastic and light in color. Cut into pieces; wrap in waxed paper or rainbow-colored cellophane; twist ends to close.

Gwen Campbell, Sterling, Va.

FRENCH POTATOES
Serves 4

1-1/2 pounds potatoes, peeled and very thinly sliced
1 medium-size onion, sliced into rings
3 tablespoons butter
Salt
Pepper
6 tablespoons milk
Paprika

Put potato slices to soak in cold water. Put the onion rings in a bowl. Cover with plastic wrap and pierce. Microwave on full power or HIGH for 1 minute. Grease a 5-cup microwave dish with a little of the butter. Layer drained potatoes and onions in dish, starting and finishing with potatoes. Season each layer well with salt and pepper.

Pour milk over potatoes and dot with the rest of the butter. Sprinkle the top with paprika. Cover with plastic wrap and pierce. Microwave on full power or HIGH for 13 minutes, giving the dish 1/2 turn twice during cooking. Allow to stand, covered, for 5 minutes before serving.

Flo Burtnett, Gage, Okla.

PIZZA HAMBURGER PIE
Serves 4

1 pound ground beef
1-1/2 teaspoons garlic salt
Salt and pepper
1-1/2 teaspoons horseradish
1 teaspoon Worcestershire sauce
1-1/2 teaspoons mustard
1 (8-ounce) can tomato sauce
2 teaspoons chopped onion
1/2 teaspoon oregano
1/2 teaspoon red pepper
1 cup mozzarella cheese

Lightly toss beef with garlic salt, salt, pepper, horseradish, Worcestershire sauce and mustard. Press meat against sides and bottom of an 8- or 9-inch pie plate; spread tomato sauce over top surface. Sprinkle with a little onion, oregano, red pepper and cheese. Cook at 70 percent power for 8–10 minutes.

Sheila Symonowicz, Hubbardston, Mass.

LASAGNA ROLLS
Serves 2

1/2 pound bulk Italian sausage
1/4 cup chopped onion
1 egg, beaten
1/2 cup cream-style cottage cheese
2 tablespoons grated Parmesan cheese
4 lasagna noodles, cooked
1 (8-ounce) can pizza sauce
1 tablespoon water or dry red wine
1/4 cup shredded mozzarella cheese

Crumble sausage into a 1-quart casserole dish. Stir in onion. Microwave, uncovered, on 100 percent power or HIGH for 3–4 minutes, or until sausage is done and the onion is tender. Drain off fat. Stir in the beaten egg, cottage cheese and Parmesan cheese. Spread each lasagna noodle with some of the cheese-meat mixture. Roll each noodle, jelly-roll style. Place seam side down in a small greased baking dish.

Stir together pizza sauce and water or wine. Pour over rolls. Microwave, covered, on 100 percent power or HIGH for 4–5 minutes, or until heated through. Sprinkle mozzarella over rolls. Microwave, uncovered on 100 percent power or HIGH until cheese is melted.

Laura Hicks, Troy, Mont.

MICROWAVE PRALINES
Makes 3 dozen

3/4 cup Milnot milk
2 cups brown sugar, packed
1/8 teaspoon salt
3 tablespoons butter *or* margarine
1-1/2 cups pecans
1 teaspoon vanilla flavoring

Mix Milnot, sugar, salt and butter in a 2-1/2–3-quart dish or casserole. Microwave on HIGH for 8–10 minutes. Stir and rotate at 3-minute intervals. Allow to cool slightly, add vanilla. Beat until creamy (about 3 minutes). Stir in pecans. Drop from teaspoonfuls onto waxed paper. Allow to cool at room temperature.

Sarah Burkett, Centralia, Ill.

REUBEN CASSEROLE

Serves 6–8

1 (16-ounce) can sauerkraut, un-
    drained
12 ounces corned beef, canned *or*
    sliced, crumbled
2 cups Swiss cheese, shredded
1/2 cup light mayonnaise
1/4 cup Thousand Island dressing
2 fresh tomatoes, sliced
2 tablespoons melted butter
1/4 cup pumpernickel *or* rye bread
    crumbs

Place sauerkraut in 1-1/2-quart baking dish. Top with layer of beef, then
cheese. Combine both dressings; spread
over cheese. Top with tomato slices; set
aside. Combine butter and bread crumbs
in small bowl; sprinkle over tomato
slices. Microwave at 70 percent power
for 12–14 minutes, or bake at 350 degrees for 45 minutes. Let stand 5 minutes before serving.

Mrs. Merle Mishler, Hollsopple, Pa.

ONION AND CHEESE CHICKEN BAKE

Serves 6

6 chicken breast fillets
4 tablespoons butter
1 teaspoon seasoned salt
1 teaspoon pepper
1/2 pound fresh mushrooms, sliced
1 (3-ounce) can french-fried onion
    rings
1/2 cup grated Monterey Jack cheese

Melt butter in 3-quart baking dish on
MEDIUM power for 1 minute, or until
melted; add seasonings. Roll chicken
in seasoned butter to coat and arrange
in dish. Cover with waxed paper; cook
on HIGH for 5–6 minutes. Turn chicken
over; top with mushrooms. Continue to
cook on HIGH for 4 minutes. Sprinkle
with onion rings and grated cheese.
Cook on HIGH for 2–3 minutes, or
until cheese bubbles.

Kim Joslin, Enid, Okla.

WALNUT PENUCHE

1-1/2 cups toasted coarsely chopped
    walnuts*
2/3 cup butter *or* margarine
1 cup packed light brown sugar
1 (14-ounce) can sweetened con-
    densed milk
1-1/2 teaspoons vanilla

*To toast walnuts, spread in a single
layer in a 9-inch glass pie plate or a
microwave pie plate. Stirring every 2
minutes, microwave on HIGH for 6
minutes.

Place butter in a 2-quart glass measure. Microwave on HIGH for 1 minute.
Blend in light brown sugar and condensed milk. Stirring every 2 minutes,
microwave on HIGH for 8–9 minutes,
or until mixture is a medium-caramel
color. Stir in vanilla and beat with a
wooden spoon, 2–3 minutes. Fold in
walnuts. Pour into a buttered 8-inch
square dish. Cool to lukewarm; then
refrigerate until set. Cut into squares.

Joy B. Shamway, Freeport, Ill.

HONEY ORANGE CHICKEN

Serves 4

2 boneless, skinless whole chicken
    breasts
2 tablespoons honey
2 tablespoons cornstarch
1/2 cup orange marmalade
1/2 cup orange juice
1/2 cup whiskey
2 cups hot, cooked rice

Cut chicken into 4 serving pieces.
Place in a 2-quart microwave casserole. In bowl, blend together honey,
cornstarch, marmalade, orange juice
and whiskey. Pour over chicken. Cover
and microwave on HIGH for 12 minutes. Turn; stir in chicken, and microwave for 8 more minutes until chicken
is tender. Serve immediately with hot,
cooked rice.

June Harding, Royal Oak, Mich.

CHICKEN PIZZA "BURGERS"

Serves 4

1 (12-ounce) package frozen chicken
    patties
4 hamburger buns, split
1/2 cup pizza sauce (canned)
4 slices (4 ounces) mozzarella
    cheese

Place chicken patties on microwave
bacon rack or paper-towel–lined plate.
Microwave on HIGH, uncovered, for
4–5 minutes, or until heated through,
rotating plate once. Place bottom halves
of buns on microwave-safe serving
plate. Spread each with about 1 tablespoon pizza sauce. Top each with a
chicken patty and additional 1 tablespoon sauce. Top each with cheese
slice and bun tops. Microwave on
HIGH, uncovered, for 1–1-1/2 minutes, or until cheese is melted.

Mrs. A.S. Warren, Charlotte, N.C.

ONE MORE TIME

Serves 6

1 or 2 large onions
1 teaspoon sugar
1 tablespoon butter
3 cups leftover mashed potatoes
2 tablespoons Parmesan cheese
Salt and pepper
6 slices cooked roast beef
1 (17-ounce) can peas, drained
1 (10-1/4-ounce) can beef gravy

Brown onion in dry frying pan.
Sprinkle with sugar. Cook on stove,
stirring until browned. Add butter. Cook
until tender. Remove from heat. Spread
half the mashed potatoes in baking dish.
Sprinkle surface with Parmesan cheese,
salt and pepper. Arrange meat on top of
potatoes. Spread onion over meat, then
peas, and gravy. Cover with remaining
potatoes. Cook, covered, on 80 percent
power for 6–8 minutes.

Sheila Symonowicz, Hubbardston, Mass.

Party
FARE

RYE CRACKERS

1/4 cup warm (105-115 degrees) water
2 packages active dry yeast
1 teaspoon salt
1 teaspoon sugar
1 cup milk
1 1/2 teaspoons crushed caraway seed
1 3/4 cups medium rye flour, divided
About 1 1/4 cups all-purpose flour

In medium bowl, combine water, yeast, salt and sugar; leave for about 3 minutes to soften yeast. Add milk, caraway seed, 1 1/2 cups rye flour and 1 cup all-purpose flour. Beat until smooth.

On floured surface, using remaining all-purpose flour, knead dough until smooth and elastic. Cut into 8 equal pieces and shape each into a round bun. Place on a greased cookie sheet, turning to grease tops. Cover and let rise in a warm place until almost doubled (about 30 minutes).

Punch down. Remove to lightly floured cloth, and with remaining 1/4 cup rye flour and stockinette-covered rolling pin, roll out each piece into a 9-inch round. Place each rolled-out round on ungreased cookie sheets, pricking entire surface with a fork.

Bake in a preheated 400-degree oven, two sheets at a time, for 4 minutes. Flip breads over, reverse positions of sheets in oven, and bake 4 minutes more, or until light brown and crisp.

Cool on racks. Store in a dry place for up to 2 months. Serve, broken into pieces, with dips and spreads.

CHEESE TRIANGLE NIBBLERS
Makes 64 snacks

1/2 cup warm water (105-115°)
2 teaspoons active dry yeast
1 teaspoon sugar
1/4 teaspoon cayenne pepper
1/4 teaspoon salt
About 2 cups flour, divided
1/2 cup margarine, softened slightly
1/4 cup grated Parmesan cheese

In medium bowl, combine water, yeast and sugar. Let mixture sit for about 3 minutes. Add cayenne pepper, salt and 1 1/4 cups flour. Beat until well-blended and smooth. Cover; let rise in a warm, draft-free place for about 30 minutes, or until doubled in bulk. Add margarine and Parmesan cheese. Beat until well-blended. Add 1/2 cup flour, beating until smooth.

Turn dough out onto lightly floured surface; divide in half. Roll out each half into a 10-inch square. Prick with fork. With a pastry wheel or a sharp knife, cut 16 2 1/2-inch squares from each square of dough, and cut each of those squares in half diagonally to make triangles.

Place triangles 1/4 inch apart on ungreased cookie sheets. Bake in preheated 425-degree oven for 8-10 minutes, until golden brown. Remove to racks to cool. Store in a tightly covered container in a cool place. Keep up to two weeks. (When ready to serve after storing, freshen for 3-4 minutes in a 350-degree oven.)

YUMMY CHEESE BALL

2 large packages (8 ounces each) cream cheese
2 5-ounce jars cheddar cheese spread
5-ounce jar blue cheese spread
3 tablespoons vinegar
Chopped pecansa

Mix all together and chill well. Shape into large ball or individual-size balls. Roll in chopped pecans.

Mrs. Florence Satterfield
Greenfield, Ohio

SPINACH BALL

3 packages frozen chopped spinach, thawed
1 cup finely chopped onion
1 1/2 cups mayonnaise
1/2 cup chopped parsley
1 1/2 teaspoons salt

Squeeze as much liquid as possible from thawed spinach. Add remaining ingredients and mix well. Refrigerate for several hours. Shape into a ball and serve with bacon-flavored crackers.

JIFFY PIZZA

For a quick homemade version of Italian pizza, split *English muffins*, spread with *butter, grated cheese,* and *tomato* or *chili sauce*. Toast under the broiler. Delicious and easy!

Helene Levine

HAPPY PIES

1 cup sugar
2 1/2 cups flour
1 1/2 teaspoons baking soda
3/4 cup dry cocoa
1/2 teaspoon salt
1/2 cup shortening
1 cup milk
1 egg
1 1/2 teaspoons vanilla
Filling:
1 2/3 cups confectioners' sugar
3/4 cup (1 1/2 sticks) margarine
1/2 jar marshmallow creme

Sift together flour, sugars, baking soda, cocoa and salt into a bowl. Add shortening, milk and egg; beat. Add vanilla and mix. Drop by tablespoonsful onto greased cookie sheet. Bake in preheated 425-degree oven for 8 minutes.

Remove and cool.

Combine filling ingredients, beating until smooth. Fill between two cookies, sandwich style.

Lois Smith, Grants Pass, Ore.

GREEN TUNA DIP

Makes 8-10 appetizer servings

2 cans (6 1/2 to 7 ounces each) tuna in oil
8-ounce package farmer cheese, divided
1 cup milk, divided
2 cups fresh parsley, divided
1/4 teaspoon hot pepper sauce
1 teaspoon salt
1/4 cup chopped, dry-roasted mixed nuts
Raw vegetables for dip

Drain tuna and flake with fork. Combine half the farmer cheese with half the milk and 1 cup parsley in blender. Cover and process at high speed until smooth (or beat on high speed of mixer). Add tuna. Repeat process with remaining cheese, milk and parsley. Add to tuna mixture in bowl. Stir in pepper sauce, salt and nuts. Chill. Serve with raw vegetables.

Mrs. Agnes Ward, Erie, Penn.

CRAB DIP

2/3 cup margarine
1 large package (8 ounces) cream cheese, softened
1 pound crabmeat (or 1 can)
Hot pepper sauce and Worcestershire sauce to taste

Melt margarine and cheese together in top of double boiler over boiling water. Cook raw crabmeat and shred finely. Fold into cheese mixture. Season to taste. Serve warm dip with crackers and raw vegetables.

Marjorie W. Baxla, Greenfield, Ohio

COFFEE COCKTAIL DIP

Makes 1 cup

1 cup sour cream
1 tablespoon brewed cold coffee
1 tablespoon catsup
1 tablespoon spicy mustard

Combine all ingredients. Blend and chill. Sprinkle with paprika. Serve with raw vegetables and cold shrimp.

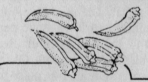

SHOCKING PINK PINTO BEAN DIP

Makes 4-6 servings

1 1/2 cups pinto beans, cooked and mashed
1 large package (8 ounces) cream cheese
6 cooked baby beets, mashed (or a jar of "baby food" beets)
1 tablespoon vinegar
2 tablespoons lemon juice
1/4 teaspoon celery salt
1/2 teaspoon salt
1 small onion, grated
Dash of hot pepper sauce
Horseradish to taste

Blend all ingredients until smooth. Store in refrigerator. Serve with chips and crackers.

Miss M.J. Witham, Fort Wayne, Ind.

TUNA SENSATION

7-ounce can tuna, drained and flaked
1 large package (8 ounces) cream cheese, softened
1/2 cup thick sour cream
1 tablespoon horseradish
1 teaspoon Worcestershire sauce
2 tablespoons minced garlic
1 clove garlic, minced
1 teaspoon crushed chervil
1/2 teaspoon salt
Dash of pepper
1/4 teaspoon Accent®

Blend cream cheese until very soft; add sour cream, horseradish, and Worcestershire sauce; beat until mixture is smooth. Blend in flaked tuna and seasonings. Cover and refrigerate several hours. Remove from refrigerator 30 minutes before serving to soften for dipping.

Mrs. Beverly Brannon, Vidor, Texas

TASTY GUACAMOLE DIP

Makes about 2 cups

2 small avocados, peeled and mashed
1 tablespoon lemon juice
1 medium onion, minced
1 small clove garlic, crushed
1 large tomato, peeled, and finely chopped
1/2 teaspoon salt
1/2 teaspoon seasoned salt
1/2 teaspoon pepper
1/2 teaspoon chili powder

Combine all ingredients; mix well. Cover. Refrigerate several hours.

DILL DIP

Makes 3 cups dip

2 cups sour cream
1 cup mayonnaise
2 heaping tablespoons dill weed
2 tablespoons dehydrated onion
2 teaspoons lemon juice

Mix all ingredients together, combining until smooth. Refrigerate.

CARAMEL POPCORN II
Makes about 4 quarts

4 quarts freshly popped popcorn
Peanuts (optional)
1 cup firmly packed brown sugar
1/2 cup margarine (1 stick)
1/2 cup corn syrup (light or dark)
1/2 teaspoon salt
1/2 teaspoon vanilla
1/2 teaspoon baking soda

Spread popcorn in large buttered roasting pan.

In heavy saucepan, stir together sugar, syrup, margarine and salt. Cook, stirring constantly, until mixture boils. Continue cooking, without stirring, for 5 more minutes. Remove from heat; stir in vanilla and baking soda. Pour syrup over popcorn, and stir to coat well.

Bake in a preheated 250-degree oven, uncovered, for 1 hour, stirring occasionally.

This recipe can be doubled; it stores well.

Fay Duman, Eugene, Ore.

BEEFY POPCORN
Makes about 3 quarts

1 jar (2 1/2 ounces) dried beef, finely chopped
1/2 cup butter (1 stick)
3 quarts unsalted popped popcorn

Cook dried beef in butter for about 3 minutes. If popcorn is not fresh, heat it in a 250-degree oven. Pour beef and butter over popcorn and toss to mix.

Serve immediately while still hot.

QUICK SNACK

1 can large pitted black or green olives
1 can (pressurized) cheese spread (like Snack Mate®)

Squirt cheese spread into olive holes and refrigerate until serving time.

Jodie McCoy, Tulsa, Okla.

MOST CEREAL SNACK
Makes about 4 cups

1/3 cup margarine, melted
1/2 teaspoon garlic salt
2 teaspoons Worcestershire sauce
2 1/2 cups Kellogg's Most® cereal
1 cup thin pretzel sticks
1/2 cup salted peanuts

Combine melted margarine, garlic salt and Worcestershire sauce in a 13x9-inch pan. Stir in cereal, pretzel sticks and peanuts, stirring gently but thoroughly to coat all pieces. Bake in a 250-degree oven for 40-45 minutes, stirring occasionally. Cool and store in an airtight container.

PINK POPCORN BALLS
Makes 10 medium popcorn balls

7 cups popped corn
3 cups miniature marshmallows
2 tablespoons butter
1/4 teaspoon salt
Few drops of red food coloring

Place popped corn in large buttered bowl. In bottom of double boiler, heat about 1 inch of water to boiling. Combine butter, marshmallows and salt in top of double boiler, over hot water. Stir until melted together. Stir in food coloring to desired shade. Pour over popcorn; stir gently to coat.

Grease hands with butter and quickly shape popcorn into 10 medium-size balls.

Mrs. Sharon Crider, Evansville, Wis.

EASY SHRIMP DIP

1 can cream of shrimp soup (frozen)
1 small package (3 ounces) cream cheese, softened
1 teaspoon lemon juice
Dash of garlic powder
Dash of paprika

Thaw frozen soup. Gradually blend soup with other ingredients. Beat until smooth. Chill.

Lois L. Smith, Grants Pass, Ore.

SPICY PUMPKIN SEEDS
Makes 2 cups

1/4 cup oil
1 teaspoon Worcestershire sauce
1/2 teaspoon paprika
1/4 teaspoon cumin
1/4 teaspoon cayenne pepper
2 dashes hot pepper sauce
2 cups hulled pumpkin seeds

Preheat oven to 300 degrees.

Combine all ingredients except seeds in a large skillet. Heat mixture well, stirring to mix. Add seeds and stir to coat well. Spread in a shallow pan and bake at 300 degrees for 10 minutes, or until crisp. Stir occasionally during the baking. Cool.

SAVORY PECANS
Makes 2 cups

2 cups pecan halves
1 tablespoon salad oil
1 tablespoon Worcestershire sauce

Combine oil and Worcestershire sauce. Place pecans in a shallow baking dish and cover with the oil mixture, stirring to coat well. Bake in a slow oven (250 degrees) for about 30 minutes, stirring once or twice. Sprinkle lightly with salt.

Store in tightly covered container.

Marjorie W. Baxla, Greenfield, Ohio

CHIVE CHEESE BALLS
Makes 30 pieces

1 small package (3 ounces) chive-flavored cream cheese
1 package (10-count) refrigerated biscuits

Divide cream cheese into 30 equal pieces. Separate biscuits and cut each into thirds. Wrap a cube of cheese inside each piece of dough, forming a small ball.

Place on lightly greased cookie sheets and bake in a preheated 350-degree oven until lightly browned.

Mrs. M. Piccinni, Ozone Park, N.Y.

Pies
FESTIVE

PRINCESS ANN TART
Serves 6–8

Crust:
- ½ cup flour
- 1 teaspoon baking powder
- 2 tablespoons sugar
- 6 tablespoons butter
- 2 tablespoons cold water
- 1 (8-ounce) jar raspberry jam

Combine flour, baking powder and sugar. Work in butter until mixture resembles cornmeal. Add water; stir into stiff dough. Roll out dough on floured surface. Place in a 9-inch pie pan. Spread jam on bottom crust.

Custard:
- 2 egg yolks
- 1 cup milk
- 1 tablespoon sugar
- 1 teaspoon flour
- 1 teaspoon vanilla

Combine all ingredients; Beat well; pour over jam in crust. Bake at 350 degrees for 30 minutes.

Meringue:
- 2 egg whites
- 4 tablespoons sugar
- ¼ teaspoon cream of tartar

Beat egg whites and cream of tartar until soft peaks form, adding sugar gradually. Beat until stiff peaks form. Pour over cooked and cooled filling. Bake at 375 degrees until browned.

June Harding, Ferndale, Mich.

PECAN PIE

- 1 (9-inch) unbaked pie crust
- 1 cup light corn syrup
- 1 cup dark brown sugar, packed
- 3 eggs, slightly beaten
- ⅓ cup butter, melted
- Pinch salt
- 1 teaspoon vanilla
- 1 cup chopped *or* halved pecans

Preheat oven to 350 degrees. In large bowl, combine corn syrup, sugar, eggs, butter, salt and vanilla. Mix well. Pour filling into prepared pie crust. Sprinkle with pecans. Bake 45–50 minutes, or until center is set. Toothpick inserted in center will come out clean when pie is done. Cool. Top with whipped cream or ice cream, if desired.

Lynn D. Jones, Gatesville, Texas

HOT FUDGE PIE

- 1/4 cup cocoa
- 1/4 cup butter
- 1 1/4 cups sugar
- 1/4 cup flour
- 3 eggs, beaten

Melt butter; add to mixture of dry ingredients. Add eggs, one at a time, mixing well after each addition. Pour into an ungreased 9-inch pie pan. Bake at 300 degrees for 30–40 minutes. Serve warm with ice cream.

Sue Thomas, Casa Grande, Ariz.

EASY COCONUT PIES

- 1-1/2 cups sugar
- 3 tablespoons flour
- 1 stick butter, melted
- 3 eggs
- 2 cups milk
- 2 teaspoons vanilla
- 1 can shredded coconut
- 2 unbaked pie shells

In large bowl combine sugar and flour. Add remaining ingredients and stir well. Pour into pie shells and bake at 450 degrees for 10 minutes. Reduce oven temperature to 325 degrees and bake for an additional 25 minutes. Let cool before slicing.

Brenda Peery, Tannersville, Va.

FRESH PEAR PIE
Serves 6–8

- Pastry for 2-crust, 9-inch pie
- 5–6 fresh pears
- 1/2 cup sugar
- 2 tablespoons quick-cooking tapioca
- 1/4 teaspoon cinnamon
- 1/4 teaspoon ginger
- 1/4 teaspoon nutmeg
- 1/8 teaspoon salt
- 1 tablespoon lemon juice

Line 9-inch pie pan with pastry. Pare, quarter and core pears. Arrange slices in pie shell. In small bowl combine sugar, tapioca, cinnamon, ginger, nutmeg and salt; pour over pear slices; sprinkle with lemon juice. Cover with top crust; seal edges; flute. Bake 40 minutes at 425 degrees.

Leota Baxter, Ingalls, Kan.

APPLE MINCEMEAT PIE
Serves 6–8

- 1 cup flour
- ¼ teaspoon salt
- 3 tablespoons butter
- 2 tablespoons shortening
- 3–4 tablespoons milk
- 4 cups cooking apples, peeled and sliced
- 2 tablespoons flour
- 2 cups prepared mincemeat
- 1 cup dairy sour cream
- 2 tablespoons confectioners' sugar
- 1 tablespoon grated orange peel

Combine 1 cup flour and salt. Cut in butter and shortening until mixture resembles small peas. Sprinkle milk over flour mixture, 1 tablespoon at a time, mixing lightly with a fork after each addition. Shape into a ball. On lightly floured surface, flatten dough slightly; roll ⅛ inch thick into a circle, 1 inch larger than diameter of a 9-inch pie plate. Fold under and flute edge. Combine apples and 2 tablespoons flour; turn into crust. Top with mincemeat. Bake at 400 degrees for 35–40 minutes. Blend together sour cream, sugar and orange peel. Place dollops of cream mixture around edge of pie; return to oven for 3–4 minutes to set topping.

Sharon Crider, Stoughton, Wis.

COCONUT DREAM PIE

- 1/2 gallon vanilla ice cream, softened
- 1-1/2 cups milk
- 1 package instant coconut pudding
- 1 prepared butter-flavored pie crust
- Whipped cream (optional)

In a large mixing bowl, combine ice cream, milk, and pudding. Blend well. Pour mixture into pie crust and freeze overnight. Before serving, spoon on whipped cream in desired amounts. Enjoy!

CREAM CHEESE RHUBARB PIE
Serves 8

- 4 cups rhubarb, cut in 1-inch pieces
- 1 cup sugar
- 3 tablespoons cornstarch
- 1/4 teaspoon salt
- 1 (9-inch) unbaked pie crust
- 1 (8-ounce) package cream cheese
- 2 eggs
- 1 cup sour cream
- 1/2 cup sugar
- Almonds for garnish

Preheat oven to 425 degrees. In saucepan over medium heat, cook rhubarb, 1 cup sugar, cornstarch, and salt, stirring often, until mixture boils and thickens. Pour into pie crust. Bake 10 minutes; remove from oven.

Meanwhile, in small bowl, with mixer at medium speed, beat cream cheese, eggs, and 1/2 cup sugar until smooth; pour over rhubarb mixture. Turn oven control to 350 degrees. Bake pie 30-35 minutes until set; cool on wire rack; chill.

To serve:
Spread sour cream on top of pie. Garnish with almonds. Just simply delicious!!

Mrs. George Franks, Millerton, Pa.

DOUBLE-CRUST STRAWBERRY PIE

- 1 cup sugar
- 1 tablespoon cornstarch
- 1/8 teaspoon salt
- 3 cups fresh strawberries
- 1 tablespoon margarine
- Crust for 2-crust (9-inch) pie

Mix sugar, cornstarch and salt together; add to the berries and mix gently. Pour into unbaked bottom crust and dot with margarine. Cover with top crust and cut slits in crust for steam to escape. Bake at 400 degrees for 10 minutes; reduce oven to 325 degrees and bake 30 minutes longer.

Jodie McCoy, Tulsa, Okla.

PEANUT BUTTER CREAM CHEESE PIE

- 2 (3-ounce) packages cream cheese, softened
- ¾ cup sifted confectioners' sugar
- ½ cup peanut butter
- 2 tablespoons milk
- 1 (9-ounce) carton Cool Whip
- 1 (8-inch) pie shell, baked
- Coarsely chopped roasted peanuts

In a small mixer bowl beat cream cheese and sugar together until light and fluffy. Add peanut butter and milk, beating until smooth and creamy. Fold topping gently into peanut butter mixture. Turn into prepared shell and chill 5–6 hours. Garnish with coarsely chopped peanuts.

Shari Crider, Stoughton, Wis.

DELUXE APPLE PIE
Serves 6

- 1 cup sifted all-purpose flour
- 2/3 cup granulated sugar
- 1/4 teaspoon baking powder
- 1/2 teaspoon salt
- 1/4 teaspoon vanilla
- 1/2 cup butter
- 4 cups thinly sliced apples
- 3/4 cup broken walnuts *or* pecans
- 1 teaspoon cinnamon
- Juice and grated rind of 1 lemon
- 1/4 cup white wine
- 2 egg yolks, slightly beaten
- 1 cup sour cream

Sift flour, 2 tablespoons sugar, baking powder and salt together. Stir in vanilla. Cut in butter as for pie crust. Press mixture in bottom and halfway up sides of a deep-dish (9-inch) pie pan. Combine apples, nuts, 1/2 cup sugar, cinnamon, lemon juice, rind and wine. Pile mixture in prepared crust. Bake at 425 degrees for 10 minutes. Combine egg yolks, remaining sugar and sour cream. Pour over apple mixture. Bake at 350 degrees for 35 minutes. Serve warm or cold.

Trenda Leigh, Richmond, Va.

APPLE WALNUT COBBLER PIE

1/2 cup sugar
1/2 teaspoon cinnamon
3/4 cup coarsely chopped walnuts, divided
4 cups thinly sliced, pared apples
1 cup sifted flour
1 cup sugar
1 teaspoon baking powder
1/4 teaspoon salt
1 beaten egg
1/2 cup evaporated milk
1/3 cup butter or margarine, melted

Mix 1/2 cup sugar, cinnamon, and 1/2 cup walnuts. Place apples in bottom of a greased 8-1/4x1-3/4-inch round ovenware cake dish. Sprinkle with cinnamon mixture. Sift together dry ingredients. Combine egg, milk, and butter; add dry ingredients all at once. Mix until smooth. Pour over apples; sprinkle with remaining walnuts. Bake in a slow oven at 325 degrees for about 50 minutes. Cut in wedges; serve with whipped cream or Cool Whip.

Sarah Burkett, Centralia, Ill.

PEANUT TOFFEE PIE WITH OATMEAL CRUST

Crust:
1 cup flour
2 cups quick rolled oats
1/2 cup shortening
1/2 cup cold water
1 teaspoon cinnamon

Combine dry ingredients with shortening, cutting into mixture. Add cold water slowly. Roll out and bake in pie pan for 12 minutes at 450 degrees. Remember to put dry beans in bottom so it will keep it shape.

Filling:
1-1/2 cups brown sugar
3 tablespoons flour
1-1/2 cups milk
2 egg yolks
4 tablespoons peanut butter

1/2 teaspoon vanilla extract
Whipped cream
Nut toffee or Heath bits

Mix sugar and flour in double boiler; add milk slowly. Cook until thickened. Add egg yolks and cook 3 minutes longer. Remove from heat; add peanut butter and flavoring. When cool, pour into baked crust and cover with whipped cream and shaved nut toffee or Heath bits.

PERFECTLY RICH CUSTARD PIE

10 eggs, beaten
1 cup sugar
1/2 teaspoon nutmeg
1 teaspoon vanilla
1 quart scalded milk
1 tablespoon butter

Scald milk and butter. Let cool and then add to egg mixture composed of eggs, sugar, nutmeg and vanilla. Pour mixture into pie crust-lined (deep-dish) 9-inch pie plate. Place in a 450-degree preheated oven. Bake 20 minutes only. Turn heat completely off. Let pie stand in oven for 1 hour.

Lynn Sylvester, Lewiston, Maine

PUMPKIN PECAN PIE
Serves 6-8

4 slightly-beaten eggs
2 cups canned pumpkin
1 cup sugar
1/2 cup dark corn syrup
1 teaspoon vanilla
1/2 teaspoon cinnamon
1/4 teaspoon salt
1 unbaked 9-inch pie shell
1 cup chopped pecans

Preheat oven to 350 degrees. Combine first seven ingredients. Pour into pie shell. Top with pecans. Bake 40 minutes or until set. Cool in pan on wire rack. Serve with whipped cream or ice cream.

Mrs. H. W. Walker, Richmond, Va.

OATMEAL PIE

1/4 cup butter
1/2 cup sugar
1 teaspoon cinnamon
1/4 teaspoon salt
3/4 cup dark corn syrup
1/4 cup honey
3 eggs
1 cup quick oats
1 9-inch unbaked pie shell

Cream sugar and butter. Beat in cinnamon and salt. Add syrup and honey, then eggs, one at a time. Beat until well-blended. Stir in oats. Pour in shell and bake at 350 degrees for about an hour, or until center tests done. During baking, the oatmeal rises and forms a chewy, nutty crust on top of pie.

Helen Weissinger, Levittown, Pa

STRAWBERRY-BANANA PIE

Crust:
2-1/2 cups graham cracker crumbs
1/2 cup sugar
1-1/2 sticks butter, melted

Filling:
1 (8-ounce) package cream cheese
3/4 cup confectioners' sugar
2 cups chopped walnuts
2 medium-size bananas, sliced
1 quart strawberries, sliced
1 (8-ounce) container Cool Whip

Crust: Mix crumbs, sugar, and butter together and press into 2 deep-dish, 9-inch pie pans. Bake at 325 degrees for 10 minutes.

Filling: Use beater and mix cream cheese and confectioners' sugar together. Divide between the 2 crusts evenly and spread along bottom. Sprinkle on top of the cream chees a layer of chopped walnuts. Next layer sliced bananas and then a layer of sliced strawberries.

Divide Cool Whip and spread evenly over the pies. Top with another layer of walnuts.

June Harding, Ferndale, Mich.

CHOCOLATE CREAM PIE

Serves 6

1 (9-inch) baked pie shell
2-2/3 cups milk
3 eggs, separated
3 squares chocolate, cut in quarters
3/4 cup sugar
1/4 cup cornstarch
1/4 teaspoon salt
1 tablespoon butter or margarine
1 teaspoon vanilla extract

Meringue:
3 egg whites
6 tablespoons sugar
Whipping cream, if desired

Combine 1-2/3 cups of the milk, egg yolks, chocolate, 3/4 cup sugar, cornstarch, salt, and butter or margarine in blender. Cover and blend at high speed for 15-20 seconds. Turn into saucepan. (I use a double boiler.) Add remaining milk and cook over moderate heat until thickened, stirring constantly. Remove from heat and add vanilla extract. Cool slightly. Pour into baked pie shell. Top with meringue made from egg whites and 6 tablespoons sugar. Bake at 325 degrees for 12-15 minutes, until lightly browned. Instead of meringue, you may cover the thoroughly cooled pie with sweetened whipped cream.

Meringue: Whip egg whites until very, very stiff. Add sugar and beat.
Virginia Essig, Bridgman, Mich.

PINEAPPLE PIE

1 (20-ounce) can crushed pineapple, not drained
1 box instant vanilla pudding
1/2 pint sour cream
1 (8-ounce) container Cool Whip

Put pineapple and vanilla pudding mix in bowl and stir. Add sour cream and fold in Cool Whip. Pour into 2 (8-inch) baked pie shells. Refrigerate and chill 3 hours. Delicious and easy!!
Marie Wyszynski, Timberlake, Ohio

CRANBERRY WALNUT PIE

3 eggs
1 cup Karo light corn syrup
2/3 cup sugar
2 tablespoons margarine, melted
1/8 teaspoon salt
1 cup cranberries, chopped
3/4 cup coarsely chopped walnuts
1 tablespoon grated orange rind
1 unbaked (9-inch) pie shell

In medium bowl beat eggs slightly. Stir in next 4 ingredients. Gently stir in cranberries, nuts and rind. Pour into pastry shell. Bake in 350-degree oven for 1 hour, or until knife inserted halfway between center and edge comes out clean. Cool.

CHILLED FRUIT COCKTAIL PIE

1 baked 9-inch pie shell
1 envelope unflavored gelatin
1/2 cup cold water
3 eggs, separated
1/8 teaspoon salt
1 (6-ounce) can frozen lemonade concentrate
1/2 cup sugar
1 (1-pound) can fruit cocktail, drained

In a double boiler soften gelatin in water; add slightly beaten egg yolks and salt; cook, stirring constantly, until mixture thickens. Remove from heat; stir in frozen lemonade concentrate; stir again until mixture thickens. Beat egg whites to soft-peak stage; add sugar slowly; beat until stiff peaks form. Fold into gelatin mixture; add drained fruit, reserving a small amount to place on individual servings. Chill at least 2 hours in refrigerator.
Gwen Campbell, Sterling, Va.

LIMEADE PIE WITH CHOCOLATE CRUST

1 (6-ounce) can limeade frozen concentrate
1 pint vanilla ice cream, softened
4 cups thawed whipped topping
Green food coloring
1 chocolate cookie crust

Place concentrate in large mixing bowl and beat about 30 seconds. Gradually spoon in ice cream and blend. Fold in whipped topping and 5 drops of food coloring, whipping until smooth. Freeze until mixture will mound. Then spoon into pie crust. Freeze until firm, at least 3-4 hours, and store leftovers in freezer. Can decorate with crumbled cookies or cookie halves, if desired. A lovely, refreshing summer dessert!!
Kathy Thompson, Midland, Ark.

CHOCOLATE SHOO-FLY PIE

9-inch unbaked pie shell
1/4 teaspoon soda
1 1/3 cups boiling water
1 1/2 cups (1-pound can) chocolate-flavored syrup
1 teaspoon vanilla
1 1/3 cups flour
1/2 cup sugar

1/4 teaspoon soda
1/4 teaspoon salt
1/3 cup butter or margarine
Cinnamon

Dissolve 1/4 teaspoon soda in boiling water; stir in chocolate syrup and vanilla; set aside. Combine flour, sugar, 1/4 teaspoon soda and salt; cut in butter to form coarse crumbs. Set aside 1 cup *each* of chocolate mixture and crumbs; gently combine remaining chocolate and crumbs, stirring just until crumbs are moistened. Pour reserved 1 cup chocolate mixture into pie shell. Pour chocolate-crumb mixture evenly over liquid in pie shell. Top with remaining 1 cup crumbs. Sprinkle with cinnamon.
Lisa Varner, Baton Rouge, La.

FLUFFY FROZEN PEANUT BUTTER PIE

Crust:
3/4 cup peanut butter chips, chopped
1 cup vanilla wafer crumbs
5 tablespoons water

Filling:
1-1/4 cups peanut butter chips
3 ounces cream cheese, softened
1/2 cup milk
1/2 cup powdered sugar
2 cups frozen non-dairy whipped topping

To make crust, chop peanut butter chips in blender or food processor, or with nut chopper. In 9-inch pie pan, combine chips and crumbs. Drizzle with melted butter; mix well. Press onto bottom and up sides of pie pan; freeze.

For filling, in top of double boiler over hot water, melt peanut butter chips; cool slightly. Beat cream cheese until smooth; gradually add milk, blending well. Beat in sugar and melted peanut butter chips until smooth; fold in whipped topping.

Spoon into prepared crust. Cover and freeze until firm. Chocolate curls may be used for decoration on pie.

Julie Habiger, Spearville, Kan.

CHOCOLATE CREAM PIE

1/2 cup white sugar
1/2 teaspoon salt
1 tablespoon flour
3 tablespoons cornstarch
3 cups milk
3 squares chocolate
3 egg yolks
1 teaspoon vanilla
1 tablespoon butter or margarine

Combine ingredients in saucepan and boil over medium heat until thick. Pour into baked pie shell. Cool and serve with whipped topping.

Pat Linie, Haure, Mont.

ICE-CREAM PIE
Serves 10

1 (9-inch) gingersnap *or* cookie crust
1½ cups canned pumpkin
½ cup granulated sugar
½ teaspoon cinnamon
¼ teaspoon nutmeg
¼ teaspoon salt
⅛ teaspoon ginger
⅛ teaspoon allspice
1 quart vanilla ice cream, softened
½ cup chopped pecans

In large bowl, combine pumpkin, sugar, cinnamon, nutmeg, salt, ginger and allspice; mix well. Fold pumpkin mixture into softened ice cream; stir in pecans, and spoon into *chilled* pie shell. Sprinkle with additional crumbs of crust mixture. Freeze, uncovered, for 30 minutes, or until set. Cover with plastic wrap or foil; keep frozen until ready to serve. Remove from freezer 10 minutes before serving; cut into wedges and serve icy cold.

Agnes Ward, Erie, Pa.

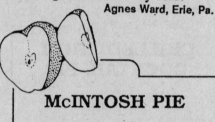

McINTOSH PIE

6 cups McIntosh apples, sliced
5/8 cup white sugar
1/4 cup golden seedless raisins
1 teaspoon cinnamon
1 package (3-1/4 ounce) dry tapioca pudding mix (not instant)
1 tablespoon butter
Crust for two-crust pie, deep dish

Prepare crust for two-crust pie, deep dish. Place apples in layer at bottom of pie crust. Mix together sugar, cinnamon and pudding powder. Toss with raisins, sprinkle half over apples. Place another layer of apples and cover with mix. Dot with butter. Place top crust on pie and bake at 400 degrees for about 15 minutes. Reduce heat to 350 degrees and finish baking 25 minutes.

Pearle Goodwin, South Ryegate, Vt.

MYSTERY PECAN PIE

1 (8-ounce) package cream cheese
1/3 cup sugar
1/4 teaspoon salt
2 teaspoons vanilla, divided
4 eggs
1 (10-inch) pie shell, unbaked
1-1/4 cups chopped pecans
1 cup light corn syrup
1/4 cup sugar

Preheat oven to 375 degrees. Combine the 1/3 cup sugar, salt, cream cheese, 1 teaspoon vanilla, and 1 egg. Mix well. Pour into pie crust. Sprinkle pecans on top. Combine remaining eggs, sugar, vanilla, and syrup. Mix well. Pour over pecans. Bake 35-40 minutes, or until center is firm.

Diantha Susan Hibbard, Rochester, N.Y.

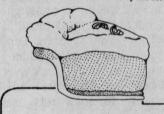

LAYERED PECAN CREAM PIE
Serves 8

1 (10-inch) unbaked pastry shell
1 (8-ounce) package cream cheese, softened
⅓ cup sugar
1 egg
1 teaspoon lemon flavoring
¼ teaspoon salt
1¼ cups chopped pecans
3 eggs
1 cup dark corn syrup
¼ cup sugar
1 teaspoon vanilla

Combine cream cheese, sugar, 1 egg, lemon flavoring and salt; blend until smooth and creamy. Spread in pastry shell; sprinkle with pecans. Combine remaining ingredients; beat until well-blended. Pour over cream cheese mixture and pecans. Preheat oven to 375 degrees. Bake for 35 minutes, or until center is firm to touch.

Erma Jackson, Huntsville, Ala.

BROWN-SUGAR PIE

1 (9-inch) unbaked pie shell
3 eggs, beaten together
2 cups brown sugar
1/2 cup butter or margarine, soft
1/2 cup rich cream or evaporated milk

Mix cream, sugar, and beaten eggs together. Melt butter or margarine; cool a little and beat into egg mixture. Pour into the unbaked pie shell. Bake in 425-degree oven for 10 minutes, then reduce oven temperature to 350 degrees and bake 30 additional minutes or until pie filling is brown on top and shakes like jelly in the center. Rich, but oh, so good!

Sarah Drury, Brandenburg, Ky.

PEANUT BUTTER ICE CREAM PIE
Serves 8

1 quart vanilla ice cream, slightly softened
1/2 cup chunky peanut butter
1/2 cup crushed unsalted peanuts
1-1/2 tablespoons vanilla
1 (10-inch) graham cracker crust
Whipped cream and maraschino cherries for garnish

Combine ice cream, peanut butter, 1/4 cup peanuts, and vanilla in large bowl; mix well. Turn into crust and sprinkle with remaining peanuts. Freeze. Decorate with cream and cherries.

Kit Rollins, Cedarburg, WI

NO-BAKE PEANUT ICE CREAM PIE

4 cups Corn Chex cereal, crushed to 1 cup
1/4 cup firmly-packed brown sugar
1/3 cup butter or margarine, melted
1/4 cup flaked coconut

1/4 cup light corn syrup
1/4 cup peanut butter
3 tablespoons chopped salted nuts (peanuts)
1 tablespoon chopped peanuts (for topping)
1 quart vanilla ice cream, softened

Preheat oven to 300 degrees. Butter 9-inch pie plate. Combine cereal and sugar; add butter; mix well. Press this mixture evenly on bottom and sides of pie plate. Bake 10 minutes; cool. Combine next 4 ingredients. Mix with ice cream until rippled throughout. Turn into pie shell.

Sprinkle peanuts on top. Freeze 3 hours or until firm. Let stand 10-15 minutes at room temperature, before serving.

Monica Turk, Milwaukee, Wis.

"BREATH OF SPRING" PARFAIT PIE

Graham Cracker Crust:
1-1/2 cups graham cracker crumbs (about 20 crackers)
3 tablespoons sugar
1/3 cup melted butter or margarine

Combine all ingredients. Press mixture firmly and evenly against bottom and sides of pie pan. Bake at 350 degrees for 10 minutes. Cool.

Lime Parfait Pie:
1 (3-ounce) package lime gelatin
1 cup boiling water
1/4 cup frozen lemonade concentrate, thawed
1 pint vanilla ice cream

Dissolve gelatin in boiling water. Add lemonade. Add ice cream and stir until melted and smooth. Chill mixture until it begins to thicken, about 20 minutes. Pour into pie shell. Chill at least 3 hours before cutting.

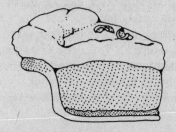

MOCHA SUNDAE PIE
Serves 6-8

Crust:
1-1/4 cups crushed chocolate wafers (about 20)
1 tablespoon sugar
1/4 cup melted butter or margarine

Filling:
1 cup evaporated milk
1 cup miniature marshmallows
1 cup semi-sweet chocolate pieces
Dash salt
1 quart coffee ice cream, softened and divided

Combine wafers, sugar, and butter. Press firmly into 9-inch pie plate. Bake in preheated 300 degree oven for 12-15 minutes. Cool, then chill. Over low heat, stir evaporated milk, marshmallows, chocolate pieces, and salt until melted and thick. Cool. Spoon half the ice cream into crust; drizzle with half the filling (chocolate sauce); spoon on remaining ice cream; drizzle with remaining filling. Freeze at least 4 hours.

Pauline Dean, Uxbridge, MA

MELT AWAY PIE

2 cups (24) crushed cream-filled chocolate cookies
1/4 cup margarine, melted
1/4 cup milk
1 (7-ounce) jar marshmallow creme
Few drops strawberry extract
Few drops red food coloring
2 cups whipping cream, whipped

Combine crumbs and margarine; reserve 1/2 cup for topping. Press remaining crumb mixture onto bottom of 9-inch spring form pan or pie plate. Chill. Gradually add milk to marshmallow creme, mixing until well blended. Add extract and food coloring; fold in whipped cream. Pour into pan; freeze until firm. Sprinkle with remaining crumbs.

A frozen pie that's quick and easy.

Barbara Nowakowski, No. Tonawanda, NY

MACAROON PIE

3 egg whites, beaten stiff
1/2 teaspoon baking powder
1 cup sugar
1 teaspoon vanilla extract
1 dozen graham crackers, rolled
    fine
1/2 cup finely cut dates
1 cup pecans, chopped
Whipped cream for topping

Beat egg whites until frothy, sprinkle baking powder over whites and continue beating until stiff. Gradually beat in sugar; add vanilla. Mix together graham cracker crumbs, dates and pecans; fold into egg white mixture. Spread in 9-or 10-inch unbuttered pie pan. Bake in 300-degree oven for 30 minutes or until set and very lightly browned. When cool, spread with whipped cream.

Mrs. J.L. Marvin, Jacksonville, FL

LEMON CHESS BUTTERMILK PIE

1/4 cup butter or margarine
1 cup sugar
1 tablespoon flour
1 tablespoon corn meal
4 eggs
1/2 cup lemon juice
1 teaspoon lemon peel (optional)
1/2 cup buttermilk

Melt butter; add sugar, flour, and corn meal. Add eggs, one at a time, beating well after each addition. Add lemon juice, lemon peel, and buttermilk. Pour into unbaked 8- or 9-inch pie shell. Bake 45 minutes at 350 degrees or until a knife comes out clean and pie is golden brown.

Mrs. P. B. Brother, Richmond, VA

FROZEN CRYSTAL LEMON PIE

3 eggs, separated
1/2 cup sugar
1/4 cup fresh lemon juice
1 teaspoon lemon zest (rind)

1/2 pint whipping cream, whipped
Crushed vanilla wafers

Beat egg yolks; add sugar, lemon zest, and juice. Cook gently until thickened; cool. Fold whipped cream into custard; fold in stiffly beaten egg whites. Crush enough vanilla wafers to cover the bottom of a freezing tray, pan, or dish. Pour lemon mixture over crumbs; cover top with crumbs. Place in freezer for at least 24 hours.

Remove from freezer 10 minutes before serving; cut into squares or slices.

Gwen Campbell, Sterling, Va.

AMISH LEMON PIE

2 tablespoons margarine, softened
1 cup sugar
3 eggs, separated
3 tablespoons flour
1/2 teaspoon salt
Juice and grated rind of one lemon
1-1/2 cups hot milk
1 (9-inch) unbaked pie shell
Cool Whip or 1/2 pint heavy whipping cream, whipped

Cream margarine and sugar; add egg yolks, beating well. Add flour, salt, lemon juice, lemon rind, and milk; blend well.

Beat egg whites until stiff; fold into lemon mixture. Pour into pie shell; bake at 350 degrees for 35 minutes. Cool; top with Cool Whip or whipped cream sweetened with 3 tablespoons sifted confectioners' sugar.

This is a very simple pie to make.

Mrs. Albert H. Foley, Lemoyne, Pa.

LEMON CHIFFON PIE

1 (8- or 9-inch) graham cracker
    crumb crust
1 (14-ounce) can Eagle Brand
    sweetened condensed milk
1/2 cup lemon juice
Few drops yellow food coloring
3 egg whites
1/4 teaspoon cream of tartar
Whipped cream or Cool Whip
    topping

Lemon slices, optional

In medium bowl, combine sweetened condensed milk, lemon juice and food coloring; mix well. In a small bowl beat egg whites with cream of tartar until stiff but not dry. Gently fold into condensed milk mixture. Turn into crust. Chill 3 hours or until set. Garnish with whipped cream and lemon slices, if desired. Refrigerate leftovers.

Aldora Hohman, Manassas, Va.

FRUIT PIZZA PIE

Crust:
Mix until light -
1 stick margarine
3/4 cup sugar
1 egg

Sift together -
1-1/2 cups flour
1 teaspoon baking powder
1/2 teaspoon salt
1/2 teaspoon vanilla

Mix together- refrigerate 1 hour. Spread on lightly greased pizza pan. Bake 350 degrees for 10 minutes or until light brown. Make glaze while dough is chilling so it can cool well.

Glaze:
1/2 cup sugar
Dash of salt
2 tablespoon cornstarch
1/2 cup orange juice
2 tablespoons lemon juice
1/4 cup water

Cook until mixture thickens (about 4 minutes). Remove from heat and let cool.

When crust is cool make filling. Mix together 1 - 8 ounce cream cheese and 1 - 8 ounce cool whip. Spread on cool crust.

Fruit:
Place grapes around outer edge, strawberries next to grapes, sliced bananas next row or two, peaches next row, fill in remaining space wiht chunk pineapple. Spoon glaze over fruit. Glaze bananas first to keep from turning dark. (KEEP REFRIGERATED).

Patricia Parsons, Shinnston, W VA

ICE CREAM PARFAIT PIE

1 (3-ounce) package strawberry
  gelatin
1-1/4 cups hot water
1 pint vanilla ice cream
1 cup sliced strawberries
1 pie shell, baked
Whipped cream, optional

Dissolve gelatin in 1-1/4 cups hot water. Spoon in ice cream and stir until melted. Place in refrigerator until thickened. Let it set 15-25 minutes. Fold in strawberries. Turn filling into baked pie shell. Chill until firm, 30-60 minutes. Serve with whipped cream, if desired.

Beulah Schwallie, Cincinnati, Ohio

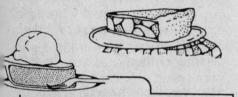

BLACK FOREST PIE

1 (9-inch) unbaked pie shell
3/4 cup sugar
1/3 cup unsweetened cocoa
2 tablespoons flour
1/4 cup margarine
1/3 cup milk
2 eggs, beaten
1 (21-ounce) can cherry pie filling
1 (9-ounce) container frozen whipped
  topping
1 (1-ounce) square unsweetened
  chocolate (coarsely grated)

In saucepan, combine sugar, cocoa, and flour; add margarine and milk. Cook until mixture begins to boil, stirring constantly. Remove from heat. Add small amount of hot mixture to eggs; return mixture to pan. Fold half the can of pie filling into mixture. Pour into crust-lined pan. Bake at 350 degrees for 35-45 minutes or until center is set but still shiny. Cool. Chill one hour. Combine 2 cups topping and grated chocolate; spread over pie. Place remaining pie filling around edge of pie. Cool.

Suzanne Dawson, Cypress, TX

AMISH VANILLA PIE

1/2 cup firmly packed brown sugar
1 tablespoon flour
1/4 cup dark corn syrup
1-1/2 teaspoons vanilla
1 egg, beaten
1 cup water
1 cup flour
1/2 cup firmly packed brown sugar
1/2 teaspoon cream of tartar
1/2 teaspoon baking soda
1/8 teaspoon salt
1/4 cup butter
1 unbaked 9-inch pie shell

Combine first 5 ingredients in 2-quart saucepan. Slowly stir in water. Cook over medium heat until mixture comes to a boil, stirring constantly. Let cool. Combine rest of ingredients (except pie shell) and mix until crumbly. Pour cooled mixture into pie shell and top with crumbs.

Bake at 350 degrees for 40 minutes or until golden brown.

Helen Weissinger, Levittown, Pa.

HAWAIIAN WEDDING PIE

1 (9-inch) baked pie shell
1/2 cup sugar
1/3 cup cornstarch
1-1/2 cups milk
3 beaten egg yolks
1 tablespoon butter or margarine
1-1/2 teaspoons vanilla
1 small can crushed pineapple, well
  drained
1/2-3/4 cup coconut
Whipped cream for topping
Toasted coconut for garnish

Combine sugar, cornstarch, and milk; mix well. Add beaten egg yolks. Cook over medium heat, stirring constantly, until mixture begins to boil and is thickened. Remove from heat. Add butter, vanilla, crushed pineapple, and coconut, thoroughly combining all. Pour mixture into pie shell and chill. When chilled, cover top with whipped cream. Sprinkle with toasted coconut.

Carme Venella, Laurel Springs, NJ

PENNSYLVANIA DUTCH SHOOFLY PIE

2 (8-inch) pastry shells, unbaked
2 cups flour
1 cup sugar
1 teaspoon baking powder
1 stick butter or margarine
1 cup dark molasses
1 teaspoon baking soda
1 cup boiling water
Pinch of salt
1 egg, beaten

Sift together flour, sugar, and baking powder. Cut in butter. In a separate bowl, mix molasses, baking soda, and water. Stir in salt, egg, and 2 cups of the flour-butter mixture. Pour into prepared pie shells and sprinkle with remaining crumbs. Bake at 375 degrees for 45 minutes.

Dorothy Garms, Anaheim, Calif.

4TH OF JULY PIE

1 pint blueberries
20-25 strawberries, hulled
Whipped cream
1 (3-1/4 ounce) package regular
  vanilla pudding mix
2 cups milk
1 (8-ounce) package cream cheese,
  softened
1/2 teaspoon vanilla
1 8-inch graham–cracker pie crust

Combine pudding mix and 2 cups milk in saucepan. Bring to full boil over medium heat, stirring constantly. Remove from heat. Add cream cheese and stir until smooth. Add vanilla. Let mixture cool for 5 minutes, stirring twice. Pour pudding mixture into pie crust. Refrigerate 3 hours or overnight. Place strawberries in circle on outer edge of pie. Place one in center. Place blueberries over remaining pudding.

Serve chilled, with whipped cream on top.

Chris Bryant, Johnson City, Tenn.

FRUIT SALAD PIE

1-1/4 cups water
3/4 cup white sugar
3 tablespoons pineapple juice
3 tablespoons maraschino cherry
    juice
3 tablespoons cornstarch
1/4 teaspoon red food coloring

Cook above ingredients until thick and then let cool.
Add:
2 large bananas, sliced
1/2 cup drained, crushed pineapple
1 (3-ounce) bottle maraschino
    cherries, drained and sliced in
    half

Pour into baked pie shell. Sprinkle with 1/2 cup coconut and 1/2 cup chopped walnuts. Chill; serve topped with whipped cream.

Clare R. Bracelin, Decatur, Ill.

---

1 teaspoon lemon juice
1 tablespoon butter

Wash and peel grapes, saving skins. Cook pulp in a saucepan with no water; bring to a hard boil. Rub through a strainer or food mill to remove seeds. Mix strained pulp with the reserved skins. Mix flour, sugar, and salt; stir into grapes. Add lemon juice and butter. Pour into pastry-lined 9-inch pie pan. Top with second crust. Slip top crust and seal edges. Bake at 400 degrees for about 40 minutes or until crust is brown and pie is bubbly.

Joy Shamway, Freeport, Il

RAISIN PIE

2 cups raisins (seedless or seeded)
2 cups boiling water
1/3 cup granulated sugar
1/3 cup brown sugar
2 tablespoons cornstarch
1/8 teaspoon salt
2 teaspoons grated lemon rind
1/2 teaspoon grated orange rind
2 tablespoons lemon juice
1 tablespoon orange juice
Pastry for 2-crust (9-inch) pie
2 tablespoons butter or margarine

Add raisins to water; simmer until tender (3-5 minutes). Combine sugars, cornstarch, and salt; stir into hot raisins. Cook slowly, stirring constantly, to full rolling boil; boil 1 minute. Remove from heat.

Blend in fruit rinds and juices. Pour hot filling into pastry-lined pie pan; dot top with butter. Cover with remaining pastry. Bake in 425-degree oven for 30-40 minutes. Serve slightly warm, plain, or with whipped cream.

Grace Lane, Redondo Beach, Calif.

ICE BOX CHERRY PIE

1 can red pie cherries, drained
1 cup nuts
1 can condensed milk
1/4 cup sugar
1 cup whipped cream
Juice of 2 lemons
1 graham cracker pie crust
Cool Whip

Mix milk, lemon juice, and sugar. Add cherries and nuts. Fold in whipped cream. Pour into pie crust. Top with Cool Whip. Refrigerate 4 hours or more before serving.

Monica Turk, Milwaukee, Wis.

GRAPE PIE

Serves 6-8

Pastry for 2-crust 9-inch pie
6 cups Concord grapes
1 cup sugar
1/4 cup flour
1/4 teaspoon salt

BUTTERMILK RAISIN PIE

1/4 cup cornstarch
1 cup sugar
1/4 teaspoon salt
2 cups buttermilk
1/2 cup raisins
2 tablespoons lemon juice
2 eggs, separated (use whites for
    meringue)
1 tablespoon butter

Cool baked 8- or 9-inch pie shell. Mix cornstarch, sugar, salt, and beaten egg yolks in top of double boiler; add buttermilk, raisins, and lemon juice. Cook over direct heat stirring constantly, until mixture boils and thickens. Remove from heat and stir in butter until melted. Cool slightly. Pour into baked pie shell. Beat egg whites until stiff. Gradually add 1/4 cup sugar; spread over pie. Bake at 350 degrees for 12-15 minutes until browned.

Helen Taugher, Nicholson, PA

BEST-EVER PUMPKIN PIE

Makes 2 (9-inch) pies

Pastry for 2 1-crust pies
1-1/2 cups sifted brown sugar
1 (No. 2-1/2) can pumpkin
4 eggs
3 tablespoons butter
2 tablespoons molasses
1-1/2 teaspoons cinnamon
3/4 teaspoon ginger
1/2 teaspoon nutmeg
1 teaspoon salt
1-1/2 cups milk

Line pastry in pie plates. Add sugar to the pumpkin. Beat eggs until thick and add with butter, molasses, seasonings, and milk to the pumpkin mixture; stir. Pour pumpkin mixture into pastry-lined pans. Bake at 425 degrees for 10 minutes; reduce heat to 325 degrees and bake 25 more minutes.

Lucy Dowd, Sequim, Wash.

CRANBERRY APPLE PIE

Pastry for 9-inch two-crust pie
1 cup sugar
1/3 cup all-purpose flour
1 teaspoon apple pie spice
4 cups sliced pared tart apples
2 cups Ocean Spray fresh cranberries
2 tablespoons butter or margarine

Preheat oven to 425 degrees. Prepare pastry. In a bowl, stir together sugar, flour, and spice. In pastry-lined pie pan alternate layers of apples, cranberries, and sugar mixture, beginning and ending with sugar mixture. Dot with butter. Cover with top crust. Cut slits in crust; seal and flute edges. Bake 40 to 50 minutes. Cool.

APPLESAUCE CHEESE PIE

6 graham crackers, crushed
1 tablespoon butter or margarine, melted
2 cups cottage cheese
2 eggs
1/4 cup sugar
1/4 cup flour
1 tablespoon lemon juice
1 cup thick applesauce

Mix crackers and butter; press into bottom and sides of 8- or 9-inch pie plate. Put cottage cheese through fine sieve; add eggs, one at a time, beating after each. Add sugar, flour, lemon juice, and applesauce. Beat until well blended. Pour into crumb-lined pie plate and bake in preheated 325-degree oven for 1 hour and 10 minutes or until mixture is set and lightly browned.

Kit Rollins, Cedarburg, WI

APPLE-BUTTER CINNAMON PIE

Pastry for 9-inch pie, plus strips for lattice
1/2 cup apple butter
2 eggs, beaten lightly
1/2 cup sugar
1-1/2 tablespoons cornstarch
1-1/2 teaspoons cinnamon
1/4 teaspoon mace
2 cups milk

Combine apple butter, eggs, sugar, cornstarch, cinnamon, and mace; mix well. Add milk gradually; blend well. Pour into unbaked pie shell; top with lattice made from 1/2-inch wide strips of crust. Bake 350 degrees for 35 minutes.

Gwen Campbell, Sterling, Va.

BLUEBERRY BOTTOM PIE

2 (4-serving) packages vanilla pudding and pie filling
1-1/4 cups milk
1-1/2 cups blueberries, puréed (1 cup)
1/2 teaspoon cinnamon
1 baked 9-inch pie shell, cooled
2 teaspoons grated lemon rind
3-1/2 cups frozen whipped topping (thawed)

Combine 1 package pudding mix, 1/4 cup of the milk, the puréed berries, and cinnamon in saucepan. Cook and stir until mixture comes to a full boil. Pour into crust; chill. Prepare remaining pudding mix with milk, as directed on package for pie. Add 1 teaspoon of the lemon rind; pour into bowl and cover with plastic wrap. Chill 1 hour. Fold in 1 cup of the whipped topping and spoon over blueberry layer. Combine remaining whipped topping and lemon rind. Spoon over filling. Chill in refrigerator, at least 3 hours before serving. Garnish with blueberries, if desired.

Suzanne Dawson, Cypress, Texas

DATE AND NUT PIE

1 unbaked 9-inch pie crust
1/2 cup butter, at room temperature
1 cup light brown sugar
4 eggs
1 teaspoon pure vanilla extract
1 teaspoon cinnamon
1/2 teaspoon nutmeg
3/4 cup whipping cream
1/2 cup chopped dates
1/2 cup raisins
1/2 cup chopped walnuts

Preheat oven to 350 degrees. Cream butter, then cream in the brown sugar, mixing until fluffy. Beat in eggs. Blend in vanilla, cinnamon, nutmeg, and cream, mixing well. Stir in dates, raisins, and nuts. Pour into pie crust. Bake in a preheated oven for about 45 minutes or until the surface is crisp and lightly browned.

This is worth the calories!

Lillian Smith, Montreal Quebec, Canada

FRUIT COCKTAIL PIE

1 (1 pound, 13 ounces) can fruit cocktail, well drained
32 vanilla wafers
1/2 cup sugar
1 teaspoon vanilla
2 cups sour cream

Preheat oven to 350 degrees. Place fruit cocktail in drainer; stir. Line bottom and sides of 9-inch glass pie plate with vanilla wafers. Add sugar and vanilla to sour cream; stir. Stir fruit cocktail again to be sure it is well drained. Add to sour cream mixture, folding gently. Pour into wafer-lined pie plate. Top with additional vanilla wafer crumbs, if desired. Bake at 350 degrees for 25 minutes, or until middle is set. Cool. Chill thoroughly before serving.

Marsha Miller, Hilliard, Ohio

Salads
SUPREME

TRICOLORED SLAW
Serves 6

1 small head of red or green cabbage (or half of each), shredded
2 large carrots, shredded
2 medium-size tart apples, chopped
   and unskinned
4 green onions, thinly sliced on the
   diagonal
1 cup yogurt
1/4 cup mayonnaise
3 tablespoons white wine vinegar
1 tablespoon sugar
1/2 teaspoon dry tarragon
Salt and pepper to taste

In large bowl combine cabbage, carrots, apples and onions. Cover and refrigerate. In a medium-size bowl or in food processor or blender combine yogurt, mayonnaise, vinegar, sugar and tarragon; blend well. Before serving pour dressing over cabbage mixture and toss lightly until well-coated. Add salt and pepper to taste.

ORIENTAL VEGETABLE SALAD

1/4 cup fresh cauliflower buds
1/4 cup bean sprouts
Several water chestnuts, thinly
   sliced
1/4 cup shredded cabbage
1/4 cup sliced fresh mushrooms
1/4 cup chopped green onions
Low-calorie Italian dressing

Toss vegetables. Add dressing; toss again lightly. Place in wide-mouth thermos for a tasty brown-bag lunch.

ORANGE MALLOW AMBROSIA
Makes 4 cups

1 (3-ounce) package orange gelatin
3/4 cup boiling water
2 cups ice cubes
1 cup whipped topping, thawed
1 (11-ounce) can mandarin orange
   sections, drained
1 cup miniature marshmallows,
   white or colored
1 (15 1/2-ounce) can crushed
   pineapple, drained

Dissolve gelatin in boiling water. Add ice cubes and stir constantly until it starts to thicken, about 3 minutes. Remove any unmelted ice. Add whipped topping, blending until smooth. Stir in oranges, marshmallows and pineapple. Pour into serving bowl or molds. Chill until set.

Jean Hugh, Bethel Park, Pa.

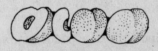

ORANGE SALAD

1 can mandarin oranges
1 large can chunk pineapple,
   drained
1 (8-ounce) carton sour cream
1 (8-ounce) carton Cool Whip,
   thawed
1 small box dry (do not make)
   orange gelatin powder
Miniature marshmallows

Combine all ingredients and chill.
Diantha Susan Hibbard, Rochester, N.Y.

CARROT SALAD
Serves 4-6

1 (8-1/2-ounce) can crushed
   pineapple
1-1/2 cups shredded carrots
3/4 cup flaked coconut
1 tablespoon sugar
2 tablespoons mayonnaise

Drain pineapple, reserving 1/2 cup juice. Combine pineapple, carrots, coconut, and sugar. Mix well. Combine mayonnaise and reserved pineapple juice; beat with wire whisk until smooth. Pour over carrot mixture and mix well. Chill.

This is a "dressed up" version of the ever-popular carrot salad that usually has only raisins.

Mrs. H.W. Walker, Richmond, Va.

HOT CABBAGE SLAW
Serves 6

4   cups coarsely shredded
    red or green cabbage
1   (16-ounce) can cut
    green beans, drained
¼   cup sugar
1   tablespoon instant
    minced onion
1   teaspoon salt
½   cup vinegar

In a large saucepan, heat all ingredients to boiling. Reduce heat; simmer, uncovered, tossing occasionally until cabbage is crisp-tender (about 5 minutes). (65 calories per serving)

Mary Bell, Cincinnati, Ohio

CHICKEN FRUIT SALAD
Serves 6

3 cups cooked, chunked chicken
3/4 cup celery, chopped
3/4 cup red grapes, halved and seeded
1 (20-ounce) can pineapple chunks, drained
1 (11-ounce) can mandarin oranges, drained

1/4 cup chopped pecans
1/4 cup salad oil
1/8 teaspoon salt
Lettuce leaves, as desired

Lightly toss chicken, celery, grapes, pineapple, oranges and 3 tablespoons pecans. Blend in salad oil and salt. Chill.

Serve on lettuce leaves. Garnish with remaining pecans.

Mrs. E. O'Brien, Richmond, Va.

TRIPLE ORANGE SALAD
Serves 10–12

2 cups boiling liquid (water *or* fruit juices)
1 (6-ounce) package orange gelatin
1 pint orange sherbet
2 (11-ounce) cans mandarin orange segments, drained
1 (13¼-ounce) can pineapple chunks, drained
1 cup flaked coconut
1 cup miniature marshmallows
1 cup sour cream *or* ½ cup chilled whipping cream, whipped

Pour boiling liquid on gelatin in bowl; stir until gelatin is dissolved. Add sherbet; stir until melted. Stir in 1 can orange segments. Pour into 6-cup ring mold; refrigerate until firm.

Mix remaining orange segments, pineapple, coconut and marshmallows. Fold in sour cream. Refrigerate at least 3 hours.

Unmold gelatin onto serving plate and fill center with fruit salad.

Vivian Nikanow, Chicago, Ill.

APPLE SALAD
Serves 10

6 apples, sweet-tart and crisp; peel, core and chop
1/2 cup chopped English walnuts
1 cup finely chopped celery
1 1/2 cups purple grapes, halved and seeds removed
1/4 cup sugar
1 heaping tablespoon Miracle Whip
1/2 pint whipping cream, stiffly whipped

Prepare fruit. Sprinkle with sugar; stir in Miracle Whip. Stir well to cover all the fruit and nuts with a light coating of sugar/dressing mixture.

Add stiffly beaten whipped cream. You can do everything, except the cream, ahead of time; refrigerate for a couple of hours, then add the whipped cream just before serving.

Linda Taylor, Gravois Mills, Mo.

FRUIT SALAD SUPREME
Serves 10

1 (16-ounce) can sliced peaches
2 (11-ounce) cans mandarin oranges
1 (16-ounce) can apricots
1 (20-ounce) can chunk pineapple
2 (10-ounce) packages frozen strawberries
1 (3½-ounce) box instant vanilla pudding

Drain peaches, oranges, apricots and pineapple very well. Pat dry on paper toweling. Place fruit in bowl and add 2 packages of thawed strawberries; do not drain. Add box of instant vanilla pudding. Stir together and place in refrigerator overnight.

Shari Crider, Stoughton, Wis.

BEET AND CABBAGE SALAD
Serves 3-4

2 (16-ounce) cans sliced beets, reserve liquid
1 cup mayonnaise
3 tablespoons milk
1 tablespoon vinegar (optional)
1 small head cabbage
1/2 cup reserved beet juice
1 small onion, chopped (optional)

Shred cabbage and place in large bowl. Add sliced beets. In a small bowl, mix together beet juice, milk, and mayonnaise. Add vinegar, if desired.

Add onion (if desired) to cabbage and beets; toss well. Pour dressing over vegetables and toss until well-coated. Prepare and refrigerate at least 1 hour before serving to allow flavors to blend.

Michaeline Duncan, Dudley, N.C.

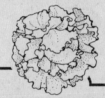

CAULIFLOWER SALAD

2 heads cauliflower, finely chopped
1 bunch green onions, finely chopped
1 bunch radishes, finely chopped
½ cup celery, finely chopped

Dressing:
1 cup mayonnaise
1 cup sour cream
1 teaspoon dill
3 teaspoons parsley
2 teaspoons beau monde spice

Combine dressing ingredients and add to vegetables. Best if refrigerated overnight.

I use my food processor to chop the vegetables.

Laura Hicks, Troy, Mont.

FRUIT COCKTAIL SALAD

1 (5-5/8 ounce) package vanilla flavored Jello instant pudding mix
1-1/3 cups buttermilk
1 (8-ounce) container Cool Whip
1 (30-ounce) can fruit cocktail, well-drained
2 cans mandarin oranges, well-drained
1 cup miniature rainbow-colored marshmallows (optional)

Blend buttermilk into pudding mix using medium speed of mixer. When smooth, blend in Cool Whip. If consistency of mixture seems too thick, add a little more buttermilk. Fold in fruit cocktail and mandarin oranges, reserving half a can of oranges for garnish. Swirl a design on top of salad with a tablespoon. Gently arrange balance of mandarin orange slices in swirled design on top of salad.

Add colored marshmallows to mixture before garnishing, if desired.
Lalla Fellows, Long Beach, Calif.

GOLDEN FRUIT SALAD

2 large Golden Delicious apples, diced
2 large Red Delicious apples, diced
4 large bananas, sliced
2 (20 ounce) cans pineapple chunks, drained (reserve juice)
2 (16 ounce) cans Mandarin oranges, drained
Whole green grapes, optional

Mix Together:
1 cup sugar
4 tablespoons corn starch
Reserved pineapple juice
2 tablespoons lemon juice
2/3 cup orange juice

Stir and boil 1 minute. Pour hot mixture over fruit. Leave uncovered until cool.

Pat Stump, Dunnell, MN

SHORTCUT FROZEN SALAD

1 small package *instant* lemon pudding
1 pint whipped topping, thawed
1/2 cup mayonnaise
2 tablespoons lemon juice
1 (1-pound) can fruit cocktail, drained
1 cup miniature marshmallows
1/4 cup chopped pecans

Prepare pudding according to package directions; blend in whipped topping, mayonnaise, and lemon juice. Fold in remaining ingredients. Turn into a 9x5x3-inch loaf pan and freeze until firm. Slice to serve.

Agnes Ward, Erie, Pa.

GUM DROP FRUIT SALAD

Serves 8

1 (#2 can) pineapple tidbits
1/4 cup sugar
2 tablespoons flour
1/4 teaspoon salt
3 tablespoons lemon juice
1-1/2 teaspoons vinegar
2 cups seedless grapes, halved
2 cups miniature white marshmallows
2/3 cup gumdrops, halved (do not use black drops)
1 (4-ounce) bottle maraschino cherries, drained and halved
1/4 cup chopped pecans
1 cup whipping cream, whipped

Drain pineapple, reserving 1/3 cup of syrup. Combine sugar, flour, and salt. Add reserved pineapple syrup, lemon juice, and vinegar. Cook over medium heat, stirring constantly until thick and boiling. Continue cooking 1 minute. Set aside and cool. Combine pineapple and remaining ingredients, except the whipped cream. Fold the cooked dressing into the whipped cream. Cover and refrigerate for 12-24 hours.

Carmen J. Bickert, Dubuque, IA

BANANA BAVARIAN CREAM

1 (6-ounce) package lemon-flavored gelatin
2 cups hot water
1/4 teaspoon salt
2/3 cup sugar
1/2 cup heavy cream
5 bananas

Dissolve gelatin in hot water. Add salt and sugar. Chill until cold and syrupy. Fold in cream, whipped only until thick and shiny, but not stiff. Crush bananas to pulp with fork, and fold at once into mixture. Chill until slightly thickened. Turn into mold. Chill until firm. Unmold. Serve with Strawberry Sauce. (Recipe below)

Strawberry Sauce:
1/3 cup butter
1 cup powdered sugar
1 egg white
2/3 cup strawberries

Cream butter and sugar, gradually add crushed strawberries and egg whites. Beat well.
Lucille Roehr, Hammond, Ind.

BUNNY SALAD

Serves 6-8

1 (3-ounce) package orange gelatin
1 cup boiling water
1 cup pineapple juice and water
1 teaspoon grated orange rind
1-1/3 cups crushed pineapple, drained
1 cup grated raw carrots

Dissolve gelatin in boiling water. Add pineapple juice/water mixture and orange rind. Chill until slightly thickened. Then fold in pineapple and carrots. Pour into 6-8 individual round molds. Chill until firm. Unmold on crisp lettuce. Add carrot strips to form ears, a large marshmallow for the head, and half a marshmallow for the tail. Serve plain or with mayonnaise, if desired.
Marcella Swigert, Monroe City, Mo.

ORANGE SHERBERT GELATIN SALAD

Serves 8

2-3 ounce packages orange gelatin
1 cup boiling water
1 pint orange sherbert
1 can mandarin oranges, drained
1 cup heavy cream, whipped

Dissolve gelatin in boiling water; add sherbert, and mix well. When partially set, add mandarin oranges and fold in whipped cream. Pour into square pan or individual molds.

Margaret Hamfeldt, Louisville, KY

CRANBERRY SALAD MOLD

1 (3 ounce) package lemon gelatin
2 cups boiling water
1-1/4 cups sugar

Dissolve and set aside to cool, but not to set.

Add:
1 small can crushed pineapple
1 cup diced celery
1 orange, cut up
1 tablespoon grated orange peel
2 cups diced apples
3 cups ground cranberries

Pour into gelatin mold; refrigerate until ready to serve. Unmold on green lettuce leaves. Stores well, and may easily be made in advance.

Fay Duman, Eugene, Ore.

BROCCOLI ASPIC

Serves 6

1 envelope unflavored gelatin
1 can condensed consommé
Salt & pepper to taste
3/4 cup mayonnaise
3 hard-cooked eggs, sliced
Juice of 1-1/2 lemons
2 cups cooked broccoli flowerets

Soften gelatin in 1/4 cup cold consommé. Add to the rest of the consommé and heat. Stir until dissolved; add salt and pepper, if needed. Let thicken until consistency of raw egg whites. Fold in mayonnaise, sliced eggs, broccoli and lemon juice. Pour into individual molds and chill until firm.

Agnes Ward, Erie, PA

STRAWBERRY-RHUBARB SALAD MOLD

3 (3-ounce) packages strawberry gelatin
3 cups hot water
2 packages frozen rhubarb
1 quart sliced fresh strawberries
Watercress or other salad greens
1 fresh whole strawberry
Chantilly Mayonnaise (recipe follows)

Dissolve 3 packages gelatin in 3 cups hot water. Drop in 2 packages of frozen rhubarb. Stir to separate the rhubarb. When jelly begins to set, add the strawberries. Pour into individual wet molds and chill until set. Unmold on watercress. Garnish each mold with whole strawberry. Serve with Chantilly Mayonnaise.

BUTTERMILK SALAD

1 (6 ounce) package apricot gelatin
1 (20 ounce) can crushed pineapple, undrained
2 cups buttermilk
1 (8 or 9 ounce) container Cool Whip

Bring pineapple to a boil in saucepan. Stir dry gelatin into pineapple and mix until dissolved. Chill until partially set. Stir in buttermilk. Chill again until partly set. Fold in Cool Whip. Refrigerate until firm.

Ruby Beheber, Ransom, IL

HOLIDAY STRAWBERRY GELATIN

1 large (6 ounce) package strawberry gelatin
2 bananas, sliced
1 can crushed pineapple with juice
1/2 cup chopped nuts
1 large package sour cream
2 packages frozen strawberries with juice

Dissolve gelatin in 1 cup boiling water; add pineapple, bananas, strawberries, and nuts. Let jell in refrigerator for about 1 hour. Pour one half mixture into 9x12 inch pan. Let jell in refrigerator about 10-15 minutes; spread sour cream on top. Pour remaining gelatin as top layer.

Refrigerate until serving; may want to garnish for the holidays.

Donna Holter, West Middlesex, Pa.

SPARKLE SALAD

1 (3 ounce) package lime gelatin
1 cup miniature marshmallows
1 cup 7-UP, heated to boiling
3/4 cup finely chopped cabbage
1/2 cup finely chopped carrots
1 cup crushed pineapple, well drained
1/2 cup chopped pecans
1 cup mayonnaise
1 cup whipped cream

Dissolve gelatin and marshmallows in 7-UP. Chill until slightly thickened. Add cabbage, carrots, pineapple, nuts, and mayonnaise. Fold in whipped cream.

Note: For convenience, use blender for cabbage and carrots.

Mrs. Charles Sharp, Newton, Kan.

BANANA YOGURT SALAD

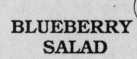

2 large bananas
2 cups yogurt
1/4 cup nuts, chopped
Orange sections
Lettuce

Peel and split bananas; place in serving dishes. Spoon one cup of yogurt onto each banana. Sprinkle with nuts; surround with orange sections and shredded lettuce.
Suzan L. Wiener, Spring Hill, Fla.

APRICOT SALAD
Serves 10-12

2 (16-ounce) cans apricots in syrup, drained. (Reserve juice)
1 (8-ounce) package cream cheese, diced
1 (3-ounce) package lemon gelatin
1 (3-ounce) package lime gelatin
1 (12-ounce) package Cool Whip

Put both gelatins in large bowl and add 2 cups boiling apricot juice, adding enough water to make 2 cups, if not enough juice. Mix until dissolved. Add diced cream cheese. Mix until smooth. Mash apricots slightly and add to gelatin mixture. Fold Cool Whip into mixture.

Pour into 13x9-inch pan. Chill overnight. May be kept in refrigerator for 2 weeks. Spoon serve, or cut into squares. This is a delicious, refreshing, simple-to-prepare salad.
Irene Adney, Eureka Springs, Ark.

BLUEBERRY SALAD

2 (3-ounce) packages grape gelatin
2 cups boiling water
1 (No. 2) can undrained crushed pineapple
1 (16-ounce) can blueberry pie filling
1 cup sour cream
1 (8-ounce) package cream cheese
1/2 cup granulated sugar
1 teaspoon vanilla

In a 9x13-inch pan, mix the gelatin and boiling water until dissolved. Add undrained pineapple and blueberry pie filling. Stir and let set in refrigerator. Mix sour cream with the softened cream cheese, sugar, and vanilla. Do not overbeat. Spread on top of the set gelatin mixture. Chill again in refrigerator. This is a great potluck dish. It can be served as salad or dessert.
Edna Mae Seelos, Niles, Ill.

TASTY APPLE SALAD

1 (20-ounce) can pineapple tidbits, drain and save juice
2 cups miniature marshmallows
1/2 cup sugar
1 tablespoon flour
1 egg, beaten
1-1/2 tablespoons vinegar
1 (8-ounce) container Cool Whip
2 cups chopped apples with skins (Red Delicious)
1-1/2 cups dry roasted peanuts, chopped

Mix pineapple juice, sugar, flour, egg, and vinegar in pan. Cook until thick. Refrigerate overnight. Next day, or 8 hours, mix together apples, nuts, Cool Whip, pineapple, marshmallows and pineapple juice; mix and refrigerate until ready to serve.
Barbara L. Henwood, Glenview, IL

SPICY PEACH SALAD

6 large canned peach halves
1/2 stick whole cinnamon
1 teaspoon whole cloves
1/2 cup white vinegar
1/2 cup sugar

1 (3-ounce) package cream cheese
1/4 cup fresh lime juice
1/4 cup pecans, chopped

Place cinnamon stick and cloves in a small cheesecloth bag; tie firmly; cook with sugar and vinegar for 3 minutes. Remove spice bag; pour over peaches; chill. Fill center of each peach with cream cheese seasoned with lime juice and chopped pecans. To serve: Arrange each peach half on a chilled, crisp lettuce leaf.
Gwen Campbell, Sterling, Va.

PEACH PARTY SALAD
Serves 12

1 (6-ounce) package orange flavored gelatin
2 cups boiling water
1 (15-1/4 ounce) can crushed pineapple, undrained
2 cups canned or fresh sliced peaches, drained
1 egg, beaten
1/4 cup sugar
1-1/2 tablespoons all-purpose flour
1-1/2 tablespoons butter or margarine, softened
1/2 cup whipping cream, whipped
1/2 cup miniature marshmallows
1/2 cup (2 ounces) shredded Cheddar cheese

Dissolve gelatin in boiling water; set aside. Drain pineapple, reserving juice; set pineapple aside. Add enough water to juice to make 1 cup. Add 3/4 cup of juice mixture to gelatin mixture; chill until consistency of unbeaten egg white. Set remaining 1/4 cup of juice mixture aside. Arrange peach slices in a lightly-oiled 12 x 8 x 2 inch dish. Pour gelatin mixture over peaches. Chill until almost firm. Combine egg, sugar, flour, butter, and remaining 1/4 cup juice mixture in a small saucepan. Cook over low heat, stirring constantly until smooth and thickened; cool. Combine pineapple, whipped cream, marshmallows, and cheese; fold in egg mixture. Spread evenly over salad. Cover; chill overnight.
Peggy Fowler Revels, Woodruff, SC

SPECIAL FRUIT SALAD

1 (3 ounce) box non- instant vanilla
  pudding
1 (3 ounce) box non-instant tapioca
  pudding
1 heaping tablespoon frozen orange
  juice concentrate
3 (11 ounce) cans mandarin oranges
3 (15 ounce) cans pineapple tidbits
3 large bananas, sliced

Drain one can of oranges and pineapple. Use the juice and add enough
water to make 3 cups of liquid. Cook
puddings and orange juice with the
liquid until thickened. Cool slightly
and add to drained fruit.

Kristy Schemrich, Shreve, Ohio

CIDER WALDORF SALAD
Serves 12

2 envelopes Knox unflavored
  gelatin
2-1/2 cups cold apple cider or apple
  juice
1 cup apple cider or juice, heated to
  boiling
2 tablespoons lemon juice
1-1/4 cups chopped apple
1/2 cup diced celery
1/2 cup raisins
1/2 cup coarsely chopped walnuts

In large bowl, sprinkle unflavored
gelatin over 1/2 cup cold cider; let
stand 1 minute. Add hot cider and stir
until gelatin is completely dissolved.
Stir in remaining cold cider and
lemon juice. Chill, stirring occasionally, until mixture is consistency of
unbeaten egg whites. Fold in remaining ingredients. Turn into 6-1/2 cup
mold or bowl; chill until firm.

Sue Hibbard, Rochester, N.Y.

FROZEN WALDORF SALAD
Serves 9-12

1 (8 ounce) can crushed pineapple
2 eggs, slightly beaten
1/2 cup sugar
1/4 cup lemon juice
1/8 teaspoon salt
2 cups unpeeled apples, diced
1 cup celery, diced
1/2 cup pecans, chopped
1/2 cup whipping cream

Drain juice from pineapple into
sauce pan. Add slightly beaten eggs,
sugar, lemon juice, and salt. Cook
over low heat, stirring constantly,
until thickened. Cool slightly. Add
pineapple, apples, celery, and pecans.
Mix to blend.

Whip cream. Fold into pineapple
mixture. Pour into an 8-inch square
dish. Freeze overnight. Before serving, place in refrigerator for about 3
hours.

Margaret Hamfeldt, Louisville, Ky.

GINGER PEAR SALAD
Serves 4-5

1 (10-1/2 -ounce) can condensed
  consomme
1/4 teaspoon ground ginger
Dash cinnamon
1 (3-ounce) package lemon-flavored
  gelatin
3/4 cup cold water
6 walnut halves
1 (1-pound) can pear halves, drained
  and diced
1/2 cup thinly sliced celery
1/3 cup coarsely chopped walnuts
Crisp salad greens
Sour cream

Combine consomme, ginger, and
cinnamon. Bring to a boil. Add gelatin and stir until dissolved. Add water. Chill until slightly thickened.
Pour a small amount into a 1-quart
mold. Arrange walnut halves and
several pieces of pear on gelatin. Stir
remaining pears, celery, and walnuts
into remaining gelatin. Spoon into

mold. Chill until firm, about 3 hours.
Unmold. Serve on crisp salad greens.
Garnish with sour cream.

MANDARIN ORANGE SALAD

60 Ritz crackers, crushed
1/4 pound butter, melted
1/4 cup sugar
1 (6 ounce) can unsweetened frozen
  orange juice, thawed
1 can Eagle Brand Sweetened Con-
  denced Milk
1 (8 ounce) container Cool Whip
2 small cans Mandarin oranges,
  drained

Crush crackers finely and add
melted butter and sugar to them.
Press mixture firmly into 9x13x2
inch baking dish. Reserve some of
crumb mixture for garnish.

Blend thawed orange juice and
milk. Stir in Cool Whip and oranges.
Fold in. Do not beat. Pour mixture
over crumb crust. Top with reserved
crumbs.

Refrigerate or freeze until serving.
This is delicious, refreshing, and
appetizing.

Patty White, Indianapolis, IN

GREEN BEAN SALAD

1 can (16 ounce) French-style sliced
  green beans
1 green onion
1/3 cup white vinegar
1/4 cup sugar
1/8 teaspoon garlic salt
4 tablespoons water
2 tablespoons oil

Drain beans well. Transfer to
medium bowl. Use scissors to snip in
green onion. Set aside.

In pint pitcher, measure vinegar.
Add sugar and garlic salt; mix well.
Add water and oil; beat with whisk or
fork. Pour over beans; toss with fork
to mix. Cover; refrigerate overnight
for flavors to blend. Serve cold.

CHERRY FROZEN SALAD

Makes 32-34 small cups

1 (16-ounce) can cherry pie filling
1 large can crushed pineapple, drained
1 can sweetened condensed milk
1 large carton Cool Whip
2 cups miniature marshmallows
1 cup chopped pecans

Mix all together in order given. Spoon into paper cups. Freeze.

This is delicious and can also be used as a dessert.

Mrs. Bruce Fowler, Woodruff, SC

SPRINGTIME SALAD

Serves 6

1 (1-pound) can grapefruit sections
4 green onions, thinly sliced
1/2 cup sliced radishes
1/2 cup cucumber, sliced or greens of your choice

Drain grapefruit. Wash and dry greens (of your choice) and tear into bite-size pieces. Add grapefruit sections, onions, radishes, and cucumber. Toss and serve with a Roquefort dressing, before serving.

Agnes Ward, Erie, Pa.

MOUNTAIN DEW SALAD

1 large package lemon gelatin
1-2/3 cups boiling water
1 cup small marshmallows
1 cup Mountain Dew soda
1 (#303 can) crushed pineapple, drain
1 can lemon pudding or pie filling
1 medium container Cool Whip

Mix gelatin in boiling water with marshmallows until dissolved. Add Mountain Dew and drained pineapple. Chill until set. Mix pudding and Cool Whip. Spread on top of gelatin which has set.

Cheryl Wellman, Quincy, IL

SILHOUETTE SALAD

Serves 4

1 envelope Knox unflavored gelatin
1 cup water, divided
1 (10-1/2 ounce) can condensed cream of chicken soup
1 tablespoon lemon juice
1/8 teaspoon pepper
1 (5-ounce) can boned chicken, diced
1/2 cup diced celery
1/4 cup chopped green pepper
2 tablespoons chopped pimiento
2 teaspoons grated onion

Sprinkle gelatin on 1/2 cup water to soften. Place over low heat and stir until gelatin is dissolved. Remove from heat; stir in soup until well-blended. Add other 1/2 cup water, lemon juice, and pepper. Chill until the consistency of unbeaten egg white. Fold in chicken, onion, green pepper, and pimiento. Turn into a 3-cup mold and chill until firm.

Joy Shamway, Freeport, IL

MOUNTAIN DEW SALAD

1 (6-ounce) package lemon gelatin
1 cup boiling water
1 can cold Mountain Dew beverage
1 (15-ounce) can pineapple chunks or tidbits, drained and juice reserved
1 package lemon pudding (cooked type)
1 cup whipping cream (whipped) or Cool Whip
1 cup colored mini marshmallows

Dissolve gelatin in boiling water; add Mountain Dew and juice drained from pineapple; chill until it begins to thicken. Cook pudding according to package instructions; cool.

Mix gelatin, lemon pudding, and whipped cream, beating together. Add drained pineapple and marshmallows. Pour into a large bowl and chill.

Betty Brennan, Faribault, Minn.

COTTAGE CHEESE DELIGHT

1 quart cottage cheese
1 can crushed pineapple, drained
1 (6-ounce) box orange gelatin
1 small package miniature marshmallows
1 large container Cool Whip

Mix cottage cheese, pineapple, and gelatin powder together. Blend in marshmallows and Cool Whip; chill before serving.

Vivian I. Parks, Mohave Valley, Ariz.

SHAMROCK SALAD

First Layer:
1 (3-ounce) package lime gelatin
1 small can undrained crushed pineapple

Dissolve gelatin in one cup hot water, then cool. Add pineapple. Pour mixture into large mold and chill until set.

Second Layer:
1 (3-ounce) package lemon gelatin
2 (3-ounce) packages cream cheese
10 marshmallows
2 cups whipping cream

Dissolve lemon gelatin in one cup hot water. Mix one package cream cheese with one cup whipping cream. Pour mixture on top of set lime gelatin. Chill until set. Mix remaining cream cheese with one cup whipped cream and the marshmallows cut into small pieces. Turn out mold on lettuce green and top with this mixture. You may decide to serve this creation as a dessert.—Whip 1/2 cup cream; add drained maraschino cherries and drained pineapple slices, arranged, to form an attractive circle on top.

St. Patrick's Day is a special one, not only because it is the beginning of spring, but because of the teasing, elfish nature of this man who makes "everything come up green" on this day. Special foods are your way of contributing to a genial atmosphere for both children and adults. On this day, we are all the same age—Happy St. Patrick's Day!

BREAD SALAD

1 large loaf sliced white sandwich
  bread
1 large onion, finely chopped
4 hard-cooked eggs, chopped
1 cup finely chopped celery
1 (7-ounce) can crab and 2 cans
  shrimp (or substitute 2 cups
  cooked chicken or turkey)
3 cups mayonnaise

Cut crusts from bread. Spread bread
lightly with butter. Cut into small
cubes. Add onions and eggs; refrigerate
overnight. Add the remaining
ingredients in the morning and chill 3
to 4 hours. Garnish with cucumbers,
tomatoes, etc.

Mrs. Martha Mehlhoff, SD.

EGG SALAD

Makes 2 cups

4 hard-cooked eggs, chopped
1/2 cup mayonnaise
1/2 cup chopped ham
2 tablespoons sliced green onions
2 teaspoons Dijon mustard
Dash freshly ground pepper

In small bowl combine eggs, mayonnaise, ham, green onion, mustard,
and pepper. Cover; chill.

Annie Cmehil , New Castle, Ind.

ORANGE SALAD

Serves 6

1 large (6-ounce) package orange
  gelatin
1 cup hot water
2 cups orange sherbet
1 cup mandarin oranges, drained
1 cup crushed pineapple, drained
1/2 pint whipping cream, whipped

Dissolve gelatin in hot water. Add
sherbet, mixing well. Add drained
oranges and pineapple. Fold in
whipped cream. Congeals quickly.
Chill.

Lucille Kavanaugh, Braymer, Mo.

RASPBERRY DELIGHT

1 (3-ounce) package raspberry
  gelatin
1 cup hot water
1 (8-ounce) can crushed pineapple
  and juice
1 (10-ounce) package frozen
  raspberries and juice
1 cup whipped topping or Cool
  Whip

Dissolve gelatin in hot water. Chill
until syrupy. Add fruits and juices.
Chill until thickened, but not quite set
hard. Fold in topping, making a
marbled effect. Chill.

Ann Sterzer, Lincoln, Neb.

EASY FRUIT WALDORF

Serves 6

1 (No. 2-1/2) can fruit cocktail
1/2 cup sliced celery
1/2 cup chopped walnuts
Salad greens
Cream Dressing (recipe follows)

Drain fruit cocktail well and mix
lightly with celery and walnuts. Serve
on salad greens and top with Cream
Dressing or mayonnaise.

Cream Dressing:
Combine *equal* parts lemon juice
and honey.

Lucille Roehr, Hammond, Ind.

BEAUTIFUL CHERRY SALAD

2 packages cherry gelatin
1 can cherry pie filling
2 cups hot water
1 cup sour cream

Dissolve gelatin in hot water. Cool
until it starts to set. Add sour cream
and cherry pie filling; pour into mold
and refrigerate. (I add pie filling first
and then just swirl sour cream through
it.)

Marcella Swigert, Monroe City, Mo.

SUMMER FRUIT FANTASY

Serves 12

3 grapefruit
3 oranges
1 pint fresh strawberries
1 pineapple, cut into cubes to yield 2
  cups cubes
2 peaches, cut into bite-size pieces
1 cup fresh blueberries
1 cup seedless grapes or remove
  seeds, use half green and half
  red
1 teaspoon orange rind
4 tablespoons orange juice
3 tablespoons sugar
3 tablespoons orange flavored
  liqueur

Mix all dressing ingredients and
set aside. Cut grapefruit and oranges
in half. Remove pulp in pieces. Hollow out shells and set aside. Cut pulp
into bite-size segments. In a large
bowl, combine grapefruit and orange
segments. Add strawberries that have
been washed, hulled, and cut in half.
Add pineapple cubes, peaches, blueberries, and grapes. Toss well. Top
with dressing. Toss carefully. Cover
and chill 30 minutes to 12 hours.
Serve in empty hollowed out grapefruit and orange shells. (You may
substitute any fresh fruit available.)

Laura Morris, Bunnell, Fla.

RASPBERRY SALAD

1 large box raspberry gelatin
2 cups hot water
2 cups applesauce
2 packages frozen raspberries, partially defrosted
1 cup sour cream
1-1/2 cups miniature marshmallows
2 teaspoons cinnamon

In oblong dish, dissolve gelatin in
hot water. Break up raspberries in
mixture. Add applesauce and cinnamon. Refrigerate until set. Combine
sour cream and marshmallows.
Spread on top of chilled gelatin. Refrigerate again for 2 hours before
serving.

Suzanne Dawson, Cypress, TX

Sandwich
TASTIES

PIZZA BUNS
Serves 8–12

1 pound lean ground beef
2 onions, chopped
1/2 pound grated cheddar cheese
1 can tomato soup, undiluted
1 teaspoon oregano
1 teaspoon minced garlic
1/4 cup oil
English muffins
Mozzarella cheese

Brown ground beef, onions and garlic; add rest of ingredients, except mozzarella cheese. Spread mixture on split English muffins and sprinkle grated mozzarella over top. Broil until brown.

Quick and easy, plus kids love these!

Jodie McCoy, Tulsa, Okla.

SWISS SANDWICH PUFFS
Makes 30 servings

1/2 cup mayonnaise
1/4 cup chopped onion
2 tablespoons snipped parsley
30 slices tiny cocktail rye
7-8 slices Swiss cheese

Combine mayonnaise, onion and parsley. Spread on bread slices, and top each with one-quarter of a slice of Swiss cheese. Broil for 2-3 minutes, watching carefully to avoid burning cheese.

TEXAS/TACO

1 (9-ounce) can bean dip (Frito Lay's)
1/2 cup sour cream
1/2 cup taco sauce
1/2 cup chopped green onions
1/2 cup sliced black olives
1/2 cup chopped tomatoes
1/2 cup browned ground beef
1/2 cup browned sausage
2 cups shredded mozzarella cheese
2 cups cheddar cheese
Meijer Nacho Chips

Spread bean dip over large pizza pan, first covered with foil. Add sour cream, taco sauce, onions, olives, tomatoes, ground beef and sausage. Top with mozzarella and cheddar cheese. Serve cold or place in 425-degree oven, or until cheese melts. Delicious served with nacho chips.

Sally Doran, Saginaw, Mich.

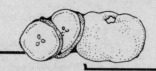

PINEAPPLE-CHEESE SANDWICH SPREAD
Makes 3/4 cup

1 (3-ounce) package cream cheese, softened
1/2 cup crushed pineapple, drained
1/4 cup finely chopped pecans

Beat cream cheese until light and fluffy; stir in pineapple and pecans. Mix well; spread on sandwich bread.

Edna Askins, Greenville, Texas

HAM SALAD
Makes 3 cups

2   cups ground ham
2   hard-boiled eggs, chopped
½   cup chopped celery
2   tablespoons or more pickle relish *or* chopped sweet pickles
    Mayonnaise

Grind ham coarsely in a meat grinder. Add chopped eggs. Add remaining ingredients and moisten with mayonnaise. Serve in sandwiches, as a salad on lettuce leaves, or stuff in fresh, hollowed-out tomatoes.

TUNA BURGERS
Serves 6

6 hamburger buns
1 (6-1/2-ounce) can tuna, drained and flaked
1/2 cup finely chopped celery
2 tablespoons minced onion
4 (3/4-ounce) slices processed American cheese, diced
1/2 cup mayonnaise or salad dressing

Combine all ingredients, except buns. Toss gently to coat. Spoon about 1/3 cup on bottom half of each hamburger bun; cover with bun tops. Wrap each sandwich in aluminum foil. Bake at 350 degrees for 18–20 minutes.

Mrs. Bruce Fowler, Woodruff, S.C.

CHOW MEIN BURGERS
Serves 8

1 pound ground beef
1/2 cup chopped onion
1 (1-pound) can chop suey vegetables, drained
3 tablespoons soy sauce
2 tablespoons cornstarch
8 hamburger buns, toasted
Chow mein noodles

Combine ground beef and onions in skillet; cook until brown. Drain off excess fat. Add vegetables. Mix 1/3 cup water, soy sauce, and cornstarch; stir into beef mixture. Cook, stirring constantly until thickened. Spoon onto bottom halves of buns. Sprinkle with chow mein noodles. Cover with bun tops.

Sharon M. Crider, Evansville, Wisc.

HAM AND CHEESE MELT-AWAYS

1 pound chipped ham
1 pound sliced Swiss cheese
1 cup soft margarine
2 tablespoons yellow mustard
1-1/2 teaspoons poppy or celery
seeds
1 tablespoon Worcestershire sauce
12 hamburger buns

Chop or cut fine the chipped ham and cheese. Cream butter until fluffy; add mustard, seeds, and Worcester-shire sauce; mix well. Add ham and cheese; mix very well. Mix all this by hand with wooden spoon or fork. Then spoon mixture onto hamburger buns. Wrap in foil. Sandwiches may be frozen, refrigerated, or baked at once in 275-degree oven for about 30 minutes.

Really a great sandwich!!

Marjorie Baxla, Greenfield, Ohio

PIZZA BURGERS

1 pound ground beef
1/2 cup chopped onion
1 (15-ounce) jar pizza sauce
1 (4-ounce) can sliced mushrooms,
drained

1 teaspoon oregano
1-1/2 cups shredded mozzarella
cheese
8 hamburger buns, sliced

Brown meat and onion; drain. Stir in sauce, mushrooms, and oregano. Refrigerate several hours. Heat oven to 400 degrees. Stir cheese into meat mixture and spoon onto sliced buns. Sprinkle each Pizza Burger with moz-zarella cheese before placing in oven to bake. Bake at 400 degrees for 10 minutes on cookie sheet.

Sandy Marqueling, Fort Wayne, Ind

SUPER TUNA MELT

1 can chunk light tuna (packed in
vegetable oil or water)
1/2 small onion, chopped
1 hard-cooked egg, chopped
1/2 teaspoon sweet pickle relish
1 or 2 tablespoons mayonnaise
according to your taste
1/4 teaspoon celery seed
Dash of salt
Dash of pepper
Velveeta cheese slices
Spicy brown mustard
Hamburger buns

Combine tuna with first 7 ingredi-ents. Mix well. Spread bottom of hamburger buns lightly with the mustard. Divide the Velveeta slices in half; place halves on top of mus-tard. Spread tuna mixture on top of cheese. Wrap hamburger buns with aluminum foil and bake in oven or toaster oven for approximately 10 minutes or until cheese is melted. Very tasty!

Cheryl Whitehouse, Robbinsville, N.Y.

GEMINI FRANKBURGERS
Makes 6

1 (10-3/4-ounce) can Campbell's
tomato soup
1-1/2 pounds ground beef
1 teaspoon salt
1-1/2 teaspoons chili powder
6 frankfurter buns, split and toasted
6 frankfurters, split lengthwise
1/2 cup chopped onion
2 tablespoons butter or margarine

1 tablespoon brown sugar
1/2-1 teaspoon vinegar

Mix 1/3 cup soup, beef, salt, 1 teaspoon chili powder; spread evenly on buns (cover edges). Firmly press frankfurters into meat. Place on broiler pan. Bake 12-15 minutes at 450 degrees. Cook onion and remain-ing chili powder in butter; add rest of soup and ingredients; heat. Serve over burgers.

This is good and especially great for teens after a game or a special Sunday-night supper.

Mrs. Melvin Habiger, Spearville, Kan.

FILLED HAMBURGERS
Serves 4

1 pound lean, ground beef
1 egg
1/4 cup fine dry bread crumbs
1 small minced onion
Salt and pepper to taste
2 teaspoons Worcestershire sauce
1 (8-ounce) can tomato sauce
1/2 teaspoon garlic powder

In a large bowl place all ingredi-ents in order. Mix well. Divide meat mixture into 8 equal portions; shape each portion into a patty 1/4 to 1/2-inch thick.

Stir together:
1 cup (4 ounces) shredded sharp
Cheddar cheese
1/4 cup shredded Swiss cheese
2 tablespoons catsup
1/2 teaspoon margarine, softened
1/2 teaspoon prepared mustard
1 tablespoon finely chopped green
onion, top included

Spread even amounts of filling over 4 of the patties to within 1/4 inch of edges. Dampen edge of each patty with a little water. Top with remain-ing patties and pinch edges of meat together to completely enclose the cheese mixture. Heat a large skillet and cook hamburgers by cooking over medium-high heat to desired done-ness. Meanwhile, have ready 4 ham-burger rolls on a bed of lettuce and set each hamburger on a roll and serve hot.

Marie Fusaro, Manasquan, NJ

Sauces & TOPPINGS

MOCK WHIPPED CREAM
Makes 2 cups

1/2 cup skim milk
1/2 cup nonfat dry milk powder
1/8 teaspoon cream of tartar
4 teaspoons lemon juice
2 teaspoons sugar (optional)
1/2 teaspoon vanilla extract (optional)

Put the skim milk in a small metal bowl; set in the freezer, and let stand just until ice crystals begin to form — about 15 minutes. Remove from the freezer and add the dry milk powder and cream of tartar. With a hand electric mixer, whip the mixture at high speed until foamy. Beat in 1 teaspoon of the lemon juice and continue beating until the mixture begins to thicken. Beat in another teaspoon of the lemon juice and, if desired, the sugar, and continue beating until the mixture peaks softly. Add the remaining 2 teaspoons lemon juice and continue whipping to stiff peaks. Fold in the vanilla extract, if desired, and serve immediately as a dessert topping.

Sally Joy, Tulsa, Okla.

HONEY BUTTER

Mix equal amounts of *soft butter* and *honey* until smooth. Add the grated *rind of 1 lemon*. Store in refrigerator in a tightly covered dish. Keeps for 4-6 weeks. Good on pancakes.

Lillian Smith, Montreal, Quebec

YOGURT-DILL SAUCE
Serves 6

1-1/2 cups non-fat, plain yogurt
2-1/2 teaspoons low-sodium dijon mustard

Combine all ingredients and mix well. Chill. Serve with cold poached salmon or fresh vegetable crudite. Note: This sauce may be served warm over fish or poultry, be careful not to heat it too quickly or the sauce will "break" (separate into water and yogurt). It heats best on a low setting in the microwave oven or over a double boiler, with constant stirring. (25 calories per serving)

SATIN FRUIT SAUCE

1 (3-1/2-ounce) package vanilla pudding (not instant)
1-1/4 cups water
2 tablespoons lemon juice
1 (10-ounce) package frozen strawberries, peaches, or raspberries
1 tablespoon butter

Pour pudding mix in saucepan; blend in water. Add frozen fruit, breaking apart with fork. Cook over medium heat until mixture comes to a boil and is thickened. Remove from heat. Stir in lemon juice and butter. Serve over cake or ice cream, either warmed or chilled.

Brenda Peery, Tannersville, Va.

MOCK "TWINKIE" FILLING

1 cup milk
1 cup sugar
1/2 cup Crisco
1 teaspoon vanilla
5 tablespoons flour
1/2 teaspoon salt
1/2 cup butter

Mix flour with milk; boil until thick then cool. After mixture has cooled, beat until fluffy (10-15 minutes). Add rest of ingredients, beating well, as you add them individually, one at a time. Spread the filling between layers of cake. Delicious!!
Note: The longer the milk and flour mixture is beaten, the fluffier the finished filling will be.

Susie Caldwell, Lima, Ohio

CHIVE-CHEESE SAUCE

1 (3-ounce) package chive cream cheese
1/4 cup mayonnaise
1/4 cup milk

Mash cheese in saucepan; stir in mayonnaise and milk. Heat over low heat, stirring until cheese is melted and sauce is smooth.

Plain cream cheese may be used instead of chive cream cheese; then add desired amount of green onions (plus some tops in 1/2-inch slices).

Serve on baked potatoes.

Edna Askins, Greenville. Texas

ZESTY MUSTARD SAUCE
Makes 1¼ cups

4 teaspoons butter
1 teaspoon instant chicken bouillon
2 tablespoons flour
2 tablespoons coarsely ground, Dijon-style prepared mustard
1 cup skim milk
3 tablespoons low-fat lemon yogurt
½ teaspoon Worcestershire sauce
¼ teaspoon sugar

Place butter and instant bouillon in a 4-cup glass measuring cup. Microwave on HIGH (100 percent) for 30–40 seconds. Stir in flour and mustard until smooth. Gradually stir in milk. Microwave on HIGH for 5–6 minutes until thick and bubbly. Stir every minute. Stir in yogurt, Worcestershire sauce and sugar. Serve warm over steamed fresh vegetables. (18 calories per serving)

Mabel Phillips, Dallas, Texas

CONEY ISLAND HOT DOG SAUCE

3 medium onions, chopped
2-1/2 pounds hamburger
1-1/2 teaspoons oregano
1-1/2 teaspoons cumin
2 tablespoons paprika
2 tablespoons chili powder
1-1/2 teaspoons celery salt
1-1/2 teaspoons garlic salt
1 tablespoon salt
1/2 teaspoon cinnamon

Chop onions and boil in enough water to cover; boil until completely cooked. Add spices. Break up hamburger into small pieces and put into onion mixture. Cook about 1 hour, stirring occasionally.

This is also great on hamburgers, as well as hot dogs!

Mrs. W.T. Gore, Aztec, N.M.

TOMATO MUSH– ROOM SAUCE

1 tablespoon olive oil
1 cup chopped onions
2 cups chopped celery
1 clove minced garlic
10 ounces sliced, fresh mushrooms
1 (6-ounce) can tomato paste
1 (32-ounce) can tomatoes

1 bay leaf
3 tablespoons snipped, fresh parsley
Pepper to taste
1/2-3/4 pound pasta
1/2 cup grated Parmesan cheese

Sauté onions, celery, and garlic in olive oil until tender. Add mushrooms and sauté lightly. Add tomato paste, tomatoes, bay leaf, parsley, and pepper; simmer for 30 minutes. Remove bay leaf. Top with Parmesan cheese.

Cheryl Santefort, South Holland, Ill.

CREAMY HOT SAUCE
Makes 1/2 cup

1/3 cup Heinz 57 Sauce
3 tablespoons dairy sour cream
1/2-3/4 teaspoon hot pepper sauce

Combine ingredients. Use as a dipping sauce for bite-size cooked chicken pieces, french fries, or tortilla chips.

Sharon Jones, Indianapolis, Ind.

WILDLY SCRUMPTIOUS BLACKBERRY SAUCE

1-1/2 cups sugar
1/3 cup cornstarch
4 cups fresh *or* frozen blackberries
1-1/2 tablespoons margarine
1 tablespoon fresh lemon juice
1 cup water

Combine all ingredients and cook over low heat. Stir with wire whip until consistency is smooth. Add more water, if desired.

MOCK CHOCOLATE SYRUP

4 cups brown sugar
2 cups cocoa
1/2 cup light corn syrup
4 cups granulated sugar
4 cups water
1/4 cup vanilla

Mix first 4 ingredients in a large pan. Add 2 cups of the water and mix well. Add remaining water. Bring to a rolling boil. Do be sure to watch this closely—it will very likely boil over. Boil for 5 minutes. Add vanilla. Pour into sterilized jars and seal. Will keep for about 8 months. Wonderful on ice cream, but you can use it to make hot cocoa or chocolate milk and much cheaper than those cans your children are always pestering you to buy!

Phyliss Dixon, Fairbanks, Alaska

SUZIE'S SWEET MUSTARD

5 tablespoons dry English mustard
10 tablespoons confectioners' sugar
Cider vinegar

Mix enough vinegar with the mustard and sugar to make a smooth paste. Stir until the sugar is completely dissolved.

Delicious on ham, cold cuts, and cheeses.

Agnes Ward, Erie, Pa.

CRANBERRY-MARMALADE SAUCE
Makes 3 cups

1 (14-ounce) can whole cranberry sauce
1 (8-ounce) jar 3-fruit marmalade (orange, lemon and grapefruit)

In a small mixing bowl, combine cranberry sauce and 3-fruit marmalade until well-blended. Cover and chill in the refrigerator before serving.

BARBECUE SAUCE

1/3 cup vinegar
1/4 cup ketchup
2 tablespoons salad oil
2 tablespoons soy sauce
1 tablespoon Worcestershire sauce
1 teaspoon mustard
1 teaspoon salt

Mix all ingredients together and allow mixture to come to a boil. This is a basic barbecue sauce to be used with all types of meats.

Jean Hugh, Pittsburgh, Pa.

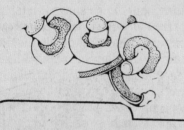

BARBECUE SAUCE

1/4 cup soy sauce
1/2 cup soybean sauce
1/2 teaspoon garlic salt
2 teaspoons sugar
1 teaspoon lemon juice
2 tablespoons cooking sherry
Dash of salt and pepper

Mix all ingredients together. Pour over 2 or 3 pieces of chicken. Refrigerate chicken in a covered dish for a few hours. Cook chicken on the barbecue grill.

M. Piccinni, Ozone Park, N.Y.

BARBECUE SAUCE

1 cup ketchup
1 chopped onion
1/2 clove garlic, finely cut
2 teaspoons chopped green chili peppers
1/2 small bay leaf
1/4 teaspoon pepper
1/3 cup lime juice
1/2 teaspoon salt
1/2 cup water
1 teaspoon dry mustard

Combine all ingredients in a 2-quart saucepan. Cover and heat to boiling; reduce heat and simmer for 40 minutes. Strain, forcing pulp through into the sauce.

MUSHROOM SAUCE
Makes 1-1/2 cups

1/2 pound fresh mushrooms, sliced
3 tablespoons melted margarine, divided
1 tablespoon all-purpose flour
3/4 cup half-and-half
1 teaspoon soy sauce

Sauté mushrooms in 2 tablespoons margarine; set aside. Combine flour and remaining margarine; place over low heat, stirring until smooth. Gradually add half-and-half; cook, stirring constantly, until smooth and thickened. Stir in soy sauce and mushrooms. Serve hot with toast or steak.

Barbara Beauregard-Smith, Northfield, S.A., Australia

MUSHROOM SAUCE
Makes 2-1/2 to 3 cups sauce

1/2 pound mushrooms, washed and thinly sliced
1 teaspoon chopped onion
1/2 teaspoon chopped parsley
6 tablespoons butter
4-5 tablespoons flour
1 cup stock or bouillon
1/4 cup sour cream
Salt to taste
1/2 teaspoon lemon juice
Butter for sautéing

Melt butter (about 2 tablespoons) and sauté onion and parsley. Add mushrooms and allow to cook for about 5 minutes. In another pan melt remaining butter; blend in flour, mixing well. Gradually add the stock and mix thoroughly. Blend in sour cream; then add salt. Pour sour cream-stock mixture into pan with mushrooms, stirring constantly, and allow to simmer gently for 15 minutes. Remove from heat and add lemon juice.

Agnes Ward, Erie, Pa.

LOW-CALORIE HOLLANDAISE SAUCE
Makes 1-1/2 cups

1 cup skim milk
2 tablespoons lemon juice
Dash red pepper
3 drops imitation butter flavoring
4 egg yolks
1/4 teaspoon salt
1-1/2 teaspoons cornstarch

Heat milk in saucepan until bubbles form around edge. Combine egg yolks, salt, red pepper, lemon juice, flavoring, and cornstarch in electric blender; cover and swirl until smooth. Slowly, add hot milk to mixture with blender on medium speed. Pour mixture into the saucepan in which milk was heated. Heat over medium heat until it reaches boiling, stirring often. Serve over Eggs Benedict or hot cooked vegetables of your choice. (45 calories per tablespoon)

Ruby Pate Bodkin, Jacksonville, Fla.

HERB AND HONEY SAUCE FOR CHICKEN

3/4 cup onion, finely chopped
1 clove garlic, minced
1/4 cup salad oil (or olive oil)
1/2 cup wine vinegar
2 tablespoons Worcestershire sauce
1 teaspoon dry mustard
1 teaspoon salt
1/4 teaspoon rosemary
1 (12-ounce) can pear nectar
1/4 cup honey
1 teaspoon prepared horseradish
1/2 teaspoon thyme
1/4 teaspoon pepper

Cook onions and garlic in hot oil until tender, but not brown. Add all remaining ingredients. Simmer uncovered for 5 minutes. Let cool, then pour over chicken and let it marinate for 3 hours minimum. When broiling chicken, use as a basting sauce. Heat leftover sauce and serve separately with chicken.

Sue Thomas, Casa Grande, Ariz.

CRAN-RASPBERRY CHOCOLATE SAUCE

7 ounces semi sweet chocolate
1 cup whipping cream
1/4 cup cran-raspberry juice concentrate, thawed, undiluted

In double boiler over medium heat, combine chocolate, whipping cream, and cran-raspberry juice concentrate until well blended and heated through. Serve hot or warm.

INSTANT HOT FUDGE SAUCE

Makes 1-1/2 cups

2 (4-ounce) bars semi sweet chocolate
3 tablespoons cream
1 to 4 tablespoons water

Melt chocolate bars over boiling water. Stir in cream, a tablespoon at a time. Stir until smooth and glossy. Remove from heat. Thin to desired consistency with 1 to 4 tablespoons water.

LEMON SAUCE

Makes 3/4 cup

Grated peel and juice of 1/2 lemon (about 1-1/2 tablespoons juice)
1 tablespoon butter
1/4 cup sugar
1 tablespoon flour
1/2 cup boiling water

Grate peel and squeeze lemon; set aside. In a small saucepan melt butter over low heat. In a custard cup thoroughly combine sugar and flour; add to melted butter. Over low heat whisk in water until smooth; stir in lemon

juice and peel. Stir over low heat until boiling; set aside to cool. Serve slightly warm. Keeps several days in refrigerator.

Dorothy E. Cornell, Elkton, Md.

PINE-COT SAUCE

Makes 2 cups

1 cup dried apricots
3/4 cup water
1/2 cup sugar
1 (8-1/2-ounce) can crushed pineapple, undrained

Place apricots and water in heavy saucepan and cook, covered, over very low heat until fruit is pulpy and falls apart when stirred. Add sugar and stir until dissolved. Add crushed pineapple with juice and bring mixture to a boil. Remove from heat. Chill. Stores well in refrigerator.

PEACH PRESERVES

Makes 6-1/2 pints

3-1/2 cups sugar
2 cups water
5 cups sliced, peeled, hard-ripe peaches
1/2 teaspoon ginger

Combine sugar and water; cook until sugar dissolves. Add peaches and cook rapidly until fruit becomes clear. Stir occasionally. Cover and let stand 12-18 hours in a cool place. Drain fruit and pack into hot jars, leaving 1/4-inch head space. Adjust caps. Process half-pints or pints, 20 minutes at 180-185 degree hot water bath.

Joy Shamway, Freeport, IL

PEAR CONSERVE

8 cups pears, sliced thin
6 cups sugar
1 small can crushed pineapple
1-1/2 cups chopped nuts
1/2 cup cherries (canned or bottled)

Peel pears and slice thin, measuring after preparation. Combine with sugar and let stand overnight. Add pineapple and simmer until pears are soft. If syrup is not as heavy as desired, remove fruit; boil down to desired consistency or add a little pectin, perhaps a teaspoon if preferred, to thicken quickly.

Add cherries and nuts to mixture. Bring to a rolling boil and put into sterilized canning jars. Seal with rings and lids that have been sterilized.

Good on breads, muffins, poultry, and meats.

Deborah Hooker, San Bernardino, CA

BLUEBERRY-PEACH CONSERVE

1 medium-size navel orange
1 lemon
2-1/2 pounds firm ripe peaches, peeled and sliced
1 pint fresh blueberries
1/3 cup granulated sugar
1/2 cup grape juice
1 tablespoon plus 1 teaspoon Sweet 'N Low® granulated sugar substitute

Peel orange and lemon; finely chop rind. Remove pits from pulp and chop pulp. Place fruit, their juices and rind in large pot. Add peaches and blueberries; sprinkle with sugar and let stand 30 minutes. Add grape juice and Sweet 'N Low. Over medium heat, bring to a boil; boil, stirring frequently, 35 to 45 minutes or until fruit is thick and translucent.

Spoon into hot sterilized jars, allowing 1/4 inch headspace (or follow jar manufacturer's instructions if different). Wipe rims with clean cloth dipped in hot water. Close according to jar manufacturer's instructions and process in boiling-water bath 15 minutes. Makes four 8-ounce jars.

Calories: 15 per tablespoon

CHIMICHURRI (ARGENTINE PARSLEY SAUCE)

Makes 1 cup

1/4 cup red wine vinegar
1/3 cup olive oil
1/2 cup minced onion
1/4 cup minced parsley
1 large clove garlic, minced
1 teaspoon oregano
1 teaspoon pepper
Cayenne to taste
Salt to taste

Combine all ingredients in a bowl. Let stand at room temperature, cover, for 2 hours. Serve sauce over broiled meats, steaks, sausages, etc. This is very delicious!
Agnes Ward, Erie, Pa.

CELERY GARLIC SAUCE FOR BROILED FISH

1 cup butter or margarine
1/3 cup finely chopped celery
2 tablespoons finely chopped onion
2 cloves garlic, crushed
3 tablespoons finely chopped parsley
Salt and Pepper

Melt butter in saucepan. Sauté celery, onion, and garlic until tender and onion is transparent. Add remaining ingredients; simmer 10-15 minutes. Brush fish with half of sauce. Broil. Turn fish. Brush with other half of sauce. Fish is done when it flakes easily with a fork.
Kit Rollins, Cedarburg, Wis.

STRAWBERRY-RASP-BERRY SAUCE

Makes 2 cups

2 cups fresh strawberries, hulled
1 (10-ounce) package frozen raspberries, thawed and drained

Combine strawberries and raspberries and purée.

BUTTERSCOTCH MARSHMALLOW SAUCE

Makes 2 cups

1 cup firmly packed light brown sugar
2 tablespoons light corn syrup
2 tablespoons unsalted butter
1/2 cup heavy cream
1/4 teaspoon salt
1 teaspoon vanilla
1 cup miniature marshmallows

In heavy saucepan combine brown sugar, corn syrup, butter, cream and salt. Bring mixture to a boil, stirring until sugar is dissolved and boil, undisturbed, until it registers 235 degrees on a candy thermometer. Stir in vanilla and let mixture cool for 10 minutes. Stir in the marshmallows and serve sauce warm over vanilla or chocolate ice cream. Sauce keeps, covered, in refrigerator up to 1 week. Reheat sauce before serving.

CHERRY SAUCE

1-1/2 pounds fresh sweet cherries, stems and pits removed
1/2 cup white grape juice
1 tablespoon lemon juice
1 whole cinnamon stick
1 teaspoon Sweet 'N Low granulated sugar substitute

In medium-size saucepan over medium heat, combine all ingredients; cook, stirring frequently, 35 to 40 minutes or until slightly thickened. Cool and pack in freezer containers or sterilized jelly jars. Seal and cool completely; freeze. Makes two 8-ounce freezer containers or jars.

Serve over ice milk, fresh fruit, angel food cake or sponge cake.
Calories: 75 per 1/4 cup.

PRALINE SAUCE

1 cup firmly packed dark brown sugar
1/2 cup chopped pecans
3 tablespoons boiling water
2 teaspoons butter
Ice cream (flavor of your choice)

Combine sugar, nuts, boiling water, and butter in small saucepan and bring to a rolling boil. Remove from heat and cool. Cover and refrigerate.

CHOCOLATE PEANUT BUTTER SAUCE

Makes 3/4 cup

1/2 cup water
1/3 cup sugar
1 (1-ounce) square unsweetened chocolate
1 tablespoon light corn syrup
1/8 teaspoon salt
1/4 cup smooth or chunky peanut butter
1/4 teaspoon vanilla
Vanilla ice cream

Combine water, sugar, chocolate, corn syrup, and salt in medium saucepan. Bring to a boil over medium heat, stirring constantly until sugar dissolves and chocolate melts. Reduce heat to low and simmer 3 minutes. Remove from heat and whisk in peanut butter and vanilla. Serve warm over vanilla ice cream.

BLENDER CARAMEL SAUCE

Makes 1-1/4 cups

3/4 cup brown sugar
2 tablespoons soft butter or margarine
1/4 teaspoon salt
1/2 cup hot evaporated milk

Put all ingredients into blender container. Cover and process at *mix* until sugar is dissolved.

PANCAKE SYRUP

2 cups sugar
3-1/3 cups Grandma's molasses
3 cups water
2 tablespoons cornstarch

Combine all ingredients together in saucepan. Bring to a boil and cook for about 2 minutes, or until slightly thickened. Inexpensive to make; ready-made syrup costs much more!!

Bernice Magnant, New Bedford, MA

MANGO-PEACH CHUTNEY

1-1/2 cups cider vinegar (5% acetic acid)
1/2 cup water
1/2 cup brown sugar, packed to measure
3 tablespoons Sweet 'N Low granulated sugar substitute, or to taste
2-1/2 pounds peaches, peeled, pitted and diced (about 5 cups)
3 mangoes (about 2-1/2 pounds), peeled and cubed (about 3-1/2 cups)
1/2 cup golden raisins
1 tablespoon lime juice
1-1/2 teaspoons ground cinnamon
1-1/2 teaspoons grated lime rind
1-1/2 teaspoons dry mustard powder
1 teaspoon salt
1/2 teaspoon ground ginger
1/4 teaspoon garlic powder

In large heavy saucepan over high heat, bring vinegar, water, brown sugar and Sweet 'N Low to a boil. Reduce heat to low; add remaining ingredients and cook, stirring, 1 to 1-1/4 hours or until mixture is thick and has texture of preserves. Taste for sweetness; add more Sweet 'N Low, if desired.

Spoon into hot sterilized jars, allowing 1/4 inch headspace (or follow jar manufacturer's instructions if different). Wipe rims with clean cloth dipped in hot water. Close according to jar manufacturer's instructions and process in boiling-water bath 20 minutes. Make 3 pints or 6 half pints.

Calories: 20 per tablespoon

SPICED PLUM SPREAD

3-1/2 pounds ripe red plums, pitted and quartered
1/2 cup unsweetened apple juice
1/4 cup honey
2 tablespoons plus 2 teaspoons Sweet 'N Low granulated sugar substitute
1 teaspoon bottled lemon juice
2 whole cinnamon sticks
8 whole cloves

In medium-size saucepan over medium heat, combine all ingredients. Cook, stirring frequently, 40 to 45 minutes or until thickened. Remove cinnamon sticks and cloves. Spoon into hot sterilized jars, allowing 1/4 inch headspace (or follow jar manufacturer's instructions if different). Wipe rims with clean cloth dipped in hot water. Close according to jar manufacturer's instructions and process in boiling-water bath 15 minutes. Makes three 8-ounce jars.

Calories: 30 per tablespoon

CHEESY CORN SPREAD

Makes 3-1/2 cups)

1 (12-ounce) package (3 cups) shredded sharp Cheddar cheese
1/2 cup dairy sour cream
1/2 cup mayonnaise or salad dressing
1/4 cup finely chopped onion
1/2 teaspoon salt
1 (12-ounce) can "Green Giant Mexicorn," drained (golden sweet corn with sweet peppers)

Bring cheese to room temperature. In large bowl, crumble cheese with fork or blend with mixer to form small bits. Mix in remaining ingredients, except corn, until well blended. Stir in corn. Cover; chill several hours or overnight. Can be stored in refrigerator up to 1 week. Serve with raw vegetables or crackers.

Agnes Ward, Erie, Pa.

CHEESE & HERB BUTTER

1/4 cup butter
1/4 teaspoon basil
1/4 teaspoon oregano
1/4 teaspoon marjoram
1/4 teaspoon thyme
Dash of Worcestershire sauce
Dash of Tabasco sauce
1 tablespoon grated Parmesan cheese

Melt butter; remove from heat and stir in remaining ingredients. Serve sauce with meat and vegetables, fish, or bread.

Stella Trulove, Somerville, Texas

ONION AND HERB BUTTER

1/4 cup butter
1 teaspoon onion powder
1 teaspoon basil
1 teaspoon chervil
1/2 teaspoon oregano

Melt butter; add onion powder. Remove from heat and stir in remaining herbs.

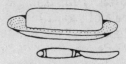

TARRAGON VINEGAR

2 cups white, cider or wine vinegar
1 teaspoon crushed dried tarragon

Bring vinegar to a boil. Add tarragon. Pour into heat-safe container, close tightly. No need to refrigerate. Let stand a few days and strain before using.

Agnes Buxton, Oklahoma City, Okla.

SWEET MUSTARD

1/4 cup mustard seed
6 tablespoons dry mustard
1 tablespoon turmeric
1-1/4 cups boiling water
1/2 cup dry white wine
1/4 cup vinegar
1 tablespoon peanut oil
1/4 cup sugar
1/2 cup finely chopped onion
2 teaspoons finely minced garlic
1/4 teaspoon allspice
1/4 teaspoon cinnamon
1/4 teaspoon ground cloves
3 tablespoons cornstarch

Combine mustard seeds, mustard, turmeric, and water in a small bowl. Let stand one hour. Meanwhile, combine vinegar, wine, oil, sugar, onion, garlic, allspice, cinnamon, and cloves in a saucepan. Bring to a boil and simmer five minutes. Pour mixture into a blender with cornstarch and blend for two minutes. Spoon and scrape the mixture back into a double boiler and cook for five minutes or until thick, stirring constantly.

HOT HONEY MUSTARD

3/4 cup cider vinegar
3/4 cup dry mustard
1/2 cup honey
2 eggs

Combine mustard and vinegar in small bowl. Blend well; cover and let stand overnight. Next day combine the mustard mixture, honey, and eggs in a small saucepan. Cook over low heat, stirring constantly, until thickened, about seven minutes. Cool. Refrigerate, covered, up to several weeks. This is great brushed on ham steak, just before broiling, or spoon thickly over brie that has had the rind removed. Sprinkle with almonds and heat at 400 degrees until the cheese is soft. Serve with French bread.

ALL-PURPOSE HERB BLEND
Makes 1/4 cup

1 tablespoon onion powder
1 teaspoon black pepper
1 tablespoon dried oregano
1 tablespoon parsley flakes
1-1/2 teaspoons tarragon
1-1/2 teaspoons basil

Blend all ingredients well. Store in tightly covered jar. Serve with poultry, meats, roasts, salads and vegetables.

SENSATIONAL SEASONING

1 (26-ounce) box of salt
1-1/2 ounce ground black pepper
2 ounces pure garlic powder
1 ounce chili powder
1 ounce MSG (or Accent)
2 ounces ground red pepper

Combine above ingredients and mix well. Store in airtight container. Use the seasoning as you would salt. Great on eggs, hamburger, and vegetables.

Sharon McClatchey, Muskogee, Okla

MUSHROOM GRAVY
(Low fat and low salt)

3 tablespoons arrowroot (thickener)
1 large chopped onion
1 pound sliced mushrooms
4 cups water
1 package no-oil salad dressing mix (preferably one with garlic and cheese)
2 tablespoons low-sodium soy sauce

Make a paste by stirring some of the cold water into the thickener until a creamy consistency is reached. Sauté onion in water in a non-stick pan and add the mushrooms. Stir until browned or beginning to cook. Cover with remaining water; add the salad dressing mix and soy sauce. When very hot, stir in the thickener. Continue to stir until smooth. Allow to

boil lightly. Remove from heat and cover.

Susan L. Wiener, Spring Hill, FL

CALICO RELISH
Makes 2-1/2 quarts

2 cups sliced cauliflower flowerets
2 carrots, cut into julienne strips
1 green pepper, cut into strips
10-12 green beans
1 zucchini, sliced
1 small jar stuffed olives
3/4 cup wine vinegar
1/4 cup olive oil
1 tablespoon sugar
1 teaspoon salt
1/2 teaspoon oregano
1/4 teaspoon pepper
1/4 cup water
Cherry tomatoes (optional)

In large pan, combine all ingredients except tomatoes. Bring to a boil and simmer covered, 5 minutes. Cool and let marinate at least 24 hours. Store in refrigerator. Cherry tomatoes may be added just before serving.

Marcella Swigert, Monroe City, MO

UNCOOKED RELISH

1 pint sweet red peppers, chopped
1 pint sweet green peppers, chopped
1 quart cabbage, chopped
1 pint white onions, chopped
2 teaspoons celery seed
4 cups sugar
1 quart cider vinegar
1 or 2 hot peppers (optional)
5 tablespoons salt

Put each vegetable through food chopper, using coarse blade. If vegetables are covered with liquid, drain off and discard liquid. Measure each vegetable after chopping. Mix vegetables with salt and let stand overnight. Next morning, drain off and discard all liquid. Add spices, sugar, and vinegar to drained vegetables and mix well. Pack into sterilized jars and seal at once. This relish is very good on hot dogs or hamburgers.

Helen Taugher, Nicholson, PA

Vegetable
DELIGHTS

CRUMB-TOPPED TOMATOES

1/2 cup butter
1 medium onion, chopped
2 cups chopped fresh or canned tomatoes
1 teaspoon salt
1 tablespoon sugar
1/2 teaspoon black pepper
2 cups unflavored bread crumbs

Preheat oven to 375 degrees. In skillet melt 2 tablespoons of the butter; add onion. Cook until clear, but not brown. In bowl mix onion, tomatoes, salt, sugar and pepper. Butter a medium-size baking dish. Place a layer of tomatoes. Mix and layer bread crumbs. Repeat, alternating layers and ending with crumbs. Dot top surface with remaining butter. Bake 40 minutes until bubbly and browned on top.

Sharon McClatchey, Muskogee, Okla.

GREEN BEAN PUFF

2 (10-ounce) packages frozen French-style green beans
1/4 cup diced celery
3/4 cup mayonnaise
1 teaspoon prepared mustard
1/4 teaspoon salt
1 teaspoon vinegar
1/4 cup milk
1 egg white, stiffly beaten
1/4 teaspoon paprika

Cook and drain beans. Combine hot beans and celery in a 5-cup casserole. Blend mayonnaise, mustard, salt, vinegar and milk. Fold egg white into mixture. Pile lightly on top of beans. Sprinkle with paprika. Bake at 400 degrees for 15 minutes, or until sauce puffs and browns.

Kit Rollins, Cedarburg, Wis.

ARTICHOKE SQUARES

2 jars marinated artichoke hearts
1 medium onion, chopped
1 clove of garlic, chopped
1-1/2 pounds cheddar cheese, grated
4 eggs, well-beaten
1/2 teaspoon salt
Pepper to taste
1/2 teaspoon oregano
Dash of Tabasco sauce
1/4 cup bread crumbs

Drain artichokes, reserving oil from one jar. Chop artichokes into small pieces. Sauté artichokes, onion, and garlic in reserved oil until tender. Combine eggs, cheese, seasonings, and artichoke mixture. Pour into 9x13-inch baking dish. Top with bread crumbs. Bake at 350 degrees for about 30 minutes or until knife inserted in center comes out clean. Cut into squares; arrange on serving tray. Serve hot.

Marcella Swigert, Monroe City, Mo.

HERBED SPINACH
Serves 4

2 tablespoons melted butter
1 (10-ounce) package frozen spinach, thawed
3 shredded lettuce leaves
1 teaspoon sugar
1/2 teaspoon chopped parsley
1/4 teaspoon salt
1/8 teaspoon pepper

In a saucepan, add spinach to butter. Cover; cook slowly for 2 minutes. Add remaining ingredients. Recover; cook slowly for 15 minutes until spinach is tender.

CORN AND CREAM CHEESE CASSEROLE
Serves 4

1   large can whole-kernel corn, undrained
1   (3-ounce) package cream cheese with chives
    Butter, as desired

Cook corn until all juice is gone. Stir in butter; add cream cheese. Heat, stirring constantly until cheese is melted.

Edna Askins, Greenville, Texas

BAKED RICE AND MUSHROOMS

1 can onion soup
1 can chicken broth
1 (4-ounce) can mushrooms
1 stick butter
1-1/2 cups regular rice (no Minute Rice)

Mix all the above ingredients together and bake at 350 degrees for 1 hour.

Brenda Peery, Tannerville, Va.

GREEN BEAN AND BACON COMBO
Serves 4

1 (9-ounce) package frozen cut green beans
4 slices bacon, cut into small pieces
2 slices bread, cut into 1/2-inch cubes
1/3 cup condensed cream of mushroom soup

Cook green beans following directions on package; drain. Put bacon into a 1-1/2-quart glass baking dish. Cover with a paper towel. Cook in microwave oven for about 2-1/2 minutes on HIGH, or until browned. Remove bacon from dish. Add bread cubes to bacon fat in dish; mix well. Cook, uncovered, in microwave oven for 2 minutes on HIGH; stir once. Mix bacon with the beans in casserole; spoon undiluted soup over beans and top with bread cubes. Cover with waxed paper. Heat in microwave oven to serving temperature, 3–4 minutes on HIGH.

Sharon Lemasters, Morgantown, W.V.

CUCUMBER COMBO

4 large cucumbers
1/4 teaspoon salt
1/8 teaspoon pepper
1/4 teaspoon nutmeg
1-1/2 teaspoons onion, grated
1 teaspoon fresh lemon juice
1 tablespoon water
1/2 cup soft bread crumbs
1 tablespoon butter or margarine

Wash and score 4 large cucumbers; do not peel. Remove seeds; cut into 1/2-inch cubes. In a generously buttered ovenproof casserole, layer cucumber cubes; mix with the next 6 ingredients. Scatter 1/2 cup soft bread crumbs over all; dot with 1 tablespoon butter. Repeat layers until casserole is full; end with bread crumbs; cover. Bake at 350 degrees for 40 minutes. Uncover; bake 15 minutes longer, or until top is nicely browned.
Gwen Campbell, Sterling, Va.

CHEESY CRUMB TOMATOES
Serves 4

4 tomatoes
1/3 cup dry bread crumbs
2 tablespoons butter
2 tablespoons grated Parmesan cheese
1/2 teaspoon salt
Dash pepper

Cut tomatoes in half crosswise; arrange cut side up on microwave-safe plate. Set aside. In small bowl, combine bread crumbs and butter; microwave on HIGH, uncovered, for 3–4 minutes, or until golden brown, stirring frequently. Stir in cheese and seasonings. Sprinkle crumb mixture over each tomato half. Microwave on HIGH, uncovered, for 3–4 minutes, or until hot.

Jen Lien, Stoughton, Wis.

TOMATO-TOPPED CAULIFLOWER
Serves 4

1 1/2–2-pound head cauliflower
Water
Salt

Sauce:
1 onion, chopped
3 tablespoons butter *or* margarine
1 clove garlic, minced
1/4 teaspoon dried basil
1/4 teaspoon dried thyme
1/2 teaspoon dried oregano
1 (16-ounce) can tomato sauce
1 cup cheddar cheese, grated
1/2 cup Parmesan cheese, grated

Place cauliflower in large pot with water and salt; simmer 15 minutes. In a saucepan, melt butter; add onion, garlic, herbs and tomato sauce; cook until thickened. Place cauliflower on warmed serving dish; pour hot sauce over top; sprinkle with cheeses.

Gwen Campbell, Sterling, Va.

SPINACH–ONION QUICHE
Serves 6

2 cups finely chopped sweet onions
1/4 cup butter
1 (10-ounce) package frozen chopped spinach
3/4 cup grated Swiss cheese
3 eggs
1 cup milk
1 teaspoon salt

1/8 teaspoon pepper
Dash nutmeg
1 unbaked 9-inch pie shell

Sauté onions slowly in butter. Cook spinach according to package directions. Drain thoroughly. Combine onion, spinach, and Swiss cheese. Beat eggs. Blend in milk and seasonings. Combine with spinach mixture. Bake pie shell. Pour in egg-vegetable mixture. Bake in 375 degree-oven, 35-40 minutes, or until knife inserted in center comes out clean.

BRUSSELS SPROUTS ROYAL

2 (10-ounce) packages brussels sprouts, halved
1 (5-ounce) can water chestnuts, drained (save liquid)
½ cup snip parsley
1 teaspoon sugar
½ cup margarine

Add sufficient water to liquid to make 1 cup. Pour sugar and parsley into saucepan with liquid. Bring to boil; add brussels sprouts. Simmer, covered, for 8–10 minutes. Drain. Add margarine and diced water chestnuts. Add pearl onions and soft buttered bread crumbs, if desired. No one will ever dare say they do not care for brussels sprouts.

HAM, EGG, AND VEGETABLE BAKE
Serves 6

2 medium potatoes, peeled, cooked, and thinly sliced
1/4 cup cooked, minced ham
3 hard-cooked eggs, sliced
1 small head cauliflower, cooked and liquid reserved
1 tablespoon flour
1 tablespoon butter
Salt and pepper to taste
1/4 cup grated cheese

Grease a baking pan. Spread a layer of potato slices over bottom. Sprinkle with minced ham. Spread egg slices over ham. Cover with crumbled cauliflower and one more layer of potatoes. In a small saucepan soften the butter and stir in flour. Mix cauliflower liquid and skim milk to make one cup. Add gradually, stirring constantly. Cook over low heat until sauce thickens slightly. Season to taste and pour over mixture in baking pan. Sprinkle with grated cheese and bake in 350–degree oven for 30 minutes. (145 calories per serving)

Judy Codenys, LaGrange, Texas

SUMMER VEGETABLE MEDLEY
Serves 6

2-3 medium zucchini, washed and coin-sliced
1 cup fresh mushrooms, washed and sliced
1/4 cup chopped onion
1/4 cup chopped green pepper
3 tablespoons butter or margarine
2 tomatoes, coarsely chopped
2 tablespoons grated Parmesan cheese
1/4 teaspoon garlic powder
Salt and pepper to taste

Combine zucchini, mushrooms, onion, green pepper and butter in 1-1/2–quart glass/ceramic casserole. Cover and microwave 8-9 minutes, or until vegetables are tender–crisp, stirring once during cooking. Add toma-toes, cheese, and seasonings. Cover and microwave 2-3 minutes or until heated through.

Mrs. Olen Begly, West Salem, Ohio

CRUSTY BREAD GRATIN OF VEGETABLES
Serves 8

1 tablespoon vegetable oil
1 tablespoon olive oil
1 onion, chopped
1/2 teaspoon garlic, minced
1 pound zucchini, cut into 1/2-inch slices
2 cups cauliflower florets
3 medium-size fresh tomatoes
1 (28-ounce) can crushed tomatoes
1/4 teaspoon salt
1/4 teaspoon pepper
1/2 cup Fontina cheese, shredded
4 slices French bread, halved and buttered

Heat oils in skillet; saute onion and garlic until tender. Add zucchini and cauliflower; saute 5 minutes. Add fresh and crushed tomatoes, salt, and pepper. Cook covered, until vegetables are tender. Pour vegetable mixture into oven baking dish; place halves of buttered French bread along edge of pan; cut side down, buttered side in. Sprinkle cheese on top of vegetable mixture; return to 350-degree oven for 5 minutes to melt cheese.

Gwen Campbell, Sterling, VA

GREEN VEGGIE BAKE
Serves 6-8

2 tablespoons butter or margarine
1/2 cup chopped onion
1 teaspoon salt
1/4 teaspoon pepper
4 ounces sour cream
1 to 1-1/2 tablespoons cornstarch
1 cup broccoli
1 cup green beans
1 cup peas
1 cup American or cheddar cheese, grated
2 tablespoons butter or margarine, melted
1 cup Ritz (salad) crackers

Cook onion in 2 tablespoons butter until tender. Add cornstarch, salt, pepper, and sour cream; mix well. Stir in green vegetables. Put in casserole dish, top with grated cheese. Combine remaining 2 tablespoons butter and cracker crumbs; place on top of cheese. Bake at 350 degrees for 30 minutes. This recipe was created for those "timid" green–vegetable eaters. Also great for leftovers.

Beth Zellars, Franklin, Ind.

TWEEDLE DEE BEETS

2 teaspoons cornstarch
1 teaspoon sugar
1/4 teaspoon salt
Dash ground cloves
3/4 cup canned orange juice
1 tablespoon margarine or butter
1 (16-ounce) can slivered beets, drained

Measure cornstarch, sugar, salt, and cloves into a medium size saucepan. Stir in orange juice. Add margarine and heat to boiling, stirring constantly to keep sauce smooth. Add beets to sauce. Heat slowly 5 minutes.

Roberta Neely, Riviera, Texas

SAVORY BEETS
2 servings

1 tablespoon butter or margarine
2 teaspoons cider vinegar
1/4 teaspoon salt
1/4 cup sugar
1/8 teaspoon dry mustard
Few drops Worcestershire sauce
3 or 4 medium beets, cooked and skinned

In a small saucepan, melt butter. Add vinegar, salt, sugar, dry mustard and Worcestershire sauce. Set over low heat; mix well with rubber spatula. Slice in beets; toss to mix; cook until beets are heated through.

The remaining beets can be chilled whole and sliced when used. This is a flavorful way to serve precooked beets.

HARVARD CARROTS

Serves 6-8

2 pounds carrots, scraped
1/2 cup sugar
1-1/2 tablespoons cornstarch
1/4 cup vinegar
1/4 cup water
1/4 cup butter or margarine

Cut carrots into 1/2-inch crosswise slices and cook, covered, in a large saucepan with a small amount of boiling salted water for 15 minutes or until tender; drain. Combine sugar and cornstarch in a small saucepan; add vinegar and water. Cook over medium heat, stirring constantly until thickened. Add sauce and butter to carrots. Cook over low heat until butter melts and carrots are thoroughly heated.

Agnes Ward, Erie, PA

COPPER PENNIES

Serves 12-15

1 pound carrots
1 can tomato soup
1 cup sugar (or sugar substitute)
1/2 cup oil
1/2 cup vinegar
1 onion, chopped
1 green pepper, chopped

Slice and cook carrots. To cooked carrots, add onion and pepper. Add remaining ingredients. Allow flavors to blend several hours before serving. This relish will keep several weeks in refrigerator.

Elizabeth Dunn, Harrisonville, NJ

DILLED BABY CARROTS

Serves 6

3/4 cup white wine vinegar
1/4 cup water
1/4 cup honey
1/2 teaspoon dried whole dillweed
1/2 teaspoon mixed pickling spices

1 teaspoon salt
1/2 pound baby carrots, scraped
Sprigs of fresh dill (optional)

Combine first 6 ingredients in large saucepan; bring to a boil. Add carrots; cover; reduce heat and simmer 10-12 minutes or until crisp and tender. Remove from heat, and pour mixture into plastic container; set container in bowl of ice water to cool quickly. Chill, Serve with slotted spoon. Garnish with sprigs of dill, if desired.

Marcella Swigert, Monroe City, Mo.

CARROT RING SOUFFLE

Serves 8

12 medium carrots, cooked and mashed
1/2 to 2 tablespoons prepared horseradish
1/2 cup mayonnaise
2 tablespoons finely minced onion
3 eggs, well beaten
1/2 teaspoon salt

Mix all ingredients together. Pour into lightly oiled ring mold. Place mold in pan of hot water; bake at 350 degrees for 40 minutes. Turn out onto serving platter; fill center with cooked frozen peas or broccoli. Serve immediately.

Marcella Swigert, Monroe City, Mo.

ROLY-POLY CARROT MARBLES

Makes 35 balls

3 ounces cream cheese, softened
1 cup shredded Cheddar cheese
1 teaspoon honey
1 cup finely shredded carrots
3/4 cup finely chopped dry roasted peanuts

Combine the first 3 ingredients and blend. Stir in carrots. Chill 1 hour. Shape into balls using 1-1/2 teaspoons mixture for each marble. Chill until firm after rolling each marble in the chopped nuts.

RICE PILAF WITH FRESH MUSHROOMS

Serves 8

4 tablespoons butter or margarine
1 large onion, chopped
1 cup sliced mushrooms
1-1/2 cups regular long grain rice
3-1/4 cups water
1 envelope (3/4 ounce) au jus gravy mix
1/2 teaspoon salt
1/2 teaspoon oregano leaves

Melt butter in a 2 quart dutch oven. Cook onion, mushrooms, and rice in butter 4-5 minutes. Stir until rice is golden brown. Add remaining ingredients. Stir to dissolve gravy mix. Cover and bake in 350 degree oven 40 minutes or until all liquid is absorbed.
NOTE: Can be cooked, covered on top of stove over medium heat for 45 minutes. Also can be frozen in "boilable plastic bags" and reheated.

Mrs. Kit Rollins, Cedarburg, WI

MUSHROOM FRITTERS

Makes 12

1 cup packaged biscuit mix
1 cup chopped fresh mushrooms
2 tablespoons sliced green onions
1 tablespoon chopped pimiento
1/4 teaspoon salt
1/4 teaspoon celery seed
1 beaten egg yolk
1/4 cup dairy sour cream
1 egg white
Cooking oil for deep fat frying

In mixing bowl combine biscuit mix, mushrooms, onion, pimiento, salt, and celery seed. Mix together egg yolk and sour cream; stir into dry ingredients just until moistened. Beat egg white to stiff peaks; gently fold into mushroom mixture.

In heavy saucepan or deep fat fryer heat oil to 375 degrees. Drop batter by tablespoons into hot oil. Fry about 2 minutes or until golden brown, turning once. Drain on rack; serve hot.

Judy Fisk, Aberdeen, Wash.

CUCUMBERS SUPREME

2 medium cucumbers
1 large onion, sliced and separated
  into rings
1 cup Seven Seas Buttermilk
  Recipe Dressing
Green—onion tops for color

Peel and slice cucumbers. Peel, slice, and separate onions into rings. Mix and add Seven Seas Dressing. Garnish with green onion tops. Cucumbers could not be any tastier!! Also a very quick side dish to add to any meal.

Mrs. C. O. Shepardson, Apple Valley, Calif.

CABBAGE AU GRATIN

1-1/2 pounds cabbage
2 tablespoons butter
6 tablespoons flour
2 cups milk
1/4 pound grated cheese

Cut up cabbage and cook in salted water until tender. Make a white sauce with the butter, flour, and milk. Fill a greased baking dish with alternate layers of cabbage and white sauce. Cover top with cheese; bake in 350 degree oven for 20 minutes.

Joy Shamway, Freeport, IL

CRUNCHY CABBAGE

Serves 6-8

8 cups thinly sliced green cabbage
Boiling water
1 (10-3/4 ounce) can cream of
  celery soup
1/2 cup mayonnaise
1/2 cup milk
1/2 teaspoon salt
2 cups corn flakes
2 tablespoons butter or margarine,
  melted
1/2 pound shredded Cheddar
  cheese

Cook cabbage in boiling water 3-4 minutes. Drain. Combine next four ingredients in saucepan. Heat, just until hot. Toss corn flakes in the bottom of a 1-1/2 quart casserole, reserving some for top. Alternate layers of cabbage and sauce, ending with sauce layer. Top with remaining corn flakes and cheese. Bake at 375 degrees for 15 minutes. Serve hot.

Lori Gerich, Hayward, Wis.

FRENCH SKILLET CABBAGE

4-6 cups shredded cabbage
1 green pepper, shredded
2 large onions, sliced (not chopped)
2 cups diced-sliced celery
2 tomatoes, chopped
6-8 slices bacon
1/4-1/3 cup bacon drippings

Fry bacon; remove from skillet and crumble; reserve drippings. Combine all vegetables in large skillet with bacon drippings. Cover; cook over medium heat for 7-10 minutes or until vegetables are still crisp-cooked. Add bacon just before serving. Do not substitute for bacon or the drippings.

Alice Dick, Montpelier, Ohio

MARINATED CARROTS

Serves 8

1 bag large carrots
2 cloves garlic, sliced
1/2 teaspoon salt
1/2 teaspoon pepper
1/4 cup olive oil
2 tablespoons wine vinegar
1 teaspoon oregano

Scrape carrots; cut into thick slices. Boil in water 10 minutes, or until tender, taking care not to overcook. Drain well; place in bowl with garlic, salt, pepper, oil, vinegar, and oregano. Stir; mix well. Let stand in marinade twelve hours before serving.

Helen Robiolo, Union City, NJ

GLAZED CARROTS

Serves 6

2 cups sliced carrots
1 cup undiluted frozen orange juice
1/2 cup sugar
2 tablespoons cornstarch
Dash of nutmeg

Cook and drain carrots. Mix remaining ingredients; cook until thick. Pour sauce over carrots and let stand a short time. Serve hot.

Juanita Cecil, Mooresville, Ind.

FREEZE AHEAD GOLDEN GLAZED CARROTS

1-1/2 pounds baby carrots or 1-1/2
  pounds carrots, cut into strips
2 tablespoons all-purpose flour
1/4 cup light brown sugar
1/2 teaspoon salt
1/4 teaspoon thyme
1 tablespoon cider vinegar
1 tablespoon lemon juice
1/2 cup orange juice
Grated peel of one orange
2 tablespoons butter

Put carrots in saucepan. Pour boiling water over them and boil exactly 5 minutes. Drain thoroughly. Blend together flour, sugar, salt, and thyme. Add vinegar, juices, and orange rind. Bring to a boil while stirring, and continue stirring until creamy. Add butter and cook for 5 minutes over very low heat. Line a casserole with foil, leaving enough around the edges to cover. Add the blanched carrots to foil-lined casserole; pour sauce over them. Freeze uncovered. When frozen, cover completely with the foil. Remove package from casserole and put back into freezer. To serve, unwrap carrots, put back into same casserole. Bake, covered in a 350-degree oven for 40 minutes. Uncover for the last 15 minutes of baking. This is a very nice way to use the first baby carrots from the garden, and then when you serve them it brings back the "taste of summer."

Lillian Smith, Montreal, Que, Canada

10-MINUTE PECAN SQUASH
Serves 4-6

2 (12-ounce) packages frozen
   cooked squash
2 tablespoons butter
4 teaspoons instant breakfast drink
   (Tang)
1 teaspoon salt, if desired
Dash of pepper
6 tablespoons chopped pecans

Combine squash, butter, instant breakfast drink, salt, and pepper; cook as directed on package. Stir in pecans.
Karin Shea Fedders, Dameron, Md.

STUFFED PATTY-PAN SQUASH

4 patty-pan squash
4 slices bacon, cooked crisp
1/2 cup onion, chopped
3/4 cup bread crumbs
1/2 cup milk

Cook squash in boiling salted water for 15 minutes. Drain and cool. From the stem end cut a small slice; scoop out center, leaving 1/2-inch rim. Chop the squash which has been removed very finely. Sprinkle the squash cups lightly with salt. Sauté onion in bacon drippings; add crumbs, milk, and reserved squash. Fill cups; sprinkle crisp bacon on top. Place in flat casserole; bake at 350 degrees for 35 minutes.
Gwen Campbell, Sterling, Va.

SCALLOPED EGGPLANT
Serves 6

2 cups cooked eggplant
1/2 cup coarse cracker crumbs
4 tablespoons onion, minced
3 ounces cheese, grated
1 egg, beaten
1/2 cup milk
2 tablespoons margarine or butter

Peel eggplant and cut in 1-inch cubes. Cook in boiling salted water until tender, 8 minutes. Drain. Put eggplant, half of cracker crumbs, onion, and cheese in layers in buttered casserole. Combine egg and milk; pour over other ingredients. Dot with margarine and sprinkle with remaining cracker crumbs. Bake at 350 degrees for 30 minutes.
Suzan L. Wiener, Spring Hill, Fla.

FRENCH FRIED EGGPLANT

1 medium eggplant, peeled and sliced
   into 1/2 x 2-inch strips
1 cup pancake flour
1 egg
1/4 cup water
1/2 cup Parmesan cheese, grated
Salt
Vegetable oil

Beat egg and water together. Dip eggplant strips into egg mixture; then roll in pancake flour. Drop into hot oil and cook until golden brown, about 2 - 3 minutes. Drain on paper toweling and sprinkle lightly with salt and Parmesan cheese. Serve hot!!
Margean Gilger, Akron, OH

SAUCY ASPARAGUS

2 cans drained asparagus
1 cup cream of mushroom soup
1 can broken pieces mushrooms
1/4 pound squared American
   cheese
1-1/4 cups bread crumbs
1/2 stick butter

Grease a long flat casserole dish with butter. Place drained asparagus over bottom. Add cream of mushroom soup. Then add mushroom pieces and juice. Cover with American cheese squares. Put bread crumbs over cheese and thinly sliced butter over top. Bake 25 minutes in 350 degree oven or until it bubbles up through and crumbs are browned. Can use 2 chopped hard cooked eggs, if desired, for garnish.
Virginia Beachler, Logansport, Ind.

SAVORY SUCCOTASH
Serves 6-8

1 (1-pound) can (2 cups) French
   style green beans, drained
1 (1-pound) can (2 cups) whole
   kernel corn, drained
1/2 cup mayonnaise or salad
   dressing
1/2 cup shredded sharp cheese
1/2 cup chopped green pepper
1/2 cup chopped celery
2 tablespoons chopped onions
1 cup soft bread crumbs
2 tablespoons butter or margarine,
   melted

Combine first 7 ingredients; place in 9x9 inch casserole or 10x6x1-1/2 inch baking dish. Combine crumbs and butter; sprinkle over top. Bake in moderate oven 350 degrees for 30 minutes or until crumbs are toasted.
Helen Taugher, Nicholson, Pa.

VEGETABLE BAKE

1 can Veg-All, drained
1/2 cup chopped celery
1/2 cup chopped onion
1/2 cup sliced water chestnuts
1 cup mayonnaise
1 cup celery soup
1 cup shredded cheese
1/2 stick margarine
20 Ritz crackers

Mix together all ingredients except margarine and crackers in a 2-quart casserole. Bake for 45 minutes at 300 degrees. Melt margarine. Mix with crushed Ritz crackers. Sprinkle over the top. Bake 15 additional minutes.

This is truly a super vegetable casserole, a crowd pleaser for church potluck suppers and one which carries and travels well.
Mary Lou Allaman, Kirkwood, Ill.

BAKED GREEN BEANS IN TARRAGON CREAM

1-1/2 pounds green beans
1 tablespoon butter
1/2 teaspoon tarragon leaves
1/2 cup heavy cream
1/4 teaspoon salt
1/4 cup seasoned bread crumbs

Prepare green beans; cook in salted water about 12 minutes. Drain; arrange in shallow baking dish. Dot with butter. Mix 1/4 teaspoon tarragon leaves with heavy cream. Pour tarragon/cream mixture over all; sprinkle with seasoned bread crumbs. Bake in 350 degree oven until golden brown, about 12 minutes.

Mrs. Gwen Campbell, Sterling, VA

GLORIFIED BEANS
Serves 6

1-1/2 pounds ground beef
1-1/2 cups chopped onions
1 tablespoon dried mixed peppers
1-1/4 teaspoons salt
2 tablespoons brown sugar
1 tablespoon chili powder
1 - 12 ounce can tomato paste
1 cup water
1 can pork and beans in tomato sauce
1 can green limas
1 can red kidney beans

Brown ground beef. Combine with rest of ingredients. Bake in 350 degree oven for 1 hour.

Jeanie Blass, Richmond, VA

MOLASSES BAKED BEANS
Serves 8

1 (10-ounce) package frozen lima beans, thawed
1 (15-ounce) can kidney beans, drained
1 (15-ounce) can pinto beans, drained
1 (15-ounce) can baked beans, undrained
6 slices crispy fried bacon, crumbled
1/2 cup chopped onion
1/2 cup dark molasses
1/4 cup light brown sugar, packed
2 teaspoons dry mustard

Mix all ingredients in 2-1/2-quart casserole. Bake, uncovered, at 350 degrees for 1 hour, stirring occasionally.

Agnes Ward, Erie, PA

BAKED CREAMED SPINACH
Serves 6

1 cup heavy cream
3/4 cup grated Parmesan cheese
3 cups cooked, chopped spinach
1/2 teaspoon salt
Pepper
Nutmeg

Whip cream until stiff. Fold in 1/2 cup grated cheese. Then fold mixture into spinach and blend well. Season with salt; sprinkle pepper and nutmeg to taste. Put into buttered ovenproof pie plate. Sprinkle 1/4 cup grated cheese on top. Bake in 375 degree oven until slightly browned.

Mrs. Robert Combs, Fair Play, MO

SPECIAL SPINACH SQUARES
Serves 4

1 (10-ounce) package frozen chopped spinach
2 eggs
8 ounces sour cream
1 tablespoon onion, grated
1/2 cup Parmesan cheese, grated
1 tablespoon flour
2 tablespoons margarine
1/2 - 1 teaspoon salt
1/8 teaspoon pepper

Cook spinach as directed on package; drain well. Beat eggs; add to spinach. Blend in other ingredients. Place into greased 9 x 9-inch square dish. Bake, uncovered, at 350 degrees for 25-30 minutes. Cool slightly and cut into squares.

Mrs. George Franks, Millerton, Pa.

SPINACH LOAF
Serves 8-10

2 cups cooked spinach
1 cup soft bread crumbs
1 medium onion, minced
1/2 cup walnuts, chopped
1 teaspoon salt
1/8 teaspoon paprika
2 eggs, beaten
1/8 teaspoon pepper
1 tablespoon butter, melted
Milk or stock

Chop spinach; add crumbs, onions, nuts, seasonings and beaten eggs. Add enough milk or stock to form into a loaf. Place in a greased loaf pan and bake 30 minutes in a 375 degree oven.

Agnes Ward, Erie, PA

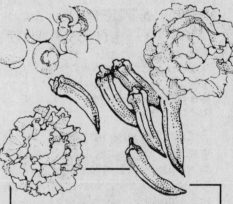

POPEYE POWER

2 (10-ounce) packages chopped frozen spinach, thawed and squeezed dry
1 cup uncooked long-grain wild rice
1 (10-1/2-ounce) can cream of celery soup
1 cup sour cream
1 medium onion, chopped
3/4 cup grated Monterey Jack cheese
1/2 cup grated mozzarella cheese
1/2 teaspoon oregano
1/2 teaspoon salt
1/2 teaspoon lemon juice
1/4 teaspoon garlic powder
1/4 teaspoon pepper

Mix all ingredients together well. Pour into a baking dish and bake at 350 degrees for 30-35 minutes or until it starts to bubble and browns around the outer edges.

Laura Hicks, Newport, Wash.

ALMANDINE ASPARAGUS
Serves 2

8 asparagus spears, shaved, cooked halfway and well drained
2-1/2 tablespoons mayonnaise
2-1/4 tablespoons sweet relish
2 pieces of fillet of sole (about 1/2 - 3/4 pounds of sole) wipe dry
1/2 tablespoon chili sauce
1/2 teaspoon margarine
2 tablespoons slivered almonds, toasted

Preheat oven to 350 degrees. In a lightly buttered baking dish lay the asparagus down gently. Mix the mayonnaise and relish; spoon over the asparagus. Place the fish fillets on top over the asparagus. Spoon the 1/2 tablespoon chili sauce over all and top with almonds. Dot with margarine. Bake for 35 minutes or until the fish flakes easily with a fork.

Marie Fusaro, Manasquan, NJ

GLORIFIED CABBAGE

1 small head cabbage, shredded
1 large onion, finely chopped
1 green pepper, finely chopped
1/4 cup green onion, chopped
2 ribs celery, sliced 1/8 inch think
2 tablespoons margarine
2 tablespoons vegetable oil
2 cloves garlic, minced
1/2 cup whipping cream
1 cup fresh bread crumbs (optional)
1-1/2 cups Cheddar cheese, shredded
2 tablespoons parsley, minced
1 teaspoon salt
1/2 teaspoon black pepper

Heat butter and oil in large saucepan; add onions, green pepper and celery; saute 5 minutes over low heat. Add cabbage and garlic; cook covered over low heat for 10 minutes or until cabbage is tender; stir in cream. Mix crumbs with 1/2 the cheese and the parsley; set aside. Add remaining cheese to cabbage mixture; stir in salt

and pepper. Turn into 1-1/2 quart buttered, shallow casserole. Top with crumbs-cheese mixture. Bake at 350 degrees for 20 minutes or until crumbs are golden and crisp.

Ella Evanicky, Fayetteville, TX

CREAMED CABBAGE VEGETABLE DISH FROM 1891
Serves 4

1 medium head cabbage
1 gill (1/2 cup) cream
1 ounce butter (walnut size)
Salt and pepper to taste
1 cup water

Slice cabbage as for slaw. Cook in 1 cup water until tender; drain. Return to saucepan. Add cream and salt and pepper. Simmer two to three minutes.
NOTE: Milk may be used by adding a little more butter.

Lou Henri Baker, Killbuck, OH

BAKED CREAM CABBAGE
Serves 6

1 medium head cabbage
1/2 cup boiling salted water
3 tablespoons flour
1/2 teaspoon salt
1-1/2 cups milk
1/4 cup bread crumbs
2 tablespoons butter

Shred cabbage very fine and cook 9 minutes in boiling, salted water. Remove cabbage; drain well. Place in buttered 1-1/2-quart casserole. Melt butter in saucepan; stir in flour and salt until smooth. Add milk gradually, continuing to stir until mixture thickens. Pour this sauce over cabbage and sprinkle breadcrumbs over top. Bake at 325 degrees for about 15 minutes or until crumbs are browned.

Karin Shea Fedders, Dameron, MD

ZUCCHINI FRITTERS
Makes 2 dozen

2 large zucchini squash
3 eggs
1/2 teaspoon salt
1/4 teaspoon pepper
1/2 teaspoon sugar
1 teaspoon dried dillweed or 1 tablespoon fresh dill
2 cloves garlic (finely diced)
5 tablespoons flour
1 onion (diced)
Salad oil and margarine

Wash zucchini, do not peel. Dice coarsely; cover with water. Add 1 teaspoon salt and bring to boil for eight minutes. Drain in colander (about 15 minutes). While draining zucchini, heat salad oil and saute onion until soft. Beat eggs; add next 7 ingredients. Stir in drained, mashed zucchini. Mix until well blended, adding sauteed onions.

Drop batter by tablespoon into skillet in which you have 2 tablespoons salad oil and 1 tablespoon margarine. Fry zucchini fritters, a few at a time, until light brown on both sides, turning once.

Place on platter with paper towel to absorb, adding more oil and margarine to skillet as needed and add more batter.

Serve plain or topped with dollop of sour cream or plain yogurt.

Carme Venella, Laurel Springs, NJ

ZUCCHINI SURPRISE
Serves 4
60 calories per serving

1 pound zucchini, sliced
8-ounce can mandarin oranges, drained
1/4 teaspoon nutmeg
Sprinkle cinnamon
1/4 cup pecans, chopped

Steam zucchini slices until tender. Add orange slices, nutmeg and cinnamon. Sprinkle with pecans; serve.

Marie Fusaro, Manasquan, NJ

ZUCCHINI QUICHE

1 cup corn muffin mix
3 cups sliced small zucchini squash
1 medium onion, chopped
1/2 cup Parmesan cheese, grated
1/3 cup cooking oil
4 eggs, well beaten
Salt and pepper to taste
1 cup rich cream or half-and-half

Mix all ingredients together. Pour into a buttered 10" pie plate or quiche dish. Bake 45 minutes at 350 degrees. Can be frozen and baked when needed. If preferred, slice tomato or green pepper rings to place on top.

Nice served with relish plate of fresh vegetables and melon or other raw fruit for a luncheon.

Marjorie W. Baxla, Greenfield, OH

ZUCCHINI ROUNDS

1/3 cup commercial biscuit mix
1/4 cup grated Parmesan cheese
Salt and pepper to taste
2 eggs, slightly beaten
2 cups shredded, unpared zucchini
2 tablespoons butter or margarine, softened

In a bowl combine biscuit mix, cheese, salt, and pepper. Stir in eggs just until mixture is moistened; fold in zucchini. For each round, drop 2 tablespoons mixture in soft butter or margarine. Fry 2-3 minutes on each side until brown.

This is an excellent summer luncheon dish or for a brunch.

Alice McNamara, Eucha, OK

ZUCCHINI APPLESAUCE

Makes 2 cups

2 medium zucchini, peeled and diced
2 apples, peeled, cored, and diced
1/4 cup sugar
2 whole cloves
1/8 teaspoon nutmeg
1/2 teaspoon salt
1 tablespoon lemon juice
1/4 teaspoon cinnamon
1/2 teaspoon vanilla extract
Water

In a large saucepan, bring to a boil the zucchini, apples, sugar, cloves, nutmeg, salt, and 1/2 cup water. Reduce heat, cover, and simmer for 20 minutes; stir occasionally. Remove cover; continue cooking until all liquid has evaporated. Discard the cloves, then mash until smooth. Stir in the lemon juice and cinnamon. Cover and refrigerate until ready to use.

Marie Fusaro, Manasquan, NJ

SQUASH PILLOWS

1 yeast cake
1/2 cup lukewarm water
2/3 cup shortening
1 teaspoon salt
1/2 cup sugar
1 cup mashed cooked squash
1 teaspoon grated lemon rind
1/8 teaspoon mace
1 cup scalded milk
2 eggs
6 to 8 cups sifted flour

Mash squash. Add sugar, shortening, salt, lemon rind, mace and eggs. Blend well. Dissolve yeast in water. Add yeast mixture to milk and add to the first mixture. Add sifted flour to make a stiff dough. Mix well. Cover and let rise in a warm place until doubled in bulk. Shape into rolls; place in greased pans. Let rise in warm place until double in bulk. Bake at 325 degrees for 25 minutes.

Mrs. Kit Rollins, Cedarburg, WI

STUFFED ACORN SQUASH

Serves 8-12

Water
4-6 acorn squash, halved crosswise and seeded
1 or 2 (6 ounce) boxes chicken-flavor stuffing mix, prepared according to package directions
Parsley sprigs (garnish)

Preheat oven to 350 degrees. Pour water into 1 large or 2 smaller baking pans to measure 1 inch deep. Arrange acorn squash in water with cut sides up, cutting a thin slice off ends so halves will stand upright. Bake, covered, for 45 minutes or until flesh is tender when pierced with fork. Fill each squash cavity with about 1/3 cup hot stuffing and garnish with parsley.

HOLIDAY STUFFED WINTER SQUASH

Serves 6

3 small acorn or butternut squash
3 green onions, chopped
1 tablespoon oil
1 cup finely-diced celery
1 bunch fresh spinach, coarsely chopped
3/4 cup whole wheat bread crumbs
1/4 teaspoon salt
1/4 cup almonds, finely ground
1 tablespoon butter

Halve and clean the squash. Bake in a 350 degree oven, for 35-40 minutes, or until tender. Sauté onions in oil until soft. Add diced celery. Cover and simmer on medium heat until just tender. Add spinach; stir to wilt. Combine bread crumbs with salt and ground almonds. Stuff the squashes with spinach; sprinkle crumb mixture on top. Dot with butter and return to oven for 10-15 minutes.

Gwen Campbell, Sterling, Va.

DEBBIE'S YUMMY BAKED BEANS

4 cans pork and beans, drained
1/2 cup minced onion
1/2 pound diced bacon
3/4 cup grape jelly
3/4 cup enchilada sauce

Fry onion and bacon; drain. Add jelly and enchilada sauce; mix well. Add beans; pour into casserole dish and bake, uncovered at 350 degrees for 1 hour. Serve hot.

Debbie Vlahovic, Mesa, AZ

Home Cooking

INDEX

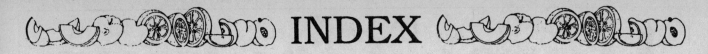